Decr 6th

D1201704

Page 53.

# A Full-Grown Nation

*Abraham Lincoln finds time to play with his son, Tad.*

# A Full-Grown Nation

## Revised Edition

☆

## Edna McGuire

Author of *Glimpses into the Long Ago · A Brave Young Land · America Then and Now*
Co-Author of *The Growth of Democracy* and *The Rise of Our Free Nation*

☆

## With Pictures by
## George M·Richards

New York
The Macmillan Company

# TABLE OF CONTENTS

## DIVISION ONE

### THE YOUNG NATION MAKES A PLACE FOR ITSELF

## DIVISION TWO

### THE NATION TURNS ITS FACE TOWARD THE WEST

## DIVISION THREE

### The Nation Struggles for Its Life

## DIVISION FOUR

### The Nation Becomes Full Grown

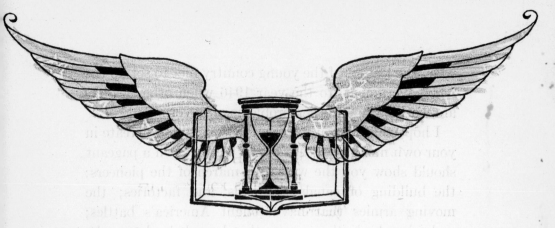

Dear Boys and Girls:

During the Century of Progress World's Fair held in Chicago a pageant called "The Wings of a Century" was presented. It showed many vivid scenes from American history. Actors dressed in the costumes of long ago rode on the great outdoor stage in covered wagons, stagecoaches, automobiles, and trains. Indians made an attack on a party of pioneers. A gay group went through an old-time dance while a fiddle played. Ladies in hoop skirts bowed to gentlemen in long-tailed coats.

Scene by scene the events of the past moved swiftly across the stage. So real did these seem that those of us who sat in the audience forgot that we were seeing a pageant. It was as though the happenings of history were marching past before our eyes.

As I watched that pageant, I determined that some day I would write a book which would make the events of the past come alive for boys and girls as the pageant had made them come alive for me. This is the book. In it you will find the story of America from that day when the leaders of the young country met to set up the new government, to the year 1946 when other leaders are working upon other problems of government.

I hope that as you read you may be able to create in your own mind a pageant of the past. Such a pageant should show you the westward march of the pioneers; the building of canals, railroads, and factories; the moving armies that have fought America's battles; and a hundred other events that have helped to make your country what it is today. If you can see these pictures and if at the same time you can understand something of the way these peoples of long ago thought and felt, you will not only have a happy time but you will have taken the first long step toward learning the history of your country.

The best way to use this book is to read a story all the way through at one time. Do not try to remember everything, but try to see the scenes as they appear. When you have finished reading, study the directions at the end of the chapter to check yourself. If you have missed parts which you need to know, you can then read again to find these. By following these directions you will also learn many new skills that will make studying easier for you.

New words are explained in a list in the back of the book. You may need to look there for some help.

After you have read a story, you will want to do some of the interesting things suggested at the end and read some of the books that are listed there.

THE AUTHOR

# DIVISION ONE

## The Young Nation Makes a Place for Itself

## THE NEW GOVERNMENT IS SET UP

September 17, 1787, was an important day in the history of the United States of America, for on that day a new plan of government was agreed upon. During the troubled years of the Revolutionary War the thirteen colonies had been held together by little except their common love of freedom. At the end of that struggle they had framed a plan of government known as the *Articles of Confederation*. After their experience as colonists these early Americans feared a strong government. Well did they remember the harsh laws made for them by the British. Because of this fear the men who framed the Articles of Confederation gave little power to the new government which they created.

It soon became clear, however, that a weak government might produce quite as many difficulties as one that was overstrong. The nation found itself unable to pay its debts. There was no one system of money. States quarreled over matters of trade. The new nation was not respected by other countries.

[1]

Matters finally became so bad that it was generally agreed that some changes must be made. Many of the leading men of the country attended a meeting held in Philadelphia in 1787. There it was decided to make a new plan of government.

The Constitution agreed upon by this convention was signed on September 17. One by one the states accepted the new plan. By the spring of 1789 the government provided under the Constitution had been set up. George Washington was chosen to be the first President and John Adams of Massachusetts was elected as the Vice President.

## The New Plan Is Launched

**George Washington takes office as President.** — To Washington the news that he must leave his farm, Mount Vernon, and take up public duties again was not welcome. He loved his beautiful Virginia home, and he was weary of public life. However, he felt that he must serve his country if he were needed.

One April day George Washington said good-by to his family and servants and set out for New York City, which was to serve for a time as the capital of the country. That the people loved and admired their great leader was proved on this journey. "In every village the people from the farms and workshops crowded the streets to watch his carriage, and the ringing of bells and the firing of guns marked his coming and going." On the whole way from Mount Vernon

[2]

to New York the people welcomed their new President, while at the end of the journey the capital city arranged to pay him great honor.

A boat with thirteen pilots, each dressed in a white uniform, waited to carry the great man across the bay. As the boat swept up to the landing, bands on the shore began to play, while church bells rang and a cannon fired a salute. A crimson cloth was spread for Washington to step upon as he left the boat. As the tall figure dressed in blue was seen walking across this crimson path, the crowds along the shore broke into such shouts that they drowned the sound of bells, cannon, and bands.

April 30 was the day chosen for the ceremony by which the newly elected President took office. This ceremony, called the inauguration, took place in the City Hall, which had been prepared for the use of the new government. Imagine yourself in the room where the Senate meets. This body, the smaller of the two houses of Congress, has invited the members of the House of Representatives to meet with them for the ceremony.

It is eleven o'clock. John Adams, who has already been inaugurated as Vice President, has taken his place in the high-backed chair facing the members of Congress. Outside, the streets are crowded with happy people. Flags flutter gaily in the breeze. Church bells, which earlier in the day called people to pray for the new government, now ring out a joyful welcome.

[4]

The shouts grow louder. The President must be near. Yes, the doors at the rear of the room swing open. Up the center aisle the tall, silent man passes, bowing to the right and left. He carries himself with the dignity of a soldier. Dressed in a brown suit and white stockings, he has a sword swinging at his side.

As he takes his place beside Adams, the Vice President leads him to the balcony outside where the oath of office is to be taken. Standing there on the balcony, high above the heads of the crowd, George Washington places his hand upon an open Bible and swears to support the Constitution of the United States of America. The man who has given him the oath turns

[5]

now to the crowd below and cries, "Long live George Washington, President of the United States!" The people take up the words and shout again and again, "Long live George Washington!"

**George Washington guides the new government.** — It was a hard task which faced the new President. The young nation was so weak that the older countries had little respect for it. There was no money with which to pay the debts that the nation owed. Many people within the United States doubted if the new government had power enough to force people to obey its laws. All of these and many other difficulties had to be met by President Washington.

One of the first steps which the President took was to appoint men to help him in the work of the new government. He asked Thomas Jefferson to take charge of matters which concerned foreign nations. This was a good choice, for the Virginian, who had already represented the United States in France, was a very able man. The President asked Alexander Hamilton of New York to find ways to raise money for the support of the government. This brilliant young man not only managed the money matters of the new government, but he was often asked by the President to give advice about other affairs as well.

Hamilton found means for raising money. Within a few years the United States changed from a country sinking under a load of debt to a nation which was willing and able to pay its debts. Other nations had

[6]

greater respect for the new country when it proved itself able to do this.

The people of France had started a revolution. They killed their king and set up a new government. Very soon Great Britain was at war with France. Many people in America, remembering the aid which France had given to the colonies in their struggle against Britain, felt that the United States should now send help to the French. These people formed societies, wore the French colors, sang songs, and tried in every way that they could to make President Washington help France.

The President knew that this tiny, new nation was in no condition to fight; so he very wisely said that the United States would not help either England or France. This disappointed the French and many Americans as well, but it was the only safe thing which Washington could do. Had the United States entered a war at that time, the freedom of the new nation would probably have been lost.

One means used for raising money was to require that a tax be paid by people who made whisky. In the western part of the country many farmers made their corn into whisky because they could take liquor to market more easily than they could haul great loads of grain over rough roads. These men objected to having to pay a tax on their whisky, and when government officers tried to collect it a group of Pennsylvanians took up arms against the government. President

Washington saw that the time had come to act. He sent 15,000 soldiers into western Pennsylvania and compelled the men to lay down their arms and obey the laws. By this firm action the new government proved that it could keep order in the country.

### THE WILDERNESS IS SETTLED

**Pathfinders lead the way across the mountains.** — The new government faced serious problems in the West. To understand these it is necessary to know what had happened there during the Revolutionary War and in the years while the states lived under the Articles of Confederation.

Even in colonial days some men began to push across the Appalachian Mountains into the great wilderness that lay beyond. Hunters, explorers, even a few settlers found their way into this new region. They carried back tales of green valleys and thickly wooded hills; of rich black soil and broad rivers. Other men, listening to these stories of a fair and fruitful land, were filled with a great longing to see it for themselves.

[8]

There were no roads leading to this wonderland beyond the mountains. He who would go must follow
the buffalo traces and the Indian paths or float down
inland rivers. He must often cut his way through
thickets and build canoes in which to cross streams.
His shelter would be only such as he could build for
himself; his food mainly the game he could kill and the
fish he could catch. Always he must be ready to defend himself from the Indians. Yet in spite of these
and many other difficulties men answered the call of
the wilderness and in many cases having seen its promise returned to guide settlers there. Thus it was that
the pathfinders led the way toward the new frontier
opening beyond the Appalachians.

**Tennessee is settled.** — In 1770 a tall, serious young
man of twenty-eight rode across the hills from his
North Carolina home into the western country. There
on the Watauga River he found land to his liking.
Choosing a piece of it, he planted corn. According to
the custom of the times this act of planting sealed his
right to the land. He remained on the Watauga to
harvest his crop, no doubt spending much of the sum-

mer in exploring the country. When his corn was gathered, the young man, whose name was James Robertson, set off for the eastern settlements. He was determined to bring his family to this new country. This he did in the spring of 1771. With the Robertsons came a small group of colonists.

The next year, in 1772, a young Virginian rode down the Holston Valley on a hunting and exploring trip. Coming finally to the little settlement on the Watauga, he found conditions that he liked. Not only was there land here, but already James Robertson's settlers were taking steps to secure law and order in their small community. All this appealed to the liberty-loving young Virginian. Then and there John Sevier cast in his lot with the settlers on the Watauga. Hurrying home, he led his entire family back to the little western settlement.

Robertson had supposed that he was settling in Virginia. However when the boundary line was surveyed it was found that the colony on the Watauga was south of Virginia. In any case the little community was far removed from the organized governments on the Atlantic coast. The settlers must keep order in their own settlement. Under Robertson's leadership a plan for self-government was made. After John Sevier came to make his home on the Watauga, he also became one of the leaders in the government of the little community.

The colonies along the Atlantic coast usually regarded their territory as extending westward to the Mississippi

[10]

River. Since the Watauga settlement had been found not to be in Virginia, it seemed that it must be in the territory claimed by North Carolina. Acting on this idea the settlement on the Watauga asked to be considered a part of North Carolina. In 1777 that colony organized a county west of the mountains. In time as settlers poured in more counties were formed.

John Sevier built a home on the Nolichucky River. This dashing stream was so called because its Indian name meant *rapid*. Thinking how like the man was to the river, his friends called John Sevier, Nolichucky Jack.

As always men felt the call of the West. In 1779 James Robertson led a party to the Cumberland River where the first settlement was made at what is now the city of Nashville. These men went by land, but it was planned that the women and children as well as some later settlers were to go out by boat. This they did, leaving from an older settlement on the Holston River. They traveled down the Holston to the Tennessee, down the Tennessee to the Ohio, on the Ohio to the Cumberland, and up this stream to the new settlement at Nashville (then called Nashborough). After many difficulties and dangers, the party completed the nine-hundred-mile river journey. The frontier had moved on from the Watauga to the Cumberland.

As the years passed, more settlers came. In 1796 a new state was created where once North Carolina had had western counties. Tennessee was admitted to the Union. John Sevier, still dashing Nolichucky Jack to those who loved him, was elected the first governor of the state.

**Kentucky is settled.** — Lying between the Ohio and Cumberland Rivers was a stretch of country used by the Indians as a hunting ground. In this region, now largely within the state of Kentucky, no Indian tribe made its home, but several regularly hunted there. To these red men the white explorers and settlers who went to Kentucky were a threat, for they cleared the forest and planted fields. This meant less game for the Indian hunters.

[12]

As early as 1740 a party of explorers had sailed down the Ohio and on into the Mississippi. They had later reported that the country along the Ohio had plenty of water, fertile soil, and fine forests.

In 1750 Thomas Walker was hired by a company that wished to open western lands, "to go to the westward in order to discover a proper place for a settlement." With five other men he rode from the older part of the Virginia colony toward the headwaters of the Holston River. Following the path beaten down by the buffalo herds, the men passed through Cumberland Gap, which formed a sort of natural gateway through the mountains. Beyond lay Kentucky, much of which they explored.

At about the same time Christopher Gist, sent by another land company, explored the West. His journey took him briefly into Kentucky. A little later John Finley spent some time there, trading with the Indians and even going with them on one of their hunts. These men, and other hunters, traders, and explorers, who went to Kentucky from time to time all agreed that it was a land much to be desired.

While some men were turning to the west others were moving from one colony to another. Among these was the Boone family that came from Pennsylvania into the valley of the Yadkin River in North Carolina. Among the several children in this family was a son, Daniel, who was about seventeen years old when the family moved to North Carolina. Before long young Daniel

[13]

married a neighbor girl, Rebecca Bryan, and the two set up housekeeping in a little cabin on the Yadkin.

Daniel Boone bought land in the valley, but more than farming he loved to roam the forest. He was a first-class hunter, an excellent trapper, and a keen-eyed woodsman. After he had explored new land, he knew it as a farmer might know his own fields.

One day the trader, John Finley, came down the Yadkin Valley Road, his goods loaded on a pack horse. He and Daniel Boone had met long before. Now he stopped for a while at the Boone cabin, and there before the fireplace he told wonderful tales of Kentucky. As he spoke of the deer, the buffalo herds, the great

flocks of wild geese and ducks, and the well-watered land, Daniel Boone felt the call of this new place. He wanted to see this "Kaintuck" for himself.

Thus it came about that Daniel Boone and four other men set out in May, 1769, with John Finley for Kentucky. Going by way of the Cumberland Gap the party reached Kentucky without difficulty. When a goodly supply of skins had been laid by, Indians came upon the white men and robbed them. However, they did the men no harm but warned them to leave this Indian hunting ground at once. Four of the men followed this advice, but Boone and one other stayed behind. They were joined by Daniel's brother Squire and a friend. Trapping and hunting were soon in full swing again. One man was killed and one returned home. When spring came Squire Boone set out with their load of skins which had to be taken back to the settlements for sale.

[15]

Daniel Boone was left entirely alone in the Kentucky wilderness, "without bread, salt, or sugar, or even a horse or dog." Having only enough powder and shot to keep himself in meat, Daniel used the time to explore the country. When Squire returned two months later with fresh supplies, no white man in the world knew Kentucky as well as Daniel Boone. In the fall Squire took a second load of skins back, but returned as soon as he could to Kentucky. In March, 1771, the two brothers headed for home, their pack horses loaded with the winter's catch. They had the bad fortune to meet a band of Indians who robbed them of their horses, skins, and guns, but the two white men were not hurt. After two years in the wilderness Daniel Boone was at last back in the little cabin on the Yadkin, but his heart was in "Kaintuck" — a land he had seen and found good.

Some two years later Daniel and Squire Boone set out with a party of settlers for Kentucky. Indians attacked a part of the group, killing a number of men and boys, among them Daniel Boone's son, James. The settlers, too frightened to go on, turned back and made their way toward their old homes.

In 1774 James Harrod, who had already visited Kentucky, made a second trip there. With him went a party of men who made a settlement that they called Harrodsburg. Indian troubles caused these settlers to withdraw but the buildings they had put up were not harmed. The next year James Harrod led his men back to Harrodsburg which from that time on remained a settlement.

A land company was formed to open a large part of Kentucky to settlement. A treaty was made between this company and the Cherokee Indians who agreed to give up their rights in Kentucky. However, other Indian tribes were not so willing to allow the whites in their hunting grounds. The company needed a woodsman to open a road over which settlers could travel to Kentucky. It was agreed that the man for the place was Daniel Boone.

On March 10, 1775, the thirty men whom Boone had chosen to help him set out to cut the Wilderness Road. Behind them came parties of settlers, the first one led by Richard Henderson, one of the men who had formed the land company. Henderson's party reached the place agreed upon for the new settlement in April. Boone's men who had arrived ahead of them had built a few cabins and laid off the near-by land into lots. Thus, Boonesborough, Kentucky, had its beginning.

A plan was made for governing the little community. New settlers arrived. Daniel Boone went back to his old home and returned with Rebecca and the children. Other settlements were made, some near Boonesborough, others as far away as the falls of the Ohio, where in 1779 George Rogers Clark built a fort. This was the beginning of the city of Louisville.

Life in the new country was hard and rough. Again and again the Indians struck, often in raids on hunting

[17]

parties, sometimes in a full attack upon a fort, and on
some occasions in pitched battle.  Men and sometimes
women and children too died at the hands of the red
men.  But the settlement of Kentucky went steadily
forward.  A new frontier was being established where
once there had been only Indian hunting grounds.

Daniel Boone had many adventures in this new
country.  But the time came when Kentucky was well
filled with settlers.  A man hadn't much "elbow room"
as Daniel put it.  The woodsman still longed for a

wilderness. Because his titles were not clear Boone
lost much of the land he had taken up when he first
settled in Kentucky. In 1799 he took his family to
Missouri where again he enjoyed the pleasures of frontier life. Missouri remained his home until his death in
1820. Daniel Boone was a master of the wilderness and
one of America's greatest pathfinders.

Kentucky was at first a county of Virginia but in
1792, while George Washington was President, it became a state. It was the first new state to be formed
west of the Appalachian Mountains.

**The Northwest Territory is made secure.** — A great stretch of land north of the Ohio River had been captured by George Rogers Clark during the Revolutionary War. It was granted to the United States when peace was made. The western boundary of the young nation was fixed at the Mississippi River. This region was known as the Northwest Territory. A famous law called the Ordinance of 1787 provided a plan of government for this region. According to this plan the territory might be formed into states as soon as enough people settled in it. The law also permitted settlers in the territory to enjoy many of the rights that belonged to citizens of the states. The Ordinance stated that slaves should never be held in the Northwest Territory.

The rich soil of this region soon drew many settlers.

Land companies were formed to send out people to make settlements. One of these, the Ohio Company, sent out a party of men in the winter of 1787–88. The party was led by Rufus Putnam, who had served as a general in the Revolutionary War. The men of his party were well fitted to found a new settlement for among them were carpenters, blacksmiths, farmers, and other skilled workmen. They followed a road across the mountains from Philadelphia to the upper waters of the Ohio. Building boats they floated down the river to the mouth of the Muskingum. Landing there in the spring of 1788 they laid out their settlement on the east bank of the Muskingum River. Other settlers came with their families in the weeks that followed. [21]

Early in July the men who directed the affairs of the Ohio Company held a meeting at the little frontier village and gave it a name. They called it Marietta in honor of the queen of France. A celebration with speechmaking and feasting was held on the Fourth of July. That same month the governor of the Northwest Territory came to make his home in Marietta. A few bold Americans had pushed into the Northwest Territory before it was properly opened to settlers. However, Marietta was the first American settlement in the territory that continued through the years. Today it is a city in the state of Ohio.

Before the end of 1788 another settlement was laid out farther down the Ohio River. This little town came to be called Cincinnati. A few years later Moses Cleaveland laid out a town on the shores of Lake Erie. Here a party of settlers from Connecticut came to make their homes. They named the town Cleveland in honor of the man who had founded it.

Ohio became a melting pot into which people poured from all the older states. Many settlers came from the northeastern states, but there were also large numbers from Virginia, the Carolinas, and Kentucky and a sprinkling from other places. Over the roads, across the lake, down the rivers came men, women, and children seeking new homes in the Northwest Territory. It is small wonder that Ohio was ready to become a state in 1803. As the westward movement continued new states were formed until at last every foot of soil

The FORT at MARIETTA, OHIO in 1791

in what had once been the Northwest Territory had become a part of some state.

But this growth of states was to come in the future. The problem which President Washington faced in the Northwest Territory was to protect the settlers from Indian attacks. As white men crowded into their country, the Indians grew angry. The settlers asked the President to send soldiers to aid them. One army which he sent was surprised by a war party of Indians who killed hundreds of soldiers.

**Peace is made with the Indians.** — The President then chose General Anthony Wayne to subdue the Indians and make a lasting peace with them. Several years of fighting were needed before the Indians were willing to talk about peace, but in 1795 after a severe defeat they accepted General Wayne's invitation to attend a great council.

Can you imagine that you are in Fort Greenville where this council is to be held? The soldiers are busy during the spring days clearing ground and building a

[24]

council house. This has a roof to keep off sun and rain, but is open at the sides so that air may pass freely through it.

With the council house ready, General Wayne turns his attention to the supplies which he has ordered from the East. The soldiers open boxes of food, rolls of clothing, and great bundles which contain all manner of gay trifles dear to an Indian's heart. The general has laid his plans carefully for this meeting.

The early days of June bring the first Indians to the council. They receive a warm welcome, made more pleasant by good food and plenty of presents. Each day sees more Indians arriving at Fort Greenville. The soldiers are busy entertaining their guests.

It is the sixteenth of June and the general council opens. General Wayne and his officers seat themselves with the chiefs of the tribes, while soldiers and Indians watch. The peace pipe goes round the group. The eight men who are to act as interpreters swear that when they change a message from one language to the

[25]

other they will repeat it as it is given to them.

Now General Wayne makes a speech in which he explains why he has called the council, and promises to wait for the other chiefs who have not yet arrived.   In

closing he says, "The heavens are bright, the roads are open. We will rest in peace and love and await the arrival of our brothers. We will on this happy occasion be merry."

Days pass, and each one brings more Indians. General Wayne explains the terms of peace which he wants to make. The red men talk together and with the general. Finally on the seventh of August, with more than eleven hundred Indians present, the treaty is agreed to by all the chiefs. The Indians have promised to withdraw from much of the Northwest Territory and to live peacefully on the lands which the white men are to recognize as belonging to the Indians.

[28]

When the time comes for the chiefs and their braves to leave Greenville, each chief makes a speech to General Wayne. It remains for the great leader of the Delaware tribe to voice the last important words of this great council. Turning to General Wayne and speaking through the interpreter, he says: "Your children well understand the meaning of the treaty which is now concluded. We experience daily proofs of your increasing kindness. I hope we may all have sense enough to enjoy our dawning happiness. . . . All who know me, know me to be a man and a warrior, and I now declare that I will for the future be as true and steady a friend of the United States as I have been an active enemy."

Thus it was that a wise and brave general finally brought peace to the Northwest Territory.

**The Mississippi is opened to western trade.** — The Mississippi River was the natural route of trade for the country west of the Appalachian Mountains. Goods could easily be shipped down this stream and sent out to the markets of the world. Since there were no good roads overland, it was next to impossible to send the products of the West to market by any other route. Spain owned New Orleans and the land west of the Mississippi River. For years the Spanish had objected to the Americans shipping on the river. President Washington was able to get Spain to agree that the Americans might use the river and land their goods at New Orleans. This right was a great aid to the western farmers.

[29]

**George Washington closes his period of service. —**
With his second term of office drawing to a close,
George Washington refused to accept a third term. He
said that eight years was long enough for one man to
stay at the head of the government. He returned to
Mount Vernon, where he hoped to take up once more his
life as a farmer, but within two years he died.

None of his many services to his country was more
important than those which George Washington gave
in the years that he was President. Under his guiding
hand the new plan of government had been safely
launched. Money had been raised to pay the debts.
The new nation had not only avoided war with foreign
nations, but had proved that it could keep peace within
its own borders. Indians had been subdued and
western lands had been made safe for settlement.

This great man, dead at sixty-seven, worn out by his
long service to his country, had earned the honor paid
to him by another famous American who said of him,
"George Washington was first in war, first in peace, and
first in the hearts of his countrymen."

## A Word Game

You should learn the meaning and the way to pronounce new words when you first meet them. Often you can tell what a new word means from the way it is used in the story. If not, you can look for it in the word list in the back of your book. If this list does not give you the meaning, look in a dictionary.

The word list and dictionary will show you how a word should be pronounced.

As you study history, you will need to use some words again and again because they carry ideas with which history deals. Such words, occurring in this chapter, are *treaty, constitution, inauguration, revolution, tax, frontier, pioneer, colonist, ordinance*. By using one or more of the methods suggested above learn the meaning of each of these words. Be sure too that you can pronounce each one. Write a sentence of your own using each word.

List these words in a notebook where you can add others as they occur in later chapters.

## A Map Study

On page 28 of this book is a map of the United States as it was in 1789 when George Washington became the first President. On this map locate each of the thirteen states;

[31]

the Northwest Territory; the region from which the new states of Kentucky and Tennessee were to be made. The first state that was added to the Union was Vermont. Find the territory which was soon to form this new state.

Locate the Cumberland Gap, the Watauga settlement, Nashville, Boonesborough, Harrodsburg, Louisville, Marietta, and Cincinnati.

Trace the route of the Wilderness Road. Explain why the settlers in cutting this and other early roads looked for and followed buffalo traces.

What natural routes of travel did pioneers have in going from the states on the Atlantic coast to the western land? What natural difficulties? Study your map before answering these questions.

## USING A BOOK

Studying is made easier if you learn how to use the helps that are contained in a book. When you start to read a new chapter, notice the chapter title. Then look quickly through the chapter and read the division headings one after another. This gives you a quick preview of the new material. If you want even a better one, read the several paragraph headings one after another. With this framework of the chapter in mind read it rapidly but carefully.

Use your word list if you come to a word that you cannot pronounce or do not know.

The index will help you find a subject quickly. It is arranged in alphabetical order. Look under the principal word of the subject about which you wish to read, *e.g.* if you should wish to locate material on the Indians who gave trouble to General Wayne, turn to your index, look under Indians, then under the listing that shows Indians who lived in the Northwest Territory.

[32]

When you have reason to use a book in the library, you will find that you can save much time by using the index and the table of contents to locate the facts you need. Suppose you try your skill in this by finding in library books new stories about George Washington, Daniel Boone, and Anthony Wayne.

If your library contains a set of encyclopedias look in these also. To find material about George Washington locate the volume that contains words beginning with W. Then turn to the words beginning Wa and follow these till you come to Washington. Where will you look for Daniel Boone? For Anthony Wayne?

SOME THINGS TO DO

1. Sometimes small events have large results. Make a floor talk in which you describe the Whisky Rebellion and explain how this one small event, as it was handled by President Washington, had large results. You may be able to find more facts about the Whisky Rebellion by using your library books.

2. Make a list of all the natural advantages that the Northwest Territory offered settlers. In a second list put down the difficulties that early settlers had to meet. Try to decide how each of these difficulties could be overcome. This was the problem that the early settlers faced. As you continue your study, try

[33]

to find how many of your solutions the settlers really used.

3. There is material in this chapter for many interesting pictures. Some scenes that you might like are the inauguration of President Washington, the Indian council at Fort Greenville, Daniel Boone in the wilderness, the settlement of Marietta.

4. Try acting both with and without words some of the scenes described in this chapter.

## SOME BOOKS TO READ

Two stories by Cornelia Meigs of the early days of this nation are *The Covered Bridge,* and *Wind in the Chimney.*

The movement to the West gave us many good stories. *The White Leader,* by Constance Lindsay Skinner is a frontier story of Tennessee just after the Revolution. Tales of pioneer adventures in Kentucky are:

*Wilderness Road,* by Katharine Clugston

*Daniel Boone,* by James Daugherty

*Journey Cake,* by Isabel M. McMeekin

*Jemima,* by Margaret Sutton

*Daniel Boone,* by Edna McGuire

*Daniel Boone, Wilderness Scout,* by Stewart E. White.

Enid L. Meadowcroft has written a story of pioneers who came to the Ohio country in *By Wagon and Flatboat.*

If you read very well, you may enjoy *Alexander Hamilton, Man of Action,* by John J. Smertenko.

Sacagawea guides the explorers across the mountains.

# THE UNITED STATES PROVES ITS INDEPENDENCE

## GREAT CHANGES COME IN AMERICA

**The rise of political parties.** — While Washington was still President, it became evident that men did not all think alike about matters of government. Because of this difference of opinion there came to be two political parties in the country. A political party is a group of people who think alike about how their country should be managed. The leader of one party was Alexander Hamilton, who believed that the wiser and better educated people should manage the affairs of government. A man who believed as he did was known as a *Federalist*.

The leader of the other party was Thomas Jefferson, who thought that all men, whether rich or poor, wise or ignorant, should have equal rights in managing the affairs of government. A person who believed as

[37]

Jefferson did called himself a *Republican*. In later years the name was changed to *Democrat*. Members of the Democratic Party of today often speak of Thomas Jefferson as the founder of their party. The Federalists and the Republicans each tried to elect their own men to office.

As the years have passed, the parties and the things which they believed have changed several times, but there have usually been at least two great political parties in the United States. Each party tries to place its men in office.

In the first election after Washington retired, the Federalists were the winners. They made John Adams President. During his term of office President Adams had to meet the same problems which Washington had faced with regard to the war between England and France. Neither nation treated the United States with respect, and each would have liked to see the young nation go to war with the other. The President realized that the country was too weak for war; so he kept the peace with both nations even though they failed to treat the United States with respect.

[38]

While Adams was President, Congress had passed some laws which were not popular with the people. This caused the Federalists to lose strength, and in the next election the Republicans were able to choose the President. Thomas Jefferson, the leader of the party, was elected the new President of the United States in 1800. His term of office saw great changes come to the young nation.

**Jefferson leads the nation.** — Thomas Jefferson was the first President to be inaugurated in the new capital. While Washington was still in office, it had been decided to build a new city to serve as the nation's capital. This city on the banks of the Potomac River was named in honor of the first President.

Just at the close of Adams' term the officers of government had moved to the new capital, which was then little more than a village. The Capitol stood in a forest, and the streets were merely roads cut through the trees. Pavements had not been laid; so men and animals made their way as best they could through the mud. Because there were no good hotels, many of the officers of government were forced to live in boarding-houses.

Perhaps the best of these boardinghouses was Conrad's. It was here that Thomas Jefferson had lived since moving to Washington. Had you been in Washington on the fourth of March, 1801, you would have wanted to look in at Conrad's, where an air of excitement could be felt.

[39]

The breakfast bell has sounded and the dining room has filled with people, all of whom chat eagerly of the great event of the day. Their fellow boarder, Thomas Jefferson, is to be inaugurated today as President of the United States. Many of these men and women can remember the inauguration of George Washington. They recall the solemn oath-taking, the speech, and the great reception which followed. They would enjoy another solemn ceremony followed by a merry gathering in the evening.

The chatter is interrupted by the entrance of the

[40]

tall Virginian. He goes quietly to his place at the foot
of the table, refusing with a smile the offer of a seat at
the head of the table near the fireplace. This man of
the people has for years held the view that all men are
equal. He will not change his stand now by accepting
favored places.

Breakfast over, Mr. Jefferson returns to his study
and his fellow boarders see him no more until almost
noon. A little before twelve o'clock he leaves the
house and walks to the Capitol. A rather strange
picture he makes as he swings along, for he is tall and
awkward, with the look of a man who has lived much

out of doors. An Englishman has called him tall and large-boned, which is perhaps a fair description. He may be awkward, but he is at the same time a kind and able man.

At twelve o'clock the guns fire a salute. The new President takes his oath of office and a little later reads his address. No ceremony marks this day upon which Thomas Jefferson takes up the reins of government. A new order of things has begun. Those who sigh for the glories of earlier days may take what comfort they can from the knowledge that the simple ways of Jefferson are well suited to life in the rude, half-finished little capital city.

The most important event which occurred while Thomas Jefferson was President was the purchase of the territory known as *Louisiana*. This great stretch of country reached from the Mississippi River west to some unknown boundary line in the Rocky Mountains. It had first belonged to France, but had been given by that country to Spain before the United States became a nation.

The only way in which the American farmers west of the Appalachian Mountains could get their produce to market was to float it down the Mississippi River and ship it from New Orleans. The Spanish, you remember, had once agreed to allow them this privilege, but by the time Jefferson became President they again refused this right to western farmers. This condition, of course, brought new complaints from these settlers.

In 1801 Jefferson heard that Spain had given Louisiana back to France in exchange for certain privileges in Europe. Fearing that the French would not permit Americans to ship through New Orleans, the President sent two men to Europe with orders to buy the city and also East and West Florida, if France would sell. In giving these orders the President took it for granted that the Floridas as well as Louisiana had passed from the Spanish to the French, although this had not really happened.

Before the Americans had time to make their offer, they were amazed to hear that the French would sell not only New Orleans but all of Louisiana. The ruler of France needed money to carry on his wars more than he needed this vast territory in the New World. The two Americans had no power to purchase this region, but they felt it was too good a bargain to miss. After some debate about the price they agreed that the United States would purchase all of Louisiana. The total cost to this country was to be about fifteen million dollars.

An old story says that after the two Americans had signed their names to the agreement one of them remarked, "We have lived long, but this is the noblest work of our lives. . . . From this day the United States take their place among the powers of the first rank." Whether or not this remark was made at the time we cannot be sure, but we do know that it expresses a great truth. With the purchase of Louisiana

[43]

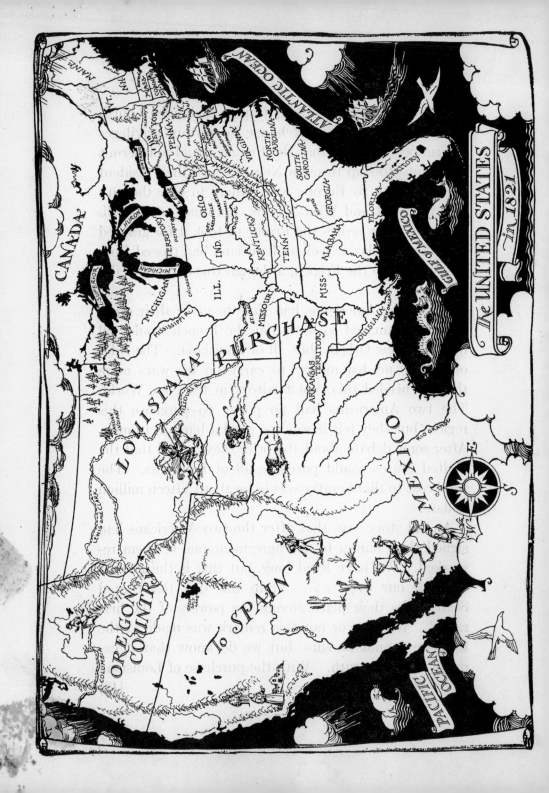

The United States in 1821

the United States grew suddenly great not only in size but in its dreams of future progress. The vast, unknown sweep of forest and prairie west as well as east of the Mississippi River called Americans to new adventures.

**Lewis and Clark explore the new region.** — Because so little was known about Louisiana, President Jefferson decided to send a party to explore the region. He chose Captain Meriwether Lewis and Captain William Clark as the two leaders for this party. The men were instructed to explore the Missouri River and the principal streams flowing into it, together with the country through which these flowed. They were to observe plants and animals in the region. They were expected to remain on friendly terms with the Indians and to learn all that they could about how the natives lived. Each man was told to make notes on all that he saw and did.

The two leaders took their men to a winter camp on the Mississippi River near the mouth of the Missouri. There they made ready for the long journey which was to begin in the spring. Will you try to catch glimpses of these explorers as they make their way toward the West?

It is May 14, 1804. The party of more than forty men is setting out today on the first step of the long journey. Soldiers and backwoodsmen work together loading the keelboat and the two smaller boats in which they are to travel. The keelboat has a square-rigged

[45]

sail, twenty-two oars, and a tow line. These men are prepared to travel no matter what the conditions. On the shore are the horses which will help tow the boats or carry hunters in search of game.

The river, swollen by spring rains, is a mass of swirling yellow-brown water as the small boats slip into the current. The horses are started upstream by a group of the men, while last of all the keelboat takes the water. With the Stars and Stripes flying from her prow and her hold loaded with goods for trade, this little vessel sets off on her brave adventure.

Days pass, and the party travels on toward the northwest. Lonely hunters and ragged trappers join the explorers around their campfires at night and tell tales of the forest dangers. Indians come to talk with the white men.

October finds the Americans among the Mandan villages in what is now the state of North Dakota. The Mandans are friendly Indians; so the leaders decide to spend the winter here. Captain Lewis at

once sets out to have a fort built. Here the explorers meet fur traders from Canada. Though friendly, these traders look upon the journey of the Americans with dread. They well know that before many years other Americans will be coming to take a part of their rich trade.

The fort is finished, and on Christmas morning the Stars and Stripes are run up above Fort Mandan. Friendly visits are exchanged between white men and red. The Americans join the Indians on buffalo hunts. In the late winter the men begin to build small boats to be used as they go farther upstream.

Lewis and Clark know that they must have guides who are acquainted with the country and with the language of the people who live in it. Here at Fort Mandan they find an old French trapper whose Indian wife, Sacagawea, had been stolen years before from a tribe living in the Rocky Mountains. This trapper and his wife agree to take the explorers into the new country.

One April day the boats push off again on the difficult journey upstream. Each day travel becomes harder. Food is so scarce that hunters must constantly roam the forests in search of game. The water grows so swift as the banks narrow that the boats must be pulled by tow lines. The men can scarcely find foothold along the shore. They strain and pull at the ropes. Their moccasins wear out faster than they can be mended.

[48]

It is a day in late May. Captain Lewis is marching along on shore, climbing swiftly to the top of a high cliff that is in his path. Suddenly he stops, for spread out before him lie the snow-covered Rocky Mountains, gleaming and dazzling in the sunshine. Only one other white man has ever traveled overland so far west, and he was forced to turn back. Not so with this daring American. He has seen the Rockies; now he must cross them and journey on to the Pacific.

Days pass, and adventures continue. The men find the Great Falls of which the Indians have told them. They mount the boats on rude wheels cut from tree trunks and drag them around the falls. On they go into the mountains, following one of the three forks which join to form the upper Missouri, until they come at last to the spring from which the river flows.

Sacagawea knows the land now as the country of her childhood. One day as Captain Clark speaks to an Indian chief, the woman falls upon him with cries of delight. This chief of the Snake Tribe is her brother, whom she has not seen since she was stolen as a child.

Having crossed the mountains, the Americans take to boats for the journey down the Columbia River. November 8, 1805, is a happy day for this little party. As the heavy fog rises they see before them the broad, blue waters of the Pacific Ocean. The shouts of the men rise above the roar of the waves breaking on the shore.

A winter on the damp, rainy coast proves as hard on

these explorers as the difficult journey across the continent.  With spring they gladly turn their faces toward the east, but they have so little in the way of goods for trade that the soldiers use the brass buttons from their uniforms to get food and horses.  Even so, dog meat is a luxury.

On the return journey Captain Lewis and a part of his men are forced to ride at breakneck speed for more than twenty-four hours to escape a party of Indians who are on the warpath.  Sore and weary they finally reach safety.

[50]

Arriving at the Mandan tribe, the men say good-by to Sacagawea and her trapper husband. To these two faithful guides they owe much of the success of their journey.

It is the twenty-third of September, 1806, when a little company of boats draws quietly up to the landing in St. Louis. People gaze in wonder at the men who step on shore, for their faces are like brown leather and their clothes hang in rags. As the citizens of the city realize who they are, a mighty shout goes up for these bold explorers — the pathfinders of a new nation.

[51]

**American seamen are seized.** — The events of these years did not all end so successfully as did the journey of Lewis and Clark. President Jefferson was troubled by the old problems which grew out of the war between France and England.

Great Britain needed sailors to man its ships, and it was not too particular about how these were secured. For years it had been the practice to seize men on the streets of English cities and carry them away to serve in the navy. It was only a step from this practice to the seizing of men from ships at sea. A British vessel would come alongside an American ship and under threat of gunfire would send officers on board the latter to search for English sailors. Sometimes men who had deserted from the British navy were found, but quite as often native-born Americans were seized and carried away to serve on English ships.

This impressment of seamen, as it was called, was continued openly for years in spite of many protests by the American Government. It is not surprising that the people of the United States grew angry over such treatment. From many parts of the country came the demand that the nation fight "for a free sea."

Because President Jefferson loved peace, he tried several laws which he hoped might cause Great Britain to stop seizing sailors and interrupting American trade. None of his measures was successful, however, and when he gave up the office to President Madison in 1808 the war clouds were growing thicker.

[52]

## A SECOND WAR FOR INDEPENDENCE

**The nation goes to war.** — The years dragged on and the troubles with both Great Britain and France continued. It was by the British, however, that the Americans felt themselves to be most deeply wronged. In 1811 it was admitted openly in the English House of Commons that as many as 1600 American seamen had been dragged from the decks of American vessels and forced to fight on British ships.

Not only did this impressment of seamen continue, but in the West the people had another cause for not liking the British. The Indians were almost always causing trouble at some point along the western settlements. The Americans felt that the British traders on the Canadian border kept the Indians stirred up against the white settlers. While it cannot be proved that the English government really favored such a practice, it was true that the red men got their guns and supplies for war from the British traders. In any

[53]

case it helped the cause of the fur traders to keep American settlers out of the West.

Within the Republican Party there began to be many men who favored war, although the great leaders of this party had always stood for peace. Most of these "war hawks," as they were called, were from the West and South. Henry Clay, a young Kentucky lawyer who was serving as Speaker of the House of Representatives, was one of the leaders of the war hawks. It was Clay who when he was asked, "What are we to gain by war?" answered, "What are we not to lose by peace? Commerce, character, a nation's best treasure, honor!"

In the end the war hawks had their way. War against Great Britain was declared in 1812. Although Clay and his friends had boasted of how quickly Canada would be conquered and England made humble, the United States was really poorly prepared for war. For years peace-loving Presidents had done little to make either the Army or the Navy strong. As in the Revolution, soldiers joined the Army for short periods of time only. Many states refused to send their troops outside their own borders. The generals who commanded such soldiers as there were seem to have been for the most part very poor officers. There was little money for carrying on a war. James Madison was an able man who had served his country in many ways, but he loved peace too well to make a good war President.

[54]

The cry of the war hawks had been "On to Canada!" so it was along the Canadian border and on the Great Lakes that the first American attack was made. Detroit was surrendered by the American general without the firing of a gun. Other losses followed until the people grew heartsick and discouraged.

Among the many defeats suffered by the Americans a few victories stood out to show that American fighting men could win battles even with heavy odds against them. One of the most famous of these was the victory won by Captain Oliver Perry on Lake Erie.

To this young American officer of twenty-eight was given the task of building a fleet of ships which could destroy the British control of Lake Erie. Through the winter and spring of 1813 Captain Perry's men toiled to build the tiny fleet. Trees of the forest furnished the lumber. The iron, canvas, and other necessary articles were hauled by horses and oxen from points more than a hundred miles away. When all was ready, Captain Perry floated his vessels out of the harbor where they

had been built and launched them on the lake. With little more than half the number of men needed, the fleet put out to face its enemy.

It is the tenth of September, and at last Captain Perry has his fleet in battle line. The British vessels are fewer in numbers but they have better guns. From his flagship, the *Lawrence*, Captain Perry watches the enemy approach. The two flagships draw close together as the guns of the British vessel open fire.

For two long hours the fire from the enemy pours in upon the *Lawrence*. Her sister ship has fallen away and is giving her no aid. The masts are shot away. All but one of her guns are silenced. More than half

her crew lie dead or wounded on the deck. The American flag still flies, but the ship can no longer be steered.

Captain Perry jumps into a small boat and orders the men to row for the *Niagara*, another vessel in his fleet. Leaping on board, he takes command and bears down upon the British flagship. Again and again the American guns pour shot upon the enemy. One by one the British vessels signal the Americans that they will surrender, until at last even the flagship "strikes her colors," as the sailors say when a ship surrenders.

As night falls on the scene of battle Captain Perry sends a message to his commanding officer. It reads,

"We have met the enemy and they are ours. Two ships, two brigs, one schooner, and one sloop."

The greatest success of the War of 1812 was won by the Navy. Of all the battles fought on the ocean, the meeting between the *Constitution* and the *Guerrière* was perhaps the most important. This battle took place one August day in 1812 when the two ships met off the coast of Nova Scotia. When the *Constitution* sighted the British ship, the *Guerrière*, the commander, Captain Hull, immediately made ready for battle. If you had been on board the *Constitution*, what would you have seen?

The men are running to their places as the fifes and

drums play.  Boys hurry about pouring sand upon the deck or placing the sacks of powder beside the guns. The battle flag is run up, and almost at once is greeted by the battle flag which appears on the *Guerrière*.

The ships approach each other, but Captain Hull withholds his fire until they are a few yards apart. His Yankee gunners have been trained to hit their mark, however, and within half an hour the British ship is a complete wreck.  The captain strikes his colors, and the Americans board the *Guerrière*.  They find Captain Dacres wounded and many of his men killed or injured.  The ship is so badly wrecked that it is fit only to be burned.

[59]

Although they are joyful over their victory, the Americans cannot but feel sorry for the British who have suffered such a terrible loss. As the wounded captain climbs up the side of the *Constitution* a prisoner of war, Captain Hull runs to him and says, "Give me your hand, Dacres. I know you are hurt."

The *Constitution* saw many years of service after this battle and earned for herself the nickname "Old Ironsides." When too old any longer to ride the waves, she was given a place of honor in the Boston Navy Yard.

The victories won by American ships caused great rejoicing in the United States, because Great Britain had always been regarded as *Mistress of the Seas*. To humble a British vessel seemed to the Americans to be a great deed.

The American Navy was not large enough to prevent the British from landing soldiers along the Atlantic coast. Many towns and cities were entered, but the event which most hurt American pride was the attack on Washington. Nothing had been done to protect the capital; so it is not surprising that a party of English soldiers one day marched into the city. They burned the Capitol, the President's home, and several other public buildings. President Madison and the other officers of government fled to Virginia until the British left.

The War of 1812 gave the United States its national song. One night the British along the coast made an

[60]

attack upon <u>Fort McHenry</u>. Through the long, dark hours the American soldiers within the fort returned their fire. A young American named Francis Scott Key had gone on board a British ship to arrange an exchange of prisoners. He was kept on board during this night attack. Can you think how anxiously he would have listened for the answering guns of the fort, and how as the first rays of light appeared he must have watched to see whether or not the Stars and Stripes were still flying? It was then that he wrote,

O, say! can you see by the dawn's early light,
   What so proudly we hail'd at the twilight's last
      gleaming,
Whose broad stripes and bright stars, through the
      perilous fight,
   O'er the ramparts we watch'd were so gallantly
      streaming?

The morning light showed the Star-Spangled Banner still waving. Fort McHenry had not surrendered.

**Peace comes to America.** — The year 1814 found the war still in progress but with both the United States and Great Britain weary of fighting. A group of Americans met a company of Englishmen in one of the cities of Europe, and after months of debate these men made a treaty of peace which the two nations accepted. It was a strange treaty, for it failed to mention some of the very matters over which the war had been fought. Not a word was said, for instance, about the impressment of seamen. Yet never again did Englishmen try to seize American sailors.

The United States gained no land and no treasure from the War of 1812, but it gained something much more important. The young country became really an independent nation as a result of this struggle. Up to that time European countries had looked upon the United States as little better than a colony. They had shown but slight respect for the rights of the new nation. But when the plucky Americans were willing to fight for those rights and when they showed themselves able to win victories from the Mistress of the Seas, Europeans looked at the United States with new respect. The War of 1812 may very rightly be called the Second War of Independence.

It is a strange fact that the one great land victory of the Americans was won after peace was made. The treaty was signed in Europe on Christmas Eve in 1814, but the news had to be carried to America by ship. Before the slow-moving vessel reached the United

States, Andrew Jackson, a rough-and-ready fighter from Tennessee, had led an army against the British in New Orleans.

It was a queer lot of fighting men which this bold general commanded. A company of Louisiana gentlemen in bright uniforms, a band of pirates with their heads bound in crimson handkerchiefs, a group of American sailors, a few regular soldiers, a company of Negroes, long lines of backwoodsmen dressed in hunting shirts and coonskin caps — these made up Jackson's army. How well this wild crowd could fight, the British learned to their sorrow. Andrew Jackson, nicknamed "Old Hickory," had told his men before the battle that they could "lick their weight in wild-cats." They agreed with him, and gave the British their worst defeat of the war.

The years which followed the making of peace were a time of good feeling in the United States. Political quarrels became less severe. Florida was purchased from Spain for five million dollars. Settlers poured in large numbers from the older states toward the new lands in the West.

For the first quarter century of its life the United States had faced toward Europe, while it struggled with the problem of making a place for itself in the family of nations. Now with its independence fully established the young nation turned its face toward the West, where forests and prairies called its people to new adventures.

[63]

## A Word Game

Find the phrase which belongs with each word.

reception      the ship of the officer who commands a
impressment    fleet
flagship       seizing by force
               a party usually attended by a large number
               of people

Add *oath of office* and *political* to the list of history terms
that you are keeping in your notebook.

## A Map Study

On page 44 is a map which shows the United States as it
was in 1821. On this locate the Louisiana Purchase.

Trace the route followed by Lewis and Clark on their
exploring trip. What natural features of the country aided
them in their journey? What ones hindered them?

Which direction is north on your map? South? East?
West? In what directions did Lewis and Clark travel?

On this same map locate Lake Erie. Try to decide for
yourself why it was important to the Americans to gain
control of this lake. Was British control of Lake Erie a
greater threat to the American cause than British control of
the other Great Lakes? Why or why not?

## Drawing Conclusions

Results always follow causes. One purpose of studying
history is to learn what results may be expected if certain
causes have been at work. For example, when a great many
citizens come to feel that a President of a country has not
served their interests, what result is likely to follow?

In this chapter events and conditions are described that
led to very direct results or conclusions. You are to com-

[64]

plete each of the unfinished statements below telling what result followed the condition mentioned in the first part of the statement. The first conclusion is stated to show you how this exercise goes.

1. People in the United States during early years did not think alike about political matters, therefore two political parties were formed.

2. Thomas Jefferson believed that all men were equal, therefore _____. (There are several possible conclusions to this one.)

3. Lewis and Clark found an Indian woman who knew her way over the mountains and thus they _____ _____.

4. The early presidents of the United States were peace-loving men, therefore _____.

5. Britain had a mighty navy, the United States a very small one, therefore the victories won in the War of 1812 by the Americans _____.

6. In the War of 1812 Britain and France learned that the Americans would fight for their rights, therefore _____.

## SOME THINGS TO DO

1. Look in your library for a longer story about the exploring trip made by Meriwether Lewis and William Clark. Tell some new and interesting events of this journey to your classmates.

2. On a long strip of paper make a group of pictures to tell the story of the Lewis and Clark exploring trip. Such a group of pictures is called a *frieze*.

3. Draw a picture of "Old Ironsides."

4. If you do not already know them, learn all the words of the "Star-Spangled Banner."

5. Write a paragraph of at least three or four sentences, beginning with this one, "Captain Oliver Perry proved that he was a hero." In the other sentences tell of events which you think show that Captain Perry was really a hero.

6. Before you leave this first division, spend a little while thinking of the problems that the new government had had to meet. Make two lists, one to show the gains which the new government had made, and the other to show the problems which had still to be met; for example —

| Gains | Problems |
|---|---|
| Great Britain and France show increased respect for the new nation. | How can settlers who go to the new western territory be supplied with the articles that they need? |

### Some Books to Read

*The Birth of a Nation's Song*, by K. L. Bakeless is an interesting story of "The Star-Spangled Banner."

Among the stories you will want to read about the Lewis and Clark expedition is a very easy one by Bonnie C. Howard, *On the Trail with Lewis and Clark*. Others that are more difficult to read are: *Young Shannon, Scout with Lewis and Clark*, by Grace V. Curl and *No Other White Man*, by Julia Davis.

In *Here I Stay*, Elizabeth Coatsworth has told of a girl who stayed in her old Vermont home while neighbors joined the westward movement.

Andrew Jackson, later to become President of the United States, had an exciting boyhood in the early days of the nation. It is told in *Andy Jackson, Boy Soldier*, by Augusta Stevenson.

[66]

# DIVISION TWO

*The
Nation Turns Its Face
Toward the West*

★

A pioneer family journeys toward a new home in the West.

## THE FRONTIER MOVES TOWARD THE PACIFIC

The story of the United States has been a tale of westward-moving people. From the time that the first settlers built homes and planted fields on the Atlantic coast to that day some two hundred years later when Americans reached the Pacific coast, people were forever turning toward the West. A pioneer is one who goes before and prepares the way for others. When you look at your map and think how great the distance is between the Atlantic and the Pacific, can you understand why America had many pioneers?

The last edge of settled country is called the *frontier*. In America the frontier moved from time to time as the waves of settlers pushed west. In very early days the frontier was at the tidewater, which was that point in the broad rivers of the Atlantic coast to which the ocean tide reached as it flowed inland.

Sturdy settlers soon pushed the frontier up to the foothills of the Appalachian Mountains. Here it remained for a few years, held by the mountains, but before the close of the Revolution the restless feet of Daniel Boone and other daring pioneers had taken the passes through the mountains to the rich lands beyond. Streams of settlers followed these men into Kentucky and Tennessee. When at the close of the Revolution the Northwest Territory became a part of the United States, it, too, quickly filled with American settlers anxious to build homes in the new region and to plant crops in its rich soil.

With the purchase of Louisiana a great new stretch of country again invited the daring and hardy to seek wealth and adventure. The frontier moved across the Mississippi to the broad prairies beyond. From there it made a long swing almost halfway across the continent to the Pacific coast. How settlers were drawn across the dry plains and high mountains by tales of gold and rich farming land is a story which you will read very soon. By the thousands they traveled the long, dusty trails to the West and quickly occupied the Pacific coast.

It was only when the rich western coast was well settled that people turned back toward the dusty plains and high mountains that earlier pioneers had crossed. America's last frontier was on these dry plains and in the mountain valleys.

Pioneers were of two kinds. The first men who pushed out into a new country might be called the trail-makers. These were strong, bold fellows who spent

[70]

most of their lives in the forests, where they hunted wild animals and traded with the Indians. When settlers wanted to go into new country these trader-hunters made excellent guides, for they knew every buffalo trail and Indian path. Because they did not like to live close to other people, the trail-makers usually pushed farther west when a region became thickly settled.

Following the traders and hunters were the men and women who went west to make new homes. With all their goods loaded on a flatboat, they could float down a river, or if they had to travel by land a covered wagon carried tools and perhaps a few pieces of furniture. At the end of the journey a rude little house was built and crops were planted, for a pioneer must provide for his own needs.

The next stories will tell you how the pioneers lived on some of these American frontiers.

**Following a pioneer family into Ohio.** — One spring day in 1818 a Pennsylvania farmer set out for Ohio. With his wife and three children he was going to settle on new land in the West. If you can imagine that you are able to follow this family on their journey, you may better understand some of the experiences of the pioneer.

The covered wagon which will carry them on the first part of the trip stands loaded before the door of their old farmhouse in eastern Pennsylvania. It contains those things which are hard to buy on the frontier. Most important of these are the tools, the guns, and

the gunpowder. There is food for the long journey and enough to last through the first few months in the new home. Flour, meal, bacon, salt, and a little sugar have been packed. A spinning wheel, an iron kettle, and a chest for clothing each finds a place in the wagon. Most of the furniture has had to be left behind because there is no room to carry it.

With the wagon loaded, the last goodbyes are said. Neighbors have gathered to see the family off. Many eyes are wet, for well do all these people know that dangers and long distances will soon separate this family from their friends in the old home.

The mother rides in the wagon, her baby in her arms and a small child on the seat with her. The father walks beside the horses. The nine-year-old boy with the help of his dog drives a cow along the road behind the wagon.

Days pass, each filled with weary hours of slow-moving travel over roads which are either rough or muddy at all times. Each night finds the travelers making camp. As the mother fries bacon and bakes biscuits by the heat of an open fire, the father feeds the horses and milks the cow, while a very tired little boy searches for firewood. Supper over, there is a short period of rest around the fire, but soon every member of the weary family is asleep.

Coming at last to Pittsburgh, the travelers meet a new problem. They must have a boat upon which to continue the journey. They might hire one, but that

[74]

would cost more than they can afford; so the father buys lumber and nails and builds a flatboat.

Upon this rough boxlike boat he loads not only his family and goods but his animals as well. Exciting days follow, for the Ohio River is full of dangers. Sand bars, logs buried in the river bed, and brush washed down by the spring rains all make flatboat travel very difficult.

In spite of these dangers the travelers arrive at Cincinnati eight days after leaving Pittsburgh. This is very rapid travel. With his journey ended the farmer is not yet through with his flatboat, for lumber and nails are scarce on the frontier. He carefully takes the boat apart, and thus has material for making many articles that will be needed in the new home.

The mother and children find shelter for a few days with a friendly family in Cincinnati while the father sets out to find a farm. He may choose the rich bottom land along the river which he will have to clear of trees, or he may go farther from the river where the land has little but grass growing on it.

The rich, black soil of the river bottom tempts this farmer. As he thinks of the great crops of corn, wheat, rye, and oats which this soil will grow, he decides to settle here, even though he and his family will probably have the ague each year. This disease, which causes the person suffering with it to shake violently, is common at certain seasons along the rivers.

When the farmer has found a piece of ground with

[75]

a good spring on it, he goes back to the town for his family. They set out at once for the new farm.

A house is the first need. The farmer cuts trees and prepares the logs for making a cabin. When enough are ready, people gather from far and near for a house-raising.

The men roll the logs to the place where the new house is to stand. They notch the great logs and lift them into place. With the help of many hands the walls rise quickly. The rafters of the roof are put in place and held by wooden pins. Today the men will cover the roof with bark, but as soon as the farmer can make them he will cut rough shingles from logs, and fasten these in place by laying small saplings across them. For the present the earth will form the only floor, but the mother is even now thinking of the time when a puncheon floor, made of split logs with the face smooth, will make her housekeeping easier.

[76]

The men are already splitting logs to make a puncheon door. When this is hung in place on its wooden hinges, it will be strong enough to protect the family from any Indian or animal that may threaten them. A shutter is made so that the window may be barred at night, but during the day it will stand open so that light may enter. When winter comes, oiled paper over the opening will keep out the cold and yet allow some light to come into the room.

With clay from the riverbank the boys fill the cracks between the logs and cover the inside of the wooden chimney. As the sun sinks in the west, the tired workers finish their tasks. A new home stands ready for another pioneer family.

The women have also been busy. At noon they fed the hungry workers, but now with the task of building completed they spread a frontier feast under the trees. A young hog has been roasted over an open fire. Corn-cakes, the first of the early summer vegetables, honey taken from the wild bees, and dried-apple pies are eagerly eaten by the tired men.

Merry talk goes on as the neighbors make this new family welcome. The men promise some of their precious seed corn to the new farmer, who may even yet have time to raise a crop before frost. The women advise their new neighbor about the best remedy for ague, give her garden seeds, and offer her their choicest quilt patterns. Men and women of the frontier are friendly folk.

As the weeks pass, the farmer and his wife work through every daylight hour. The nine-year-old boy has many tasks, and even the little five-year-old girl helps her mother in the cabin.

A clearing is made around the house. Other trees are "girdled" by having a ring of bark cut away around the trunk. Corn is planted between these, and as the branches die more and more sunlight reaches the little plants beneath. It is but a poor crop this first year, but next year, with these trees cut and corn planted in the spring, a great harvest can be gathered.

Within the cabin the farmer has built a bed by driving a large stick into the earthen floor and fastening poles from this corner post to the two walls. Saplings laced back and forth hold a tick filled with straw. This straw was the gift of a neighbor who last year grew wheat. A rough table, a bench, some three-legged stools, and a shelf along one wall have also been the work of the farmer. The places of honor are held by the chest and the spinning wheel which were brought from the old home.

The farmer's wife not only keeps her house, but she has made a "truck patch" in the clearing. Here pumpkins, squashes, melons, beans, peas, and corn are growing. With winter to prepare for, this busy woman is glad that she will have corn and pumpkins to dry. A neighbor has promised her apples which can be dried or boiled into apple butter. Honey from the wild bees is stored for winter use.

With cold days coming, this pioneer mother must think not only of food but of clothing as well. Since the family owns no sheep, her husband buys a fleece from a neighbor. Carefully the woman prepares the wool for spinning, cleaning it and rolling it into long, fluffy rolls with her wool cards. The whir of the great spinning wheel soon tells that thread is forming under her busy fingers.

A neighbor woman will weave the cloth on her loom in exchange for help given during the harvest season. The mother plans to have the woolen thread mixed with linen so that the cloth may be very strong as well as warm. Such cloth, called *linsey-woolsey*, will wear for years.

If the farmer can be lucky enough to kill a deer during the winter, the family may have not only meat but a skin as well. From this the housewife can make a hunting shirt for her husband and moccasins for the children.

Life is not all work, even in this busy pioneer home. A neighbor who has harvested a big corn crop invites everyone for miles around to a husking "bee." In the barn the merry company gathers around the great piles of corn, pulling off husks and joking as they work. When the last ear of corn is reached, there is a great shout, for now with the work done the dance can begin. The fiddlers take their places and strike up a gay tune. Quickly the young people form sets on the puncheon floor, four couples in each set. The voice of the caller calling the figures of the dance rises high above the noise of the crowd.

The older men talk of crops, religion, and political matters. The women hold sleeping babies or help

[80]

spread the supper, all the while exchanging neighborhood news. For the young people, however, the dance is the great event of the evening, and they swing through set after set to such calls as, "Balance and Swing," "Cast Off," "Right and Left," "Four Hands Around."

Not only a husking bee but a logrolling calls the neighbors together for both work and play. Even after a hard day's work spent in rolling together and burning felled trees, the men and boys must have a few foot races and wrestling matches to test their strength.

The family from the East have sadly missed the little church which it was their habit to attend each Sunday. Once during the summer a frontier preacher riding his circuit preached at the little log schoolhouse. Eagerly this father and mother listened to the good man's promise to return in the autumn. Now the word has come that the circuit rider will hold a camp meeting a few miles away from the settlement where the family lives. Work is put aside for a few days, the cow is left with a neighbor, the children are loaded into the wagon, and these pioneers are off for a week at the camp meeting.

Arriving at the camping ground, they quickly find a place for their wagon and start toward the great platform where the afternoon services are beginning. Their friend the circuit rider opens the service, but after two hours of preaching he yields his place to another man, who continues to preach until the shadows are growing long.

After a brief rest for supper the first preacher starts again, all the while pleading with the people to give up their old ways and act as Christians. As he preaches, he grows excited, pacing up and down the platform, shouting and beating his breast.

The people too become excited. Some begin to sing, while others shout. One man falls as if in a faint, another suddenly begins to dance, while a number are seized with the "jerks." This is a condition, brought on by excitement, in which the muscles of the body jerk and twitch. Men and women stream down the aisles to the mourners' bench, where those who are ready to announce themselves as changed men and women sit during such a service as this.

We leave our pioneers of the Ohio country here in the camp meeting. They have not only settled in a new home, but they have also taken their place in the work, the play, and the religious life of the neighborhood.

[82]

**The Southern planter moves west.** — When people were moving toward the West, the Southern planter as well as the Northern farmer often set out to find new land. There were two events which caused the planters to move west in large numbers. One of these was the invention of the cotton gin, and the other was the successful war which Andrew Jackson made against certain Indian tribes who lived in what was then the southwestern part of the United States.

In 1793 Eli Whitney, a young schoolteacher from Massachusetts, went to Georgia. He heard from the cotton planters there of the great difficulty which they had in separating the seed of the cotton from the lint. This work, which had to be done by hand, was so slow that even the quickest workers could separate only one or two pounds of lint from its three pounds of seed in a day. Because of the great amount of labor necessary for this work, the cost of producing cotton was very high. As a result cotton cloth was very little used.

Eli Whitney made up his mind to invent a machine which would separate the cotton seed from the lint. After a time he succeeded in making a very simple machine which performed this work. It was called the *cotton gin*.

[83]

As soon as the Southern planters learned how well this machine did its work, many gins were put in use. With the cost of producing the cotton lowered, much more of it was used. From early colonial times there had been some Negro slaves in America, but with the increase in the amount of cotton grown came a greatly increased need for slave labor in the cotton fields. The price of slaves became much higher than it had been before the cotton gin was invented.

Because they could get good prices for their cotton, the Southern planters grew it year after year on the same land. Cotton is a crop which soon wears out the soil. After some years of growing nothing but cotton a planter would find his plantation producing less and less. It was when this happened that the planter began to think of moving to new land farther west, where new soil would grow large crops.

For some years there was danger of Indian attacks in the new country to which the planters wanted to go. After Andrew Jackson defeated the Creek Indians, this danger was removed. Very shortly after this the Southern roads which led toward the West were crowded with planters and Negro slaves.

Perhaps you can catch a glimpse of a planter and his slaves as they make camp one night in 1828 on the "Federal Road" which runs from Athens, Georgia, to New Orleans. On his way to start a new plantation in Mississippi, this planter is a pioneer quite as much as was the Pennsylvania farmer who settled in Ohio.

[84]

The sun is dropping far down in the western sky as the first of the company comes into view. At the head of the procession rides the planter mounted on a splendid sorrel horse. A carriage following close behind the rider carries the planter's wife and children. Wagons loaded with furniture, tools, and supplies are next in the line. Here and there a brightly turbaned head or a little black face surrounded by many "pig-tail" braids tells that a Negro woman or child has found a place to ride on the loaded wagons.

Behind the wagons the Negro men and some of the younger women walk wearily. As they move they sing, their voices making a kind of low mournful wail. Near the end of the long line are a few Negro men who are chained together. These are field hands, rough fellows who sometimes run away. Their master is taking no chance of losing them while on this long journey.

A few white men on horseback are the last of the procession. It is their task to look after the Negroes and to direct their work.

Coming to an open field beside the road, the planter stops the line. As the slaves see that the wagons ahead of them are pulling into the field to make camp, their mournful wail changes to a higher and happier sound.

The camp for the night is quickly made. Each slave has his work to do, and with the desire for food and rest urging him on each works as well as he can. A

tent is set up at one side for the master and his family.
Campfires are lighted, and very soon the Negroes are
baking corn pone by the heat of the glowing coals and
frying bacon over the open fire.

With supper over, the drooping spirits of the slaves
rise. As they sit around the fire, many sing again.
Here and there a voice is raised in a song which tells
of the Negro's sorrow at being taken far from his old
plantation. Among the younger slaves are some who
look at this great journey as a gay adventure which
brings them a change from the round of plantation
work.

In his tent the planter and his wife talk of the new
home which they will make in Mississippi. They plan
to have a great white house, built as nearly as possible

[86]

like the one which they left behind in Georgia. They
expect much of the rich soil of this new state, where,
with the help of their slaves, they hope to grow great
quantities of cotton and perhaps a little corn.

Thus it was that pioneers of both the North and the
South carried their ways of living westward to the
frontier, which for a number of years lay between the
mountains and the Mississippi River.

## The Settlement of the Louisiana Territory

Some Americans had already entered Louisiana Territory before it was purchased by the United States. After the purchase the stories told about the region by Meriwether Lewis, William Clark, and other explorers caused more people to want to move there.

New settlers traveled west by riverboats and covered wagons, the latter being known as *prairie schooners*. In many ways the frontier that was created between the Mississippi River and the Rocky Mountains was like the earlier frontiers that lay east of the Mississippi. In the section where many trees grew people came to build log cabins and clear the land for farming, just as they had done at an earlier time in Ohio, Kentucky, and other states east of the river. In those parts of the Louisiana Territory which had both rich soil and warm climate the planters from the South came to start new plantations. In this way slaves were carried into Missouri and into all that part of the purchase which lay south of it.

The Louisiana Territory offered one new problem which settlers on earlier frontiers had not had to solve. Great prairies stretched over many parts of the new country. These had few or no trees, but were covered with tall, thick grass whose long roots reached deeply into the soil. How was the pioneer to build a house in this country, which was bare of trees? How could he plant crops where deep-rooted grass grew?

[88]

In solving these problems that they met on the prairies the pioneers who entered Iowa, Nebraska, and neighboring regions developed a kind of life suited to the place where they lived. If you will imagine that you are looking in on a neighborhood in western Iowa in the year 1840, you may learn something of how the farmers of the prairie states lived and worked in pioneer times.

**Pioneering on the prairies.** — On this day in early summer the far-stretching prairies seem to make a world of green and gold. The green grass waving gently in the wind stretches as far as the eye can see, save for a few squares of black where the farmers have plowed. Over this wide, green world the golden sunshine falls, warm and glowing. To a farmer who is slowly following his oxen back and forth, back and forth as they pull the plow through the tough sod formed by the deep-rooted prairie grass, this bright sunshine is welcome. As it falls warm on his back, it sets him dreaming.

Of what does the prairie farmer dream? He sees these acres of prairie covered with fields of grain. Corn, wheat, rye, and oats should do well in this soil which his plow is turning. He sees a big white house standing where his little "soddy" now is. Barns will be there too, giving shelter to the farm animals and housing the grain from the great harvest. He sees roads where now there is only a track worn in the prairie grass. These roads of his dreams lead to other farms, to schoolhouses, to churches, even to towns built on this wide prairie.

It is a dream such as this farmer has that gives each pioneer of the prairies courage to face the hard life before him. For instead of the big white house which he hopes to have sometime this farmer and his family live in a sod house. A sod barn shelters their oxen, a cow, and a half-dozen sheep. The track through the prairie grass leads to the homes of a few other farmers, who like this one live in sod houses. The town has had its beginning in a little settlement where one may buy flour, salt, calico, and a few other articles, and where twice a month one may go for the mail.

The sod house which is the home of the farmer plowing on the hill has been well built. Blocks of sod were cut from the prairie and piled one upon another to form the walls. Saplings were cut along a small river twenty miles away, and hauled across the prairie by the oxen. These were laid across the walls to form a support for the roof, which was made of more blocks of sod. The window and door show that the owner of this house is indeed a well-to-do man, for the window has glass panes and the door is made of smooth lumber. Inside, whitewash over the dirt walls, and a floor of wood indicate the very height of luxury in sod houses.

[90]

The farmer's wife gives thanks for her comfortable house whenever she visits one of her neighbors. This woman lives in what is little better than a cave, for the floor is four feet below the level of the ground. The sod walls rise a little above the ground. Across these walls saplings hold dried prairie grass, while over this a layer of earth has been scattered, to keep the grass in place. The window has no glass, and in winter when a blanket hangs before it to keep out the cold, the inside of the little "soddy" is pitch dark. The floor is the earth, made smooth and hard by the tramping of many feet.

In the settlement are some houses of logs, and others of logs and sod. In the latter the builder usually digs four or five feet into the earth, then raises log walls some four or five feet above. Poles put across the top hold a roof of sod. Such houses have doors of wood. The windows are usually covered with oiled paper, but sometimes they have glass in them instead. The logs for these houses, like the saplings used in the sod houses, have been hauled from the river. For a half-mile or so on each side of this small stream there is a heavy growth of trees.

In the little settlement stands a small schoolhouse built of sod and logs. To this the children of the countryside who can be spared from work in the fields come for three months in the summer. School is sometimes held during other seasons, but winters are very cold, and when snow lies deep on these Iowa prairies it is not possible for the children to get to school.

Inside the schoolhouse are benches made by splitting logs into two pieces. Holes bored in the rounded side have short sticks stuck into them to make the legs of the bench. Along the wall are a few higher benches made in the same way. These are the only desks which the pupils have. The one real desk is for the teacher.

At one end of the room is a big fireplace, at the other end the door. The windows have no covering now, but sometimes when the schoolhouse is used at colder seasons they are covered with greased paper. The floor of beaten earth is sprinkled now and then with water. The bare feet of the boys and girls keep it patted smooth and hard.

The schoolmaster "boards round" with the parents of the pupils. He takes his pay in such things as the farmers have — corn, hams, wool, and the like. At the village store he is able to trade these for other articles which he needs.

A hickory stick hangs on the wall to remind the children of what may happen to mischief makers. The teacher cuts pens from goose quills and sets writing copies on paper for the older children. The younger ones write on their slates. The pupils read from whatever books their parents have been able to find at home for them. There are a few *New England Primers*, while several children boast of owning Webster's "Blue Back" spelling book. The teacher sets examples, most of which are very long and hard, from his

own sum book. The pupils then try to solve these
on their slates.

If you will look in on this little schoolhouse some
evening, you may find it the scene of a neighborhood
gathering. The schoolmaster is also a singing master,
and here he holds singing school. By the light of
candles stuck between the logs he leads in singing
hymns or popular songs.

Here too the people sometimes gather for a spelling match. On this occasion two people choose sides and the schoolmaster gives out the words. When a person misses, he takes his seat. As fewer and fewer people are left standing, interest runs high. Great honor belongs to the man or woman who can "spell down" everyone else in the neighborhood.

[95]

## THE SPANISH SOUTHWEST BECOMES AMERICAN

**Texas wins independence.** — The Spanish explorers laid claim not only to Mexico but to all the land that is now the southwestern part of the United States. Scattered settlements were made over this vast territory. In 1821 Mexico engaged in a revolution against Spain and won its independence. Spanish North America thus became Mexican territory.

Even before Mexico became an independent country, Americans had shown a great interest in Texas, which was a part of the old Spanish territory. Many wanted to go there to settle. At about the same time that the Mexican Revolution began, Stephen F. Austin led the first organized party of settlers into Texas. He took them to land which a few years before had been granted to his father.

Other Americans followed, until Texas was dotted with their settlements. These people very naturally favored a plan of government in Texas like that which they had known in the United States. They were willing to obtain this kind of government by peaceful means if Mexico would grant them the right that they asked, but many Texans were not opposed to a show of force if this seemed necessary to gain their ends.

[96]

All the time Americans at home were watching events in Texas with keen interest. That many of them wished to see Texas a part of the United States there can be no doubt. Andrew Jackson, who was President between 1828 and 1836, certainly desired this land, but he was wise enough to know that to take it would bring on a war with Mexico. Various offers of the United States to purchase Texas were hotly refused by the Mexicans.

By 1835 the Texans were in open rebellion against the Mexican government. Sam Houston was chosen to command the Texan army. Fighting occurred at several points. One of the most terrible battles was fought at San Antonio, where a small party of Texans held an old Spanish mission called the *Alamo*. A large Mexican army under General Santa Anna demanded their surrender.

Let the words of William B. Travis, the commander of the Texan forces, show you what his reply was. In a letter to his fellow Texans asking that aid be sent him he wrote, "I am besieged by a thousand or more of the Mexicans under Santa Anna. I have sustained a continued bombardment and cannonade for twenty-four hours and have not lost a man. The enemy has demanded a surrender, otherwise the garrison are to be put to the sword if the fort is taken. I have answered the demand with a cannon shot and our flag still waves proudly from the walls. I shall never surrender or retreat."

Sam Houston led a party of soldiers to the rescue, but they arrived too late. One hundred eighty-eight Texans fought to the death against a Mexican army that outnumbered them sixteen to one. Before the battle began Santa Anna said to one of his generals, "You know that in this war there are no prisoners." The trumpets blew the signal, "No quarter." The Alamo ran red with blood, and ever after the rallying cry of Texas soldiers was to be "Remember the Alamo."

The Texans now declared themselves to be independent of Mexico. In the United States there was a

[98]

wave of popular sympathy for the Texans, but the Government took no direct action in the matter. Sam Houston not only defeated the Mexicans but took Santa Anna a prisoner.

In their first election the people of Texas chose Sam Houston as their president, and at the same time they expressed a desire to become a part of the United States. While Andrew Jackson and many other Americans desired this also, the Government delayed taking the necessary steps, although in 1837 the United States did recognize Texas as an independent nation.

**The Texas question brings war with Mexico.** — For nearly ten years the United States struggled with the problem of whether or not to annex Texas. Since slaves were held by Texans, some people favored annexing the country because it would add a slave state. Other people opposed the annexation because they did not want more slave states. Many people feared, and very rightly, that annexation would bring a war with Mexico. Finally, on March 1, 1845, the United States invited Texas to become a state of the Union. In July Texas accepted this invitation.

A dispute now followed regarding the boundary line between Texas and Mexico. Although this dispute was not yet settled, President James K. Polk ordered American soldiers under General Zachary Taylor into Texas. While these troops were camped near the Rio Grande, they had a small fight with a party of Mexican soldiers. President Polk seized upon this as an excuse for going to war. He sent a message to Congress on May 11, 1846, asking that war be declared against Mexico. Congress at once did as he asked.

Perhaps the fact that Mexico held vast stretches of land which separated the United States from the Pacific Ocean had much to do with President Polk's desire for war. He had already dreamed of an America which stretched across the continent to the western ocean.

[100]

Two American generals won fame for themselves in the Mexican War. Zachary Taylor, known as "Old Rough and Ready," was a poor general but a splendid fighter. He often made mistakes in planning battles, but he was never found lacking in the courage to fight them. At Monterrey he led his soldiers into the Mexican city after three days of terrible hand-to-hand fighting.

Going on to Buena Vista, Taylor made a mistake in planning the battle but his army was saved from defeat by the daring of officers and men. This cool courage of the Americans was too much for the Mexicans, who retreated in the night. Thereafter General Taylor was thought of as the "Hero of Buena Vista."

General Winfield Scott was given the command of an army which landed at Veracruz and made its way to Mexico City, the capital. On this march Scott's army not only had to fight the Mexicans several times, but men, horses, guns, and supplies had to be moved across the mountains. More than once by the use of ropes the Americans drew cannon up steep mountainsides where it seemed impossible to take guns.

The most famous of the attacks made by Scott's army was the storming of Chapultepec. This steep hill just outside of Mexico City had on its top an old palace which was held by a strong company of Mexican soldiers. Scott's army stormed the heights in a bloody battle. That night the American flag waved on Chapultepec.

General Scott now pushed on into the capital. The war was nearing its end. The talk about the terms of peace occupied several months. On February 2, 1848, a treaty of peace was signed. By its terms Mexico lost an empire, and the United States gained another vast stretch of territory. President Polk's dream of a country reaching to the Pacific was realized, but only at the price of Mexican hatred. For years these people felt that they had been unfairly treated.

Except for a small part of southern Arizona which was purchased from Mexico six years later (the Gadsden Purchase), the treaty established the boundary line of southwestern United States as it is today. Out of the territory which this country secured as the result of the Mexican War were later made the states of California, New Mexico, Arizona, Utah, Nevada, and part of Colorado.

**Traders follow the Santa Fe Trail.** — While the Spanish still held an empire in North America, some men had made the long trip from Santa Fe, New Mexico, to Missouri. Their journey set people to thinking of the trade which might be carried on between these two places. However, it was not until after Mexico had become an independent nation that the business was well established. When New Mexico became American territory at the close of the Mexican War, trade over the trail increased. It continued to be important until 1880, when a railroad took the place of the old wagon trail.

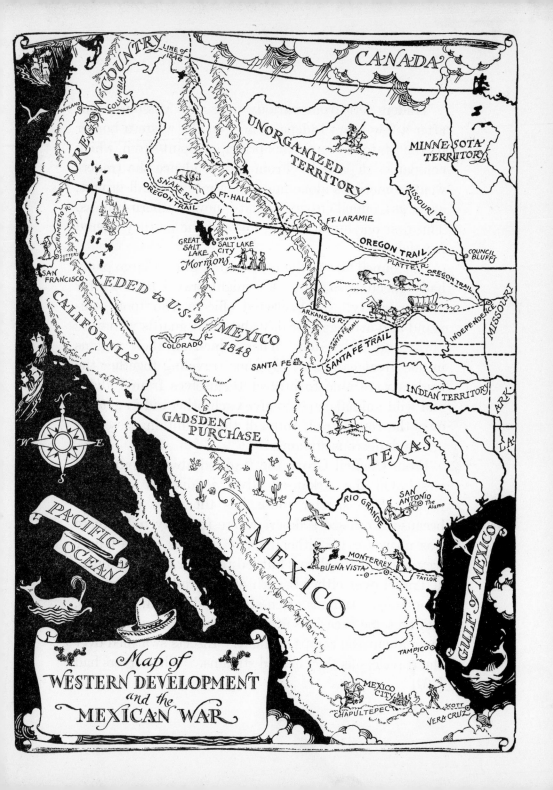

Map of
WESTERN DEVELOPMENT
and the
MEXICAN WAR

Traders left from various towns in Missouri; but after a few years Independence, on the western border of the state, became the principal point from which companies departed. From Independence the traders went, sometimes alone and sometimes in small groups, as far as Council Grove in what is now southern Kansas. This first one hundred fifty miles of the journey offered few dangers.

At Council Grove the men waited until a large party had collected, so that they might travel together for greater safety. They elected officers who took command and arranged for day and night guards who were always on the watch. They joined all their wagons in one great caravan. By thus traveling together the traders were able to protect themselves from Indians and wild animals, and to give each other aid in getting over the rough trail, through the mountain passes, or across dangerous streams.

From Council Grove the trail led always south and west. On the Arkansas River it divided into two routes. The shorter route was the more dangerous because it crossed a desert where for sixty miles there was no water for either men or animals. The longer way avoided the desert but led through the mountains.

Travel over either branch of the trail was hard and dangerous. Indians often stole goods, oxen, or mules, and on some occasions attacked the caravans. Wolves hung about the camps at night. Insects swarmed over the travelers as they neared streams. When rivers had

[104]

to be crossed, wagons sank deep into the mud. When the trail led through the desert, men sometimes suffered terribly from thirst.

In spite of all these dangers and hardships the trail drew men. Not only did it hold the golden promise of profits, but it led to Santa Fe. This old city which for so many years had known the marching feet of Spanish explorers and soldiers had a strange charm for Americans. Its people were usually poor and were often a wild, rough lot, but the very name Santa Fe suggested glory and adventure.

The great covered wagons had to be loaded with precious goods, for space could not be used to carry cheap articles. Among the most prized of such goods were woolen, cotton, and silk cloth, shawls, looking glasses, and various articles made of metal.

Had you lived in the years between 1820 and 1880, you would most certainly have wanted to make a trip over the Santa Fe Trail. Suppose that you turn back the pages of time and try to follow the traders as they make the long, hard journey from Independence to Santa Fe.

The year is 1831. The time is early spring. Wagons, some of them drawn by oxen and others by mules, are leaving Independence today in groups of two or three. From eight to twelve beasts are required to pull each wagon.

Independence is a busy place. The goods which have been brought up the Missouri River by boat are

[105]

packed for the journey. For each man in the party food is carefully measured — fifty pounds of flour, fifty pounds of bacon, ten pounds of coffee, twenty pounds of sugar, and some salt. To this will be added fresh meat killed along the trail. Guns and gunpowder, tools with which to mend broken wagons and harness, and a blanket for each man in the company must all be stored away in the wagons. Workmen examine harness and wagons to make sure that they are in good condition. Blacksmiths shoe the mules. All is hustle and bustle at this season in the little Missouri town.

As each wagon is made ready it swings out upon the trail, headed for Santa Fe more than seven hundred miles away. Arriving at Council Grove, the men make themselves comfortable in their camps and feed the animals well against the long, hard trip. Each day brings more wagons to the little settlement. The traders choose officers and make ready for the journey.

One morning from the camp of the man who has been chosen captain comes a call, "Catch up! Catch up!" At once the camps are in a stir. Drivers shout as they run to harness the mules and yoke the oxen. Each man wants to be the first one ready to leave.

"All's set!" cries one driver, who, quicker than the others, has his mules harnessed. From other throats the same cry echoes again and again, "All's set!" "All's set!"

The captain's next command comes quickly, as he

shouts "Stretch out!" Whips crack, wagons squeak, hoofs tramp as the mules and oxen are headed toward the trail.

Last of all comes the marching order, "Fall in!" The wagons form into a long line, which begins to work its way along the trail, moving slowly toward the Southwest.

Days grow into weeks. The wagons creak along the dusty track during the day. With the coming of night camp is made. Wagons are pulled into a circle. Animals are hobbled with ropes tied between their forelegs and turned on the plains to graze. Watchmen are ever on guard to protect men and animals from prowling Indians or wild beasts.

Fires are lighted, and supper is cooked. Afterward around the glowing coals old travelers on the trail spin yarns for the wonder of the newcomers. Across the night air sometimes comes the clear shrill whistle which is the signal of a certain tribe of plains Indians. Again it is the long, wailing note of the prairie wolf which sends chills along the spines of the men.

Morning always brings new bustle as the cry "Catch up!" rings out. Soon the forty wagons are again following the trail. Through the buffalo country, across the Arkansas River, over mountain passes, and across drier and drier plateaus they drive on, until one day an excited shout is heard far up at the head of the line. The men who are leading the caravan have sighted Sante Fe.

There is a pause while each man does what he can to clean himself up for the entrance to the city. Each driver fastens a new "cracker" to the lash of his whip, for when he drives through the streets he hopes to outdo all his fellows in the way he swings and cracks this whip.

On into the old Spanish city they move, as the people flock into the streets shouting, "The Americans! The Americans! The caravan is entering!" Black-eyed girls, fat mothers with babies wrapped in their shawls, Indians, merchants, soldiers — all pour into the streets to welcome the men from the North.

When the government taxes have been paid by the traders, buying and selling begin. Some Americans sell their entire load of goods to one merchant. Others set up their own stores and sell in small amounts.

[108]

A few push on from here into Mexico, where prices are better. Santa Fe hums with excitement, for these American traders not only bring rare goods, but they also bring almost the only news which these people receive from the outside world. On the night when the traders come in, Santa Fe holds a merrymaking.

**The Mormons settle in Utah.** — In the spring of 1847 a company of one hundred forty-eight men and women traveled across the plains and mountains to the shores of Great Salt Lake. They found nothing growing on those shores but sagebrush and a few sunflowers. The earth was dry and hard. There were no trees for miles. Millions of black crickets overran the land. Yet in spite of these discouraging conditions the newcomers decided to settle around the lake.

In order to understand why these people, who were called *Mormons*, were willing to move to such a barren

land you must hear the story of their earlier troubles. They were members of a church which had been started in New York about twenty years before this trip was made to Great Salt Lake. Almost from the beginning the Mormons had difficulties with their neighbors who did not belong to their church. These neighbors objected very strongly to some of their beliefs.

Searching for a place where they could live and worship as they pleased, the Mormons first moved to Ohio. However, they had so much trouble with other people that they moved on to Missouri. Here they again had quarrels with their neighbors, which led them once more to seek new homes.

The next move was to Illinois, where many of the Mormons became very prosperous. Trouble once more arose, however, and the leader of the church was killed. The new leader, Brigham Young, determined to take his people far into the wilderness. He hoped that they might find a refuge beyond the borders of the United States.

It was Brigham Young who led the little band west in 1847. Having decided to settle in the region around Great Salt Lake, Young returned for other members of his church.

During the next few years several thousand Mormons made the long trip west. They had left behind them forever their rich fields and comfortable houses in Illinois. With only such articles as they could carry in covered wagons and such animals as they could

[110]

drive before them, they set out for the barren lands in the West.

No American pioneers faced greater hardships, but toil brought its reward. Irrigation ditches were dug and water was turned into them. The fields were plowed and planted. Soon great crops of flax, hemp, sugar beets, and wheat were growing where only sage-brush had been before. Houses, barns, and a temple were built. Streets were laid out in the little settlement which was presently to grow into Salt Lake City. Skilled workmen among the Mormons tanned leather, made pottery and nails, took sugar from the sugar beets, manufactured gunpowder, and carried on many other industries.

With the close of the Mexican War the Mormons found themselves again in American territory, but this time they were not disturbed. The region where they had settled became the territory and later the state of Utah.

The Mormon pioneers were men and women of courage. By hard work they turned a barren region into a place of cultivated farms and busy towns.

**Early interest in the Pacific Northwest.** — The region lying along the Pacific coast north of California was visited in early days by people of several lands. In 1776 an English explorer set out on a long voyage, during which he visited this North Pacific coast. The Indians brought otter skins to the ship and traded them to the sailors for various small articles. The sailors used these skins for cloaks and bed coverings. Later the ship crossed the Pacific and touched at a port in China. To the great surprise of the sailors the Chinese were eager to secure the otter skins. A fur that a sailor had obtained by trading an article worth only a few pennies could be sold for a hundred dollars in the Chinese market.

Naturally when this news spread, the region along the North Pacific coast had a new interest to people. Very soon trading companies were formed in America. Ships sailed from Boston and other North Atlantic ports loaded with goods which the Indians would take in exchange for furs. After making the long journey around South America and northward along the Pacific coast the ships visited villages where the sailors traded with the Indians.

When a shipload of furs was obtained, the vessel set out for China, where the furs were sold and the vessel loaded with silks, fine shawls, carved wood, and other

[112]

Chinese goods. Then off the ship sailed for the Atlantic coast. Such trade often brought great riches to the men who engaged in it.

The British were also eager for a share in the rich fur trade of this northwest country. The Hudson's Bay Company built a fort and trading post there and for many years carried on a very good business in fur trading.

With both the United States and Great Britain claiming rights in the same region, it was only to be expected that a boundary dispute should follow. In 1818 it was agreed between the two nations that they should have equal rights of settlement and trade in Oregon. This name was used to refer to all the region which is now included in the states of Oregon, Washington, Idaho, and a small part of Montana. The plan of joint occupation of Oregon was renewed nine years later, and continued in operation until 1846, when the present boundary line was fixed between the United States and Canada.

**Americans take the trail for Oregon.** — Once more America had heard the call of a new frontier. Soon the restless feet of pioneers were beating a wide, dusty trail across the country as men and women set out for faraway Oregon.

From western Missouri the travelers followed the Santa Fe Trail for a short distance, then turned north and west toward the Platte River. Going through the valley of the Platte, the pioneers came to Fort Laramie,

[113]

which stood at the entrance to the mountains. After a difficult journey across what is now Wyoming, they reached Fort Hall. Just beyond this point the trail divided, one part going south and west toward California. The pioneers bound for Oregon turned northwest, following the valley of the Snake River. This led them to the Columbia. With the last mountains behind them the new settlers found themselves in a land where rolling valleys, rich soil, and pleasant climate promised great harvests.

In 1831 four Indians left their homes in the Northwest and traveled over this long trail to St. Louis. There they went to see General William Clark, who years before had explored their country. They told General Clark that some Christian Indians had visited their tribes and told them of the Christian religion. These red men had made the long journey to St. Louis to ask for white teachers who would tell them more about the new religion.

This appeal of the Indians stirred the churches of America to action. Missionaries were sent to Oregon, the first party going out in 1833. One of the best known of these early missionary pioneers was Dr. Marcus Whitman. This young man soon returned to the East for more supplies and helpers. While there he married Narcissa Prestiss, and in 1836 the bride set out with her husband for Oregon. Another couple traveled with the Whitmans. These two young wives were the first women who ever made the long journey over the Oregon Trail.

Not only Protestant but Catholic missionaries as well worked among the Indians of the Northwest. The most famous of the Catholics was Father De Smet, a Jesuit priest, who went to Oregon in 1840. When he needed money for mission buildings, Father De Smet appealed to the people of New Orleans, who gave generously. With these and other funds which he secured the good priest built six mission stations in Oregon.

These missionaries were not only themselves pioneers, but the story of their work in Oregon made other people think of going to the new region. All over the United States this interest spread rapidly. "On to Oregon" became the rallying cry of the pioneers, who set out from all parts of the country.

By 1847 the westward movement over the Oregon Trail was in full swing. Between four and five thousand people left Missouri that year for Oregon. Can

[115]

you imagine yourself to be traveling for one day with a party of pioneers who have reached the Platte River Valley?

At four o'clock in the morning the sleeping camp is wakened by the sound of rifle shots. The guards who have been on watch through the night are rousing the pioneers for a new day's work. Almost at once people begin to stir. Women and children pour out of the covered wagons where they have slept, while the men appear outside their tents. The smoke from the fires rises on the morning air.

While the women are preparing breakfast, the men go out to get the horses, cows, and oxen which have been grazing beside the trail. They form a circle around the animals and drive them slowly toward the camp.

[116]

A few animals have been tied to stakes driven in the ground, while some have had their legs hobbled. Those which usually graze without wandering far away have been left free. However, guards have not only watched through the night to prevent the animals from wandering off, but have kept a sharp lookout for Indians as well.

As the animals are brought into the camp, drivers begin harnessing their horses or yoking their oxen. Everyone is in a hurry now, for breakfast must be eaten, tents taken down, wagons packed, and the party ready to move when the bugle blows at seven o'clock.

Here and there a woman is milking a cow. These pioneer mothers know that fresh milk will do much to keep their children well and strong through the long, hard months on the trail. One woman who last night churned some butter is packing it now in a bag of flour where it will be somewhat protected from the heat of the day. Her neighbor has a precious store of eggs put away in a bag of flour. Many of the women have brought bags filled with dried apples, peaches, and pumpkin. These women have heard of the hardships of earlier travelers who failed to provide any food beyond meal, flour, and meat. They have planned more wisely for their own journey.

At seven o'clock the bugle blows its call. The sixty wagons fall into line in fifteen smaller companies, four wagons in each company. The company which leads today will fall in at the rear tomorrow. At the head

rides the guide who is leading the party. As the
caravan moves off along the trail, a party of young men
set out across the plains for a buffalo hunt. They will
join the wagons at the evening camp.

The summer day passes, with a brief stop at noon.
Sunset finds the caravan at another camping ground.
The guide, who knows the trail well, has gone ahead
and selected the spot. As the wagons come up he
directs the drivers so that they form a great circle.
When the animals are unhitched, the tongue of each
wagon is fastened to the wagon just ahead, while heavy
ox chains are also stretched from wagon to wagon.

Inside this circle the tents are pitched and the camp-fires made.  Upon occasions when Indians threaten, the animals are sometimes driven inside as well.

All in camp are busy.  A group of women hurry down to the near-by river to wash some clothes before dark   Other women set up their sheet-iron stoves or build fires on the ground, and begin to cook supper. The hunters have returned with enough fresh buffalo meat for the whole company.  Soon the air is filled with the delicious odor of broiling steaks.

With supper finished, groups of friends gather around the campfires.  Some speak of the abundant crops which they expect to raise in Oregon.  Others talk a bit sadly of the old home which they have left behind. One jolly young chap is strumming a banjo while his friends sing in lusty voices.

The guide who has been over this trail many times before tells tales of dangers through which he has led other parties.  He speaks of the cholera, a terrible sickness which has sent hundreds of people to lonely graves beside the trail.  He recalls the piles of goods left by the early travelers who had overloaded their wagons.  He tells of the hardships of the trail when the Platte rises in flood, or when summer heat destroys grass and dries up water.

As they listen to these tales of hardship and danger some of the people feel their hearts sinking.  However, to most of the pioneers Oregon still remains the land of promise.

## THE LURE OF GOLD DRAWS MEN TO CALIFORNIA

**A glimpse of California in 1848.** — In the valley of the Sacramento River lies a great ranch. Each year its broad acres yield rich harvests of grain and fruit. Grapevines brought from Europe grow on the hills. Thousands of cattle produce milk, cheese, meat, and hides. Fine horses graze in the meadows.

From his beautiful house built among giant shade trees John Sutter looks out across his ranch and thinks of the many adventures which life has brought him. Born in Switzerland, he came to America and lived for a time in the United States, but tales of the West drew him at last to California. Here he received from the Mexican government a grant of land which bore rich harvests. With his profits he bought more acres. Now, with the Mexican war at an end, California has become a part of the United States, and John Sutter finds himself the largest landowner in all America.

Barns, houses, granaries, and all manner of workshops dot the great ranch. One thing is lacking, however, and this the owner determines to have. A sawmill is needed. John Sutter engages James W. Marshall to build the mill. Marshall takes a party of workmen and goes up into the mountains some distance from the ranch house. There one January day Marshall notices something shining in the bottom of the ditch which forms the millrace. Reaching down through a foot or so of clear water, he picks up a couple of small pieces of yellow metal.  Neither is as large as a pea.

Turning these tiny bits over in his hand, James Marshall feels his heart pounding wildly against his ribs.  Can this be gold?  His knees tremble at the very thought!  But Marshall has much common sense.  He concludes that if this is gold it can only be a few stray grains.  Upon returning to camp he tells the men of his find.  They share his excitement but agree with him that there is little chance of securing more gold.

However, as the days pass the men watch the bed of the stream, and to their joy they do find other small bits of the shining stuff.  Marshall decides to carry the news to Sutter.

As he rides down the mountain to the ranch house, the man thinks more and more about those few ounces of metal in his pocket.  His excitement grows so that he fairly bursts into the room where Sutter sits writing.

Behind locked doors the two examine the yellow grains.  How can they make sure whether or not this is really gold?  Sutter turns to his encyclopedia, where he finds an article on gold.  Reading this suggests to them that they may weigh the metal and test it with acid.  Breathless moments of waiting are ended when Sutter turns to Marshall with the words, "You have found pure gold."

After their first excitement passes, the two men agree that the matter must be kept secret for a few weeks

[122]

until the sawmill is finished. The workmen promise to say nothing of the matter, but such news is not easily kept.

The wife of one of the men is at the camp acting as cook. When a man comes one day with a load of supplies, she tells him the story and gives him a few grains of gold to prove it. Hurrying back, the driver spreads the story among all the people who work on the ranch. Another day passes, and a man appears on the streets of San Francisco bearing a bottle containing a few yellow grains, and shouting, "Gold! Gold! Gold from the American River!"

Excitement seizes people like a madness. John Sutter's workmen rush for the mountains, leaving cows unmilked, sheep without shepherds, fields with no one to tend them. Even his house servants are up and away to the hills. One thought possesses them all — they must find gold.

Clerks from the stores in the towns leave their counters. Sailors desert the ships as they come into port. The little newspaper in San Francisco cannot be published because there is no one to write the news and set the type. Farmers leave their fields and appear at Sutter's ranch with pick, shovel, and pan. From far and wide as the news spreads men pour into the valley and up the mountain streams — all searching for the precious metal.

These men pay no attention to Sutter's rights as a landowner. They "squat" on his land and use whatever they want of his property. He must not only see his fields go without crops for lack of workers, but he has to watch them pass into the hands of other men who take them for their own. Because gold has been found on his ranch, the largest landowner in America becomes himself a poor and broken man. What a strange trick life played on John Sutter!

**The coming of the forty-niners.** — The news of the discovery of gold in California reached other parts of the country within a few months. People in distant places acted much like the Californians when they first heard of the discovery. In order to go west, men left farms, stores, factories, offices, banks, schoolrooms, and various other places where they were employed. In such a great rush as this there were men of all sorts — rich and poor, good and bad, old and young, but they had one thing in common. All wanted to find gold.

During the year of 1849 this westward rush was very large. Men who went to California at that time are often called "the forty-niners." People continued for several years to go in search of gold, and this caused such rapid increase in the population that California became a state of the Union in 1850.

When great numbers of people suddenly wanted to go to California all at one time, it was not surprising that they had difficulty in finding ways to travel. There were three choices as to routes. The safest and usually the most comfortable way to go was by

ship around South America, but this was also the longest and most costly route. A shorter but less sure way was by Panama. Travelers took ship to the Atlantic side of the narrow neck of land which joined North and South America. There they took their own chances on getting across the country to the Pacific coast, where in time a ship would probably stop for passengers. The way most often used to reach California was to cross the western part of the continent by wagon.

Overland routes varied. Some people first went south to the Mexican border and then turned west. Others took the Santa Fe Trail for the first part of the journey. By far the largest number, however, used the Oregon Trail, turning south at Fort Hall and crossing Utah and Nevada before entering California.

The experiences of the gold seekers on the overland trails were not very different from those met by other travelers. People rushing west to hunt for gold were always in a hurry, and this caused some parties to set out without proper guides and led others to attempt travel over dangerous short cuts. Cholera broke out and caused the death of hundreds.

When the gold hunter reached California, he at once looked for a place on some mountain stream. In the beginning only placer mining was used. This means that the gold was found by washing the sand and gravel taken from the bed of a stream.

At first the men simply used pans, each man working alone. Later the miners made what they called cradles. After one of these cradles was filled with "pay dirt," the owner rocked it to and fro with one hand while he poured water through it with the other. The sand and soil washed out and the grains of gold caught in the bottom of the cradle. After men began to work

in groups, they used what was called the "long tom." This box was set on the slant, with water pouring over the pay dirt which the men piled in with shovels. Pan, cradle, and long tom all required water for washing the dirt away from the grains of gold.

Fortune smiled upon a few of the gold seekers, but many were disappointed. Men working side by side had very different luck. One time two friends worked next to each other for a week. During that time one found an ounce of gold worth about twenty dollars, while the other found six thousand dollars' worth. Some men chased a Negro away from the little valley where they were panning. They told him to try the top of a near-by hill — a place where he was not likely to find gold. He did, and took out metal to the value of four thousand dollars.

As soon as the gold was discovered in California, prices went sky high. Flour and bacon each cost a dollar or more a pound. Eggs, when they could be had at all, came at a dollar each. Lumber enough to build even a small cabin cost a thousand dollars. Workmen who hired out often made more than the gold seekers. A cook deserting from a ship coming into port could be sure of getting five to six hundred dollars a month for frying bacon and cooking flapjacks. The few men who after the first excitement returned to work on farms and in mills received at least ten dollars a day.

Towns grew into cities almost overnight. In 1847 San Francisco was a prosperous little town with a good harbor. When the magic word "gold" was spoken, San Francisco was suddenly deserted as its people ran away to the mines. But only for a little while did this continue, for the wiser realized that greater fortunes could be made by selling goods to the miners than by hunting gold. By 1849 the city was growing as fast as men could build rude houses or set up tents. Time and again fire swept over great areas, but each time new and better buildings rose to take the place of the old ones.

The miners were mostly honest men, but where easy money is to be had men and women of bad character always gather. So it was in California. Every camp and town had gamblers, thieves, and other people who were only waiting for the chance to get hold of the miners' gold. These bad citizens sometimes gained control of the government of a city, and when this happened honest men had little chance to get their rights.

In San Francisco things became so bad that in 1851 and again five years later groups of honest citizens took matters into their own hands. Upon each occasion the group of citizens, who called themselves a Vigilance Committee, arrested some well-known lawbreakers, gave them a fair trial, and upon finding them guilty hanged them at once. Such quick justice showed the bad people that they could not control California.

Let us take a walk through San Francisco in April, 1850. On every side are tents and houses of thin

[129]

boards.  These serve either as homes or as places of
business, depending upon their owner's need.

Along the water front several ships lie at anchor.
Here men are rapidly loading goods into wagons for
the haul to the stores of the city.  Walking around the
plaza, or public square, we see all manner of things.
In one of the best buildings in the city is a huge gambling house.  Strains of music float through its open
[130]

doors, and men and women can be seen crowding around its tables.

The saloons are also busy places. The miners fresh from the "diggings" pass much of their hard-won gold across the bars in exchange for drinks of liquor.

Here are a group of men newly arrived who need supplies. In one of the stores each man buys himself a pick, a shovel, a pan, and a pack of food. With the bed rolls which they have used on shipboard they are ready to face life in the open.

A pawnshop is doing a good business. Watches, rings, guns, coats, and boots are only a few of the articles that are piled about on tables and shelves. Here men come when bad luck at the diggings or gambling table has taken all their gold and money.

On one side of the plaza "Father" Taylor has mounted a bench in front of a big gambling house. As he sings a hymn, men pour out of doors along the street. By the time he has begun to preach, a huge crowd has gathered. Here in the midst of the hurry and bustle men listen for an hour to this fiery Methodist preacher who is calling on them to live better lives.

A group of young fellows are standing on the street in front of the bunkhouse where they have found sleeping quarters for the night — ten men to a room. On their way to the diggings for the first time they are so sure of their luck that they are singing in gay young voices,

"Oh! Susanna,
Oh don't you cry for me,
For I'm off to California
With my washbowl on my knee."

## A Word Game

Here are more history terms to add to your list. Be sure that you understand the meaning of each one before you write it in your notebook.

*annex*                   *independence*                   *boundary dispute*
*westward movement*   *vigilance committee*       *joint occupation*

Here are some words which you will need to know. Try to learn the meaning from the way the word is used in the story. If you cannot do this, look up the word in the word list at the back of the book.

| | | |
|---|---|---|
| buffalo | puncheon | plantation |
| flatboat | linsey-woolsey | prairie |
| ague | husk | sod |
| besieged | circuit rider | slate |
| bombardment | caravan | hobbled |
| cannonade | missionary | squat |
| surrender | rallying cry | cholera |
| sapling | cotton gin | flapjack |

## A Map Study

On page 103 is a map which shows the western part of the United States as this region was in pioneer times. On this map locate Texas and the area obtained from Mexico as a result of the Mexican War.   Locate the Gadsden Purchase.

Trace the routes of the Oregon and the Santa Fe Trails. Why did both of these trails start from western Missouri? What advantage did that give to the towns in this area?

What natural difficulties did the pioneers traveling these trails have to overcome?

On a map of the United States that has a scale of miles, measure roughly the distance of each of these two trails.

The map in your text has tiny pictures on it.   Explain the meaning of each of these pictures.   How are mountains shown?   What type of mark shows trails?

### A Time Table

The westward movement spread over many years of time. Below are listed some important events of that movement, but they are not listed in the order in which they occurred. Rewrite the list putting them in order from the earliest to the latest.   After each event write the date when it occurred.

To find some dates you will have to look back in earlier chapters.   When your list is completed, look at it to see whether one event may have brought about another.

The Louisiana purchase
The settlement of Marietta
The settlement of Harrodsburg
The Mexican War
The Lewis and Clark expedition
The entrance of Texas into the Union
The discovery of gold in California
The settlement on the Watauga
The invention of the cotton gin
The settlement of Mormons in Utah
The settlement of Oregon boundary dispute
The settlement of Boonesborough

## Some Things to Do

1. There were many well-known pioneers about whom very little has been told in this book. You may find interesting stories about some of them in your library. Choose one man, read about his deeds, and make a talk to your classmates about him. Among these pioneers were Daniel Boone, James Harrod, James Robertson, John C. Frémont, Kit Carson, Zebulon Pike, and Davy Crockett.

2. Collect pictures showing pioneer scenes. Place some of the best of these on the bulletin board with a title written under each.

3. There are old people still living who had pioneer experiences when they were young. Perhaps you can invite such a person to tell stories of his early days to your class.

4. One boy while studying about the pioneers who went to Oregon wrote this verse:

### Pioneer Dreams

Far stretches the long white caravan
Like great ghosts creeping through the dust and sand.
The bull whacker driving with long loose reins
Is wearily dreaming of his new homestead.
His wife though crooning a low lullaby
Has fear of the Indians that everyone dreads.
So onward they push, these brave pioneers,
To the goal of their dreams, The Oregon Land.

George Hammett, 7A.

Have you read of any frontier events about which you would like to write in verse? Try to put the pictures that are in your mind into words.

5. Learn some of the country dances and singing games. Among these are "Old Dan Tucker," "Jolly Is the Miller," "Pop Goes the Weasel."

6. Sing some of the songs which were popular on the frontier. Some well-known songs were "Old Zip Coon," "Oh! Susanna," "Buffalo Gal," "Old-Time Religion."

7. Build a pioneer home on the sand table. Select one type of frontier life and keep all the facts true to this type. For example, a log cabin could be placed in a clearing in the forest, but a sod house should be shown on a grass-covered prairie.

8. Make furniture to put in the pioneer house and a covered wagon to stand before the door. Perhaps you would like also to make a pioneer family to live in the house. Keep the sizes of figures, wagon, and furniture right for the size of the house. Plan clothes for the family that suit the frontier.

9. There are several things which were done by pioneer housewives that you might do in your schoolroom, for example, dipping candles, making apple butter, braiding rugs, weaving rugs, carding wool, piecing quilts.

10. If anyone in your neighborhood weaves rag rugs, make a trip to see the loom in use. Perhaps someone who owns a spinning wheel will show you how spinning was done.

11. Have an exhibit of old things which were used by pioneers. Some things that you may find are candle molds, dishes of lusterware or glazed earthenware, guns, cradles, flatirons, kettles, bed warmers, and spinning wheels.

12. You could divide the class into committees and have

each committee tell a part of the story of the pioneers. One committee might draw a frieze and another a reel for a "movie," while a third group might give a play or a series of pantomimes. You could show the work and play of a pioneer family in Ohio, a scene in a prairie sod house, a caravan on either the Santa Fe or the Oregon Trail, gold seekers arriving at Sutter's mill. What other ideas for scenes can you find by reading this story again?

### Some Books to Read

The westward movement furnished much exciting material for stories. Among those that deal with real men and women who did daring deeds are:

*Davy Crockett*, and *Kit Carson*, by Frank L. Beals
*Narcissa Whitman, Pioneer of Oregon*, by Jeanette Eaton
*Kit Carson, Trail Blazer and Scout*, by Shannon Garst
*As the Crow Flies*, by Cornelia Meigs
*Sam Houston, Boy Chieftain*, by Augusta Stevenson
*Trapper Days, Tales of the Prairies*, by Ralph V. Hunkins and Regina H. Allen

Stories, both interesting and easy to read, that center about the life of some pioneer boy or girl are:

*Skip-Come-A-Lou*, by Ada Claire Darby
*The Butterfly Shawl*, and *The Nuggets of Singing Creek*, by Grace S. Dawson

[137]

*High Prairie*, by Walter and Marion Havighurst

*Delecta Ann, the Circuit Rider's Daughter*, by Myna Lockwood

*When Abigail was Seven*, and *A Little Girl of Long Ago*, by Eliza O. White

*Susan and Arabella, Pioneers*, by Rhoda Morris

*The Treasure in the Little Trunk*, and *Secret of the Rosewood Box*, by Helen Fuller Orton

*Lonnies Landing*, and *The Faraway Trail*, by Charlie M. Simon

*With Fife and Drum*, by Florence W. Taylor

*Children of the Covered Wagon*, by Mary J. Carr

*Hello, the Boat*, and *Walking on Gold*, by Phyllis Crawford

*Drusilla*, by Emma Brock

*Away Goes Sally*, by Elizabeth Coatsworth

The pioneer adventures of the Ingalls family is told in a series of seven interesting books by Laura Ingalls Wilder. The first book of the series is *Little House in the Big Woods*. Look for the others in your library.

Other, more difficult stories of the westward movement, are:

*On the Golden Trail*, and *Wheels toward the West*, by Hildegarde Hawthorne

*Swift Rivers*, by Cornelia Meigs

*Wagons Westward, A Story of the Old Trail to Santa Fe*, by Armstrong Sperry

*Rolling Wheels*, by Katherine Grey

*Caddie Woodlawn*, by Carol Brink

*The Pony Express is heading for California.*

## BETTER WAYS OF LIVING FOLLOW THE FRONTIER

As the frontier moved westward, people made many changes in their manner of living. When hundreds of pioneers were leaving each year for the West, there came to be a great need for better ways to travel. As these pioneers settled in new homes, they wished to receive news from their friends and relatives in the old homes farther east. This desire brought about a need for ways of carrying news rapidly from one part of the country to another. As the men and women of the frontier carried on the hard work which was necessary if they were to have a living, they felt the need for tools and machines which would make their work less difficult.

A part of the story of how young America became a full-grown nation concerns the way in which these needs were met. Just as the frontier moved always toward the West, so better ways of living followed the frontier.

[141]

## Men Find Better Ways to Travel

**Roads are built.** — In the early days in America roads were very bad. They were often so narrow that only travelers on foot or horseback could pass over them. They were always muddy in wet weather and usually rough in dry weather. Often they wound around stumps and rocks. Some passed over low spots where wagons frequently stuck in the mud.

It was because roads were so very bad that nearly all travelers in colonial times either used boats or rode on horseback. During this period such goods as could not be sent by water were often loaded on to the backs of pack horses.

The first paved road in the United States was built in 1794 between Philadelphia and Lancaster, Pennsylvania. This length of sixty-two miles of the Lancaster Pike remained for · years the wonder of the country. People came from distant places simply to ride over its smooth surface, which was made of crushed rock packed down by travel.

When the westward movement of the pioneers created a need for a good road to connect the East and the West, Congress made a plan for building it. This road ran from Cumberland on the Potomac River to Wheeling on the Ohio River, a distance of one hundred forty-one miles. It was known both as the National and as the Cumberland Road. The route was chosen in 1806, but there were many delays and it was 1815 before much work was really done. By 1818 the mail coaches were traveling over the new road from Washington to Wheeling.

Built thirty feet wide in the mountains and sixty-six feet wide in other places, this new road was much better than any earlier one. It was covered with crushed rock. The bridges were so solidly built of stone that many are still in use today. A ditch on either side carried away water. All of these improved features made the road cost more than thirteen thousand dollars per mile.

[143]

In order to get money to keep the National Road in repair, toll gates were established. Travelers passing along the road paid a small sum called a *toll* at each of these gates.

The National Road was gradually extended west. At the same time some other paved roads were built although the number of these was never large. Often roads were constructed by private companies which then charged toll in order to get paid for their undertaking.

It is not surprising that better stagecoaches were made after roads were improved. The early boxlike vehicle known as a stage wagon gave place to one with an egg-shaped body suggesting the stream-lined automobiles and trains of today. This in turn was followed by the style known as the Concord coach, which was used for many years. As the frontier pushed west, the Concord coach was never far behind.

There were companies that owned stage lines just as there are companies today that own railroad lines.

Stages ran both day and night over some of the roads. Usually a coach was drawn by four horses which were changed about every twelve miles. In this way coaches traveled at what was thought then to be very rapid speed. While they averaged about ten miles per hour, they did upon occasion make much better time.

The stage driver was an important person. His was no easy task. He must take his coach through all kinds of weather. When his route led him off the main roads, he was likely to have to drive through mudholes into which the coach might easily sink. Many a driver had his coach turned over on sharp curves. At such times the passengers usually climbed out and helped the driver lift the coach back in place. Where there were no bridges, the coach was driven through the water if it were not too deep. When thus crossing a stream the driver not only had to guide his horses carefully, but he often had to quiet excited passengers as well.

Not only passengers but supplies of all sorts were carried to and from the West. After roads were improved, wagons usually took the place of the pack horses that had been used at an earlier time.

A style of wagon that had a curved bed came into use in Pennsylvania during colonial days. Because it was first used in the valley of the Conestoga River, this was called a *Conestoga wagon*. It served its purpose so well that it was used in America for a hundred years. Freighting companies used Conestoga wagons for sending goods to Western cities, while pioneers traveled in them all the way to the Pacific coast.

Over the top of a Conestoga wagon were bows which supported a white canvas cover, drawn down at each end with cords. Since the front and back bows were higher than those in the middle, the top of the cover curved down to match the curve in the bed. The body of the wagon was always painted blue and the side boards bright red.

The men who drove the wagons for the freighting companies were a sturdy lot. With six thousand pounds or more packed into their great wagons a driver could make a journey of about fifteen miles in a day. From four to seven horses drew each wagon. The driver rode the left-hand horse of the first pair in front of the wagon. Bells on the harness often made a merry jingle as the horses moved along the road.

[146]

**A night in a Western tavern.** — There were many taverns on the main-traveled roads. Stage companies used them as stations. Passengers on the coaches depended upon them for food and shelter. Drivers of freighting wagons fed their horses in the tavern yards and slept quite soundly on the barroom floors. Some of these taverns had very comfortable quarters for their guests, but many did not. The farther one traveled into new country, the poorer the taverns were likely to be.

Will you suppose that you are looking in on a Western tavern one spring evening in 1836? Along the road before the door pass coaches and wagons bound for the frontier beyond.

The toot of a horn brings the landlord and half a dozen guests running from the front door of the tavern. Down the road races a stagecoach. The horses, seeming to sense the importance of the occasion, toss their heads and put forth their best efforts. As the coach nears the tavern, the driver sets his brakes and pulls on the reins. In a cloud of dust the vehicle stops exactly before the door.

The poor shaken passengers climb down, all the while settling hats and bonnets into place. The tavern helper takes bags and boxes from the place where they are carried at the rear of the coach. The landlord bustles about welcoming the five men and three women who have arrived. The horses are led away to the barn.

[147]

This is the supper stop; so driver and passengers make their way eagerly into the tavern. The barroom, which they enter first, has a large fireplace at one end and a bar at the other. Guests sit about the fireplace, where a cheerful little blaze takes the chill from the air.

The women who arrived on the coach are shown into a side room, where they may lay aside their bonnets and make themselves tidy for supper. The men find a tin pan and a pitcher on a bench at one side of the barroom. A comb on a shelf under a tiny looking glass serves any traveler who cares to use it.

The ringing of a bell soon calls the people to supper. In a room beyond the barroom the guests find a table set. On it fried pork, potatoes, corn bread, eggs, applesauce, and honey are set out in large dishes. A red and white checked cloth covers the table, but napkins are entirely lacking. Steel knives and forks with bone handles are at each place. A few spoons are scattered along the board. No words are wasted while the hungry travelers attend to the business of eating.

Supper over, the men return to the barroom, which is now quite filled because a group of wagon drivers have arrived. These fellows toss aside their blankets and hurry into the dining room for a bite of supper.

The landlord has a full house tonight. The women guests share the side room with his two daughters. All the men except the wagon drivers are shown to

[148]

the one room upstairs, where they find that the only pieces of furniture are two stools and three beds. The wagon drivers roll up in their blankets and lie down on the barroom floor with their feet toward the blazing fire.

**Steamboats sail the rivers.** — At the same time that some Americans were taking a great interest in the building of paved roads, other people were turning their thoughts to making a new and better style of boat. From the time when the first pioneers along the Atlantic coast had pushed their way up the broad rivers in the East, boats had played an important part in the growth of the country. Flatboats and keelboats had been two of the most popular styles, both for moving people and for carrying goods.

A flatboat had oars by which it could be rowed, but when going downstream it was carried by the current. A keelboat had oars and a sail, but when the water was shallow enough it was poled, and in times of great difficulty even towed by a mule or horse that walked along the bank of the stream and pulled a rope which was attached to the boat. When a boat was poled, each of the boatmen thrust a long pole into the bed of the river and then walked from front to rear along

[150]

the side of the boat. Taking out his pole, he walked back to the front and repeated the act. This pushing movement carried the boat forward.

By the latter part of the eighteenth century men were attempting to build steamboats. One of the most successful of these builders was John Fitch. As early as 1786 he made a boat which ran, although it did not work very smoothly. He improved his first model until he was able in 1790 to carry passengers up and down the Delaware River. Fitch's difficulty was that he was ahead of his time. Most people were not yet ready to accept the idea of a steamboat and so would not put money into building one. Since Fitch himself was very poor, he could not carry on this work alone. He finally grew so discouraged that he went away to the Kentucky wilderness and gave up trying to build steamboats.

The idea was not lost, however, but for a few years no one made much use of it. Then in the early part of the nineteenth century Robert Fulton showed the world that steamboats could be used successfully. He was aided by Robert Livingston, a wealthy and able man who had long been interested in boatbuilding. They got a steam engine from England and had a steamboat built at New York City.

This boat, named the *Clermont*, made a trip to Albany and back in 1807. News that the boat was to attempt such a journey brought hundreds of men and women to line the banks of the Hudson River.

[151]

Can you see them there watching anxiously for the
*Clermont* to appear?

The people on the riverbank are talking rather
wildly as they wait for the strange boat to come into
view. "It must be a sea monster," cries one man.

"No, not a sea monster but a sign from Heaven,"
replies his neighbor, adding, "It means that the end
of the world is coming soon."

At the sound of a whistle all talking ceases as everyone strains forward to see the strange sight. How
queer to see one tall, straight smokestack where masts
have always been on sailing ships! The splashing
[152]

and foaming of the water which is being churned by the huge paddle wheels is almost enough to make one believe in sea monsters indeed.

Black clouds of smoke which are pouring from the smokestack settle over the people. A couple of fishermen who have been watching from the shore suddenly give a yell and take to their heels in terror.

As the *Clermont* steams along on an upstream trip which requires but thirty-two hours to reach Albany, a man on shore speaks of "Fulton's Folly." The nickname is repeated from mouth to mouth until everyone along the bank is ready to call this boat "Fulton's Folly."

Yet strangely enough this trip proved the worth of steamboats. After 1807 they were improved and built in ways better suited to particular needs, but never after that did people doubt their value.

The boats used on Western rivers were usually built in a style that was well suited to river sailing. Great quantities of goods and many people made all or part of the journey to a Western frontier on a steamboat. This kind of travel grew heavier year by year until it reached its height in the fifties and sixties. Then the larger use of railroads caused some falling off in the amount of business done by steamboats.

Not only did boats carry passengers and goods, but some were used as "showboats." These floating theaters went up and down the Mississippi and others of the larger rivers of the West. Each night a showboat tied up at some river town and gave a play in the little theater which was built into the boat. Poor as were the plays thus given, they were warmly welcomed by the Western people, who had no other chance to attend a theater.

The early steamboats had many accidents, for which there were several causes. Boats were poorly built, and since the captains frequently raced each other up or down a river it was quite common for a boiler to blow up. Because the boats were built of wood, they often caught fire from the sparks which poured out of the smokestacks. Snags and sand bars in the river bed also caused accidents.

[154]

One of the most interesting sights to be seen along a riverbank was the loading or unloading of a steamboat. This work as well as the cleaning and carrying of the wood used for fuel was done by men who were called roustabouts, or, more briefly, rousters.

Some of the roustabouts were old river men who at an earlier time had run the flatboats and keelboats. There were also many men who had only recently come to this country. However, the greater number of the rousters were Negroes. These happy, carefree workers were a very important part of the life along the rivers. They sang as they worked, timing their movements to the rhythm of the song. These songs, known as *coonjine*, which were made up by the Negro roustabouts, gave good pictures of life along the rivers.

**Canals are built.** — Many of the cities along the eastern coast of the United States desired to share in the trade that was carried on with the new settlements in the West. As long as most of this trade followed the rivers, it was evident that only cities fortunate enough to be located on large streams could benefit from it. With the building of the National Road a few more cities gained a share in the trade, but many others still had to watch the growth of New Orleans and other centers on the great rivers without themselves receiving any benefits. It was this condition of affairs which set men to thinking of canals.

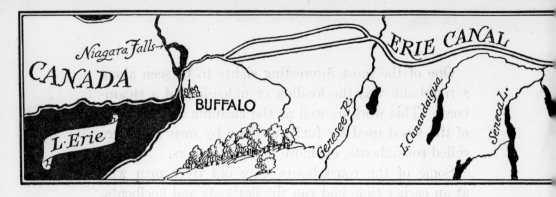

This dream of building canals to connect all the principal rivers of the country held people for more than a quarter of a century. First talked about early in the nineteenth century, the plan of canal building continued to be a pet idea in America until the late thirties. It was only when railroads had proved their value that the notion of building canals was dropped.

New York was one of the cities which was most concerned because it could not share in the Western trade. Citizens of the city, looking about for some way to remedy the trouble, hit upon the plan of building a canal which would connect Lake Erie and the Hudson River. This meant digging a ditch three hundred sixty-five miles long through the forests of New York state. It seemed to be a foolish plan, yet strangely enough it was successfully carried out.

After talking about the plan for nearly ten years, the legislature of New York in 1817 ordered the work begun. It was the hope of the state that Congress would give aid in paying the cost, but in this New York was disappointed. The whole sum of about five million dollars was paid by the state alone.

[156]

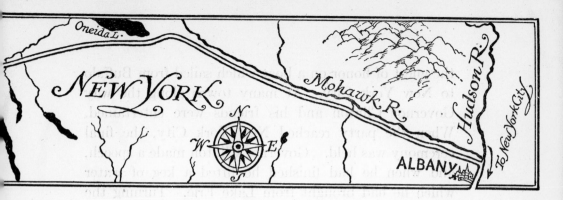

The Erie Canal was built in spite of the most severe hardships. With little except shovels, plows, and scrapers to aid them the workmen dug the great ditch. Some new pieces of machinery were invented to aid in removing the great trees and stumps which blocked the path. Supplies had to be hauled while the ground was frozen in winter. Fever and ague made hundreds of the workmen ill. Since Lake Erie was more than five hundred feet higher than the Hudson River at Albany, it was necessary to build locks in order to raise and lower the water level for the boats passing through the canal.

Yet in spite of all these difficulties the Erie Canal was finished in 1825. A great celebration was held when it was completed. Cannon were set up along the canal within hearing distance of one another. When all was ready the cannon at Buffalo on Lake Erie was fired. One after another all the others along the route were fired in turn, until the news of the opening of the canal was carried to Albany.

Governor De Witt Clinton of New York, who had done much to secure the building of the canal, was the guest of honor on a boat which sailed from Buffalo to New York City. At many towns along the way Governor Clinton and his friends were entertained. When the party reached New York City, the final ceremony was held. Governor Clinton made a speech, and when he had finished he lifted a keg of water which he had brought from Lake Erie. Turning the keg, he poured into New York Bay the water which it held. By this ceremony he united the water of lake and ocean, as in its way the Erie Canal also united these two great bodies of water.

The new canal brought cheaper shipping rates to the West and greatly increased the business of New York City. Indeed the lead in size and wealth which this city has over all others on the Atlantic coast may be traced to the added business brought by the Erie Canal. "Clinton's Big Ditch" proved to be worth all it cost.

The Erie Canal was not the only one which was successfully used. Many were built, among which two of the more important were the Ohio Canal and the Illinois and Michigan Canal. The first of these joined the Ohio River with Lake Erie, while the second connected the Illinois River with Lake Michigan. It is interesting to know that while this latter route was being planned a little town was laid out along the shores of Lake Michigan near Fort Dearborn. This little town was one day to grow into the great city of Chicago.

[158]

Canals served not only as a means of shipping goods but also as a way of travel. Hundreds of pioneers made part of their trip to the West by canalboat. There were two types of boat which carried passengers. *Line boats* carried people during the day from one place to another along the canals. *Packet boats*, which traveled both by day and by night, were much faster than line boats and offered more comforts to passengers. A cook prepared and served meals on board, and there were bunks in which some at least of the passengers could sleep.

If you had lived in America in 1830, you would have thought a trip on a packet boat a great luxury. Will you suppose that you are now on board such a boat, having a pleasant trip on a summer day?

Everyone is gathered on deck, which is more pleasant in warm weather than the cabins within. Here are a group of men having a lively game of cards. Near by an old lady who looks as if she did not approve of such pastime is gazing at the scenes along the bank. With the boat moving only four miles an hour, she has a good chance to see all the sights. Several other women have brought their sewing on deck. One young lad holds a drawing board on his knee while he draws some of the passing scenes. Several men are reading.

Suddenly the steersman shouts, "Low bridge!" At once the people all duck, while a few careful souls drop flat on the deck. The boat passes slowly under a

bridge, after which the passengers once more straighten
their backs and return to their work or play.

Along the towpath beside the canal walk the horses
which pull the boat. Several of the men from the
boat are now walking beside the driver on the towpath. It is in this way that passengers get exercise.

The cook appears on deck, a dinner bell in hand.
Very quickly the company goes inside to the large
cabin in the center of the boat where dinner is spread
on boards which will later be removed. It is in this
cabin that the men sleep at night. When all the

bunks are in use, other passengers find blankets and lie on the floor. This is also the gathering place when bad weather forces the passengers to leave the deck.

Dinner finished, a number of the ladies retire to the small cabin where they may smooth their hair and arrange their ruffles safe from the eyes of the men. A few settle themselves for afternoon naps. Most of the men return to the deck, where talk of political matters and Western trade is soon mixed with the laughter of the card players and the call of the steersman as he shouts, "Low bridge!"

[161]

**Railroads are begun.** — The very first railroads were built and used in the mines of England, where cars of ore were hauled by small mules. One day it occurred to someone that if a plank were laid down for the cars to run upon they would move more easily. The plan was tried and found to be so successful that the idea was put into use. The one plank became two wooden rails. The wheels of the cars were so arranged that they could not get off the rails. Then another man had the thought that perhaps steam engines could be made to draw the cars in place of the faithful little mules.

An engine which worked successfully was put into use by George Stephenson as early as 1815. Roads were now extended beyond the mines to connect various cities. In 1829 Stephenson built an engine called the *Rocket* which won a prize offered by a railroad company for a better engine. The improvements which were included in the *Rocket* were soon copied by other builders.

[162]

In America, too, men began to think of using steam engines to draw trains. In 1813 a book was published in which the writer said, "The time will come when people will travel in stages moved by steam engines from one city to another, almost as fast as birds can fly, fifteen or twenty miles an hour." At that time it was hard to believe that such speed could ever be reached.

However, the first railway cars used in the United States were drawn by horses and mules. The first line was built in 1826 in Massachusetts. It was four miles long and was used to carry blocks of granite to a dock where they could be loaded on boats.

The next year a line nine miles long was built in Pennsylvania. It was used to carry coal from a mine to a boat landing on the river. Since the mines were on a level much higher than the river, the road was so constructed that the cars could move downhill by their own weight. Mules, which were needed to draw the empty cars uphill again, were allowed to ride down in one of the cars. It is said that the mules enjoyed the sport of riding so much that they simply refused to walk downhill.

The first engine which drew a train in this country was brought from England and tried on a railroad in Pennsylvania in 1829. Over this road, seventeen miles long, the little engine raced at the great speed of ten miles an hour. The engine had proved its worth, but the wooden rails over which it ran were so poor that its use could not be continued.

These were the years when canal building was going forward rapidly. Towns that were reached by canals did not favor the building of railroads except as a means of bringing passengers and goods to the canals. On the other hand, cities which did not have the benefits of canal service began to take a great interest in railroads.

Peter Cooper bought an interest in a small railroad called the Baltimore and Ohio. The railroad cars were drawn by horses. The owners wanted to try the new steam engines, but there was such a sharp curve in the road that it was feared an engine could not be kept on the track. Peter Cooper, who was handy with tools, said he believed that he could build an engine which would do the work.

The result of his effort was a little engine which he called the *Tom Thumb* because of its tiny size. It worked successfully, and the owners of the road were so delighted that they were about to put steam engines into use when an accident caused them to wait.

[164]

The owners of a stage line, fearing that the new railroad would get much of their business, dared Peter Cooper to race against one of their drivers. He accepted, and one day the horse train and the steam train started off on two tracks which ran side by side.

The horse sprang forward at the word "Go" and gained a quarter of a mile while the *Tom Thumb* was getting up steam. Passengers in the horse train shouted their joy. Then *Tom Thumb* began to gain speed, and soon the two were racing neck-and-neck. The driver used his whip, while Peter Cooper gave his little engine all the steam that it had. *Tom Thumb* gained until with a great shout from the passengers it left the horse train far behind.

Now came the accident. A belt slipped on the engine. *Tom Thumb* began to slow down. The driver, seeing what had happened, urged his horse forward, passed Cooper as he repaired his engine, and drove into town ahead of the steam train.

[165]

The results of this race so discouraged the owners of the railroad that they did not begin using steam engines until 1831. Thus it happened that although the *Tom Thumb* was the first American-built engine which worked successfully, the first railroad to use such engines in regular service was the Charleston and Hamburg line. Trains drawn by engines ran over this South Carolina road in 1830.

In 1831 the Mohawk and Hudson Railroad in New York used a steam engine for the first time on their line. This engine, named the *De Witt Clinton*, made its first run on August 9, going from Albany to Schenectady, a distance of seventeen miles. Had you been able to travel on that train, you would have met some of the difficulties and dangers of early railroad travel. Shall we suppose that we have each bought one of the tickets that are on sale at the taverns in Albany, and are ready to climb aboard?

Our train stands waiting on the track. Behind the *De Witt Clinton* is a car called a *tender* in which water and wood are carried. Back of the tender are three cars shaped like stagecoaches, and behind these several flatcars. Both cars and coaches are rapidly filling with people. We quickly find places in the last coach.

Around the train a crowd is gathered. Men, women, and children examine the stout little engine and look with envy at those of us who have tickets for the trip.

The conductor stands on a platform outside the coach and collects our tickets. When he has secured

[166]

all of them he climbs into the tender and blows a great blast on a horn. Hurrah! Now we shall be off! The people around the train join their voices with ours in a great cheer.

Biff! Bang! Slam! Instead of being off to Schenectady we are off our seats, sprawling over each other on the floor. Each car is fastened to the one in front of it by a chain of three links. The tender in turn is fastened to the engine in the same way. When the engine started, the tender was jerked against the engine, the first coach against the tender, and each car behind in turn against its neighbor ahead. Each jerk sent a new lot of passengers sprawling.

Picking ourselves up and finding no bones broken, we brush off our clothes and settle down for a peaceful ride. We are no more than in our places when great, black clouds of smoke from the wood-burning engine pour over us. This smoke is followed by a shower of sparks. At once we are all stirring as tiny flames flare. Our clothing is catching on fire from the sparks! We slap each other, beating and rubbing our own clothing in between slaps at our neighbors'. Back of us on the flatcars those who have umbrellas have raised them. A good idea, we say. But no, an umbrella is blazing. Now another bursts into flames and still another. Soon all that the owners have are the metal frames of their umbrellas.

We are coming to a stop and once more we are jerked out of our seats. While the *De Witt Clinton*

[167]

takes in water, we get out and make a rush for a rail fence beside the road. The men carry rails to the train and cut them the necessary length to fit between the cars. We all lend a hand when these are lifted and tied in place. At least we shall not be jerked out of our seats when we start and stop.

Back on the train once more, we have nothing to do but fight sparks and watch the passing scene. As we approach Schenectady we see a great crowd awaiting us at the end of the line. Many carriages, coaches,

[168]

and wagons are drawn up along the track. The horses have never seen a steam engine before. As we come to a stop with a loud toot of the whistle the poor beasts become so frightened that they all rear and plunge, while some even pull loose and run away.

We climb down from the coach in Schenectady, safe and well in spite of having been thoroughly jerked about and almost burned alive. The *De Witt Clinton* has won a place for itself on the Mohawk and Hudson Railroad.

[169]

During the early years of building railroads many problems had to be solved. No one knew what made the best roadbeds. Some lines tried stone, which was so hard that it jarred the passengers badly, while others tried softer materials, which wore out very quickly. The width of the early roads varied from three to six feet, which meant that cars made to run on one line could not be used on another. Rails were at first made of wood, but these wore so badly that strips of iron were nailed over them. Later, rails of solid iron took the place of these, and after some years steel rails were used.

The first railroad coaches were shaped like the bodies of stagecoaches, but before long boxlike cars took the place of these early coaches. A stove at one end furnished too much heat for those sitting near it and usually not enough for passengers at the other end of the car.

People had some very interesting ideas about traveling at such high rates of speed as fifteen and twenty miles an hour. Some held it to be dangerous, fearing that such rapid movement might scramble the brains of the traveler. There were others who believed that it was wicked to go so fast. They said that had God wanted men to move at such a pace He would have given them either wings or longer legs.

As the pioneers pushed westward and created new needs for shipping goods to the frontier, more and more railroads were built. At first many of these were intended to connect with river routes, but as time went on the railroads often put the steamboats out of business. The forties and fifties saw much railroad building in both the East and the West. It was during this period that Chicago, at the southern tip of Lake Michigan began to be a leading railroad center. By 1860 the United States had about thirty thousand miles of railroad tracks, and one line had been built as far west as St. Joseph, Missouri.

Land travel was by this time faster than ever before in America. To the pack horse, Conestoga wagon, and stagecoach had been added the railroad train drawn by a sturdy little steam engine.

**The telegraph.** — On board a ship that is crossing the Atlantic Ocean a group of men are talking about electricity. In this year of 1832 many people do not know a great deal about this wonderful force; so eager questions are being put to one man on board who does know. The talk turns now to the question of how far and how fast electricity can travel. The man of science replies that electricity travels instantly over any known length of wire.

At this reply one of the passengers sits up with a start, his face lighted up by the new thought which has just come to him. Why not send messages by electricity? If started at one end of a wire they would be received instantly at the other end, though that be many miles distant. Samuel Finley Breese Morse has the idea of a telegraph.

Long before, while attending college at Yale, Morse had been interested in electricity, but he had become an artist rather than a student of science. However, from the time that the idea of the telegraph came to him he gave his best efforts to the invention. During the remainder of the voyage he worked on plans for carrying out his idea. Upon landing in New York he set about building h s first telegraph instrument. Since he was poor, he had to give many hours each day to painting or to teaching others to paint, in order to make his living. Sometimes he was hungry because

[172]

he had no money with which to buy food, but he never for a minute gave up his efforts to invent a successful telegraph.

During these hard years two men were convinced that Morse had a good idea. These two, Leonard D. Gale and Alfred Vail, became Morse's partners and gave him much help.

When he was sure that his telegraph was a success, Morse asked Congress for enough money to build a short line so that he might show how it worked. He was to be disappointed, however, for Congress took no action at that time.

A few months later we find Morse once more in Washington, where he is again asking Congress to help him. Weeks pass as the anxious inventor goes day after day to the Capitol. At last comes a day in February, 1843, when he sits in the gallery of the House of Representatives and sees the vote taken on a bill which provides thirty thousand dollars for building a telegraph line between Washington and Baltimore. Some members of the House treat the matter as a great joke, but to Samuel Morse it is a matter of the most serious nature. Vote after vote is recorded. Will the bill pass or fail? At last the count is finished! The bill has passed. Morse can only say, "The long agony is over."

The inventor speaks too soon, however, for the Senate must also pass the bill before it can become a law. Days pass, bringing ever nearer the third of

March, upon which date Congress must come to an
end.   Early in the morning of the third Morse takes
his place in the gallery of the Senate to hear the vote
on his bill.   Hours drag by, dozens of bills are considered, but not the one which concerns the telegraph.
Night comes, and still the weary man in the gallery
waits.

At last a friend, feeling sorry for him, explains that
since it is almost midnight when Congress must close
there is now no chance of the bill being considered.
Morse stares at him, unable at first to believe the words
he has heard.   Convinced at last, he makes his way
slowly out of the gallery and returns to his hotel, a
disappointed, heartbroken man.   More than ten years
of labor seem lost.

The next morning young Annie Ellsworth enters
the hotel as Morse comes downstairs.

[174]

"I have come to congratulate you," she cries.

"For what, my dear young friend?" the surprised man asks.

"On the passage of your bill. It was put through last night only a minute or two before midnight."

Joy and surprise leave Morse without words at first, but when he recovers he promises Annie Ellsworth that she may choose the first message which will be sent over the new telegraph line.

After delays and difficulties the trial line was finished in May, 1844. In Washington, Morse sat before the instrument while at Baltimore Vail was ready to receive and send messages. Annie Ellsworth handed Morse a paper on which were written the words, "What hath God wrought?" Morse flashed the message to Vail, who at once sent it back again. The telegraph had proved itself a success.

A number of men before Morse had thought of using some such plan as the telegraph for sending messages. One or two had even set up simple systems. However, it remained for the poor painter to put the best of all the ideas together and thus to make a telegraph which really worked.

During the next few years Morse had to defend his right to the invention. Several men tried to use his idea to make money for themselves. In the end Morse won his fight against these men, and both he and his partners lived to receive wealth and honor for their invention.

**The Atlantic cable.** — As telegraph wires were stretched from place to place on land, some people began to dream of a time when wires would also reach across the ocean. One man, Cyrus West Field, determined to lay a cable containing wires between North America and Europe. He formed companies to carry on the work, and the first cable was laid in 1857.

This attempt was ended when the cable broke after more than a thousand miles had been laid. The work was started again in 1858, and this time a complete line was put down. The Queen of England sent a message to the President of the United States. A few days later the cable suddenly ceased to work.

A number of years passed before another line was laid between the two continents. Field kept up his efforts, and in 1866 he had his reward, for during that year a successful cable line was established. Ever since that

time messages have flashed back and forth between Europe and America.

Within a few years the use of the cable had spread to other oceans, and the use of the telegraph to other lands. Not only people in America but people everywhere had faster ways to carry news.

**The overland mail.** — From its beginning the government of the United States had provided a postal system which carried the mail to various parts of the country. As the frontier pushed west, there was naturally a need to extend this system so that mail could be carried to the pioneers in the new regions.

Many different means were used for delivering the mail. It was carried on horseback, in wagons, in stagecoaches, and even at times on the backs of men. Newly opened frontiers were nearly always without any Government postal service at first, and during this time some sturdy pioneer would usually make trips to and from the nearest post office, charging each person for whom he carried mail. But always, sooner or later, Congress was brought to see that the new region must have regular postal service provided by the Government. Mail once a month in good weather and less often in bad was considered a luxury on a new frontier, but as settlers became more numerous they always demanded that the Government provide more frequent deliveries of mail.

The story of the overland mail is one of the most interesting bits of this history of the postal service.

[178]

When the opening of Oregon and the discovery of gold in California sent hundreds of settlers to the Pacific coast, there naturally arose a need for mail service to this far-western frontier. Since great stretches of plains and mountains had to be crossed to reach the Pacific coast, the matter of providing frequent and regular deliveries of mail offered many difficulties.

The first mail to California went by ship to Panama or some other point along the narrow isthmus that connects North and South America. It was sent across the isthmus to the Pacific coast, where it was picked up by another ship which took it on to San Francisco. Mail coming in this way usually reached the pioneers on the west coast twice a month. The time necessary for a letter to travel from New York to San Francisco by this route was usually about three weeks.

The Californians were not content with this mail service, and through their Representatives and Senators in Congress they insisted that the Government arrange to have mail sent by an overland route. At the same time settlers in Utah and other western territories were asking for regular mail service.

During the early fifties several mail routes were established between points in the West, but it was not until 1858 that a route was actually laid out from the Mississippi River to the Pacific coast. The route as finally chosen by the Postmaster General of the

United States went through Texas and southern California, then northward along the coast to San Francisco. Many people were disappointed with this route because they had wanted the mail to travel over the old trail through the central part of the country.

The first contract for carrying the mail to the Pacific coast was given to a company headed by John Butterfield. For this reason the service was often called the Butterfield Overland Mail.

At first Concord spring wagons were used, but later regular Concord coaches were provided. Nine or more passengers could be carried as well as the mail. Indeed the carrying of passengers was an important part of the business to the Butterfield Company, for the fare for the journey from St. Louis to San Francisco was about two hundred dollars for each person. This did not include meals, which were bought along the way. Since the journey required about twenty-five days, it

is easy to understand that travelers must have been very weary when they reached their journey's end, after having traveled day and night for weeks in a crowded coach.

Along the mail route there were stations every ten or fifteen miles. Every fifty miles or so there were "home stations," where the drivers were changed and where passengers ate their meals. The stops in between were at "swing stations," where fresh horses were secured. At certain points there were blacksmith and harness shops, as well as places where coaches could be repaired. A horseshoer and harness repairer also traveled from station to station doing his work.

A number of other mail routes were opened after the southern route. The people who wanted the mail to travel through the central part of the country did not give up their fight until this route was opened in 1861. The Butterfield Company then moved north and carried the mail over the new route.

[181]

In the middle sixties the overland mail reached its greatest size and importance. It continued to serve the West, however, until the first railroad which crossed the continent was completed in 1869. Even after this time stagecoaches were used for many years to carry mail to places in the West that were not reached by railroads.

The Concord coach played an important part in the development of this country. As it rolled along over the plains or climbed narrow mountain roads with its load of passengers and mail, it bound the far-distant parts of the United States together. Before telegraph wires and railroad tracks had stretched across America, the sturdy Concord coach was the chief means of carrying news from the older regions to the new frontiers.

**The pony express.** — When a central route was being urged for the overland mail, a Senator from California decided to show Congress that this was a route over which mail could be sent rapidly and safely. He asked a man who had freight and stage lines across this part of the country to establish a fast express service which would carry mail to the Pacific coast. The man agreed to set up such a plan, and two months later the pony express was ready to begin its work.

The mail was carried by men who rode fast horses. Stations were built every twelve or fifteen miles so that horses could be changed. Each rider rode from seventy-five to one hundred miles a day. He then

[182]

rested at the "home station" until another rider brought in the mail from the opposite direction, when he rode back to the station where he had first picked up the mail. The pony express was really a huge relay race run by men on horseback.

The route began at St. Joseph, Missouri, which was at that time the farthest point west reached by a railroad. The western end of the great race course was at Sacramento, California. The only city of any size along the way was Salt Lake City, Utah.

Rapid travel required a light load. Riders usually weighed less than one hundred twenty-five pounds. The mail was carried in four leather boxes, called *cantinas*, which were fastened to a square of leather known as the *mochila*. This mochila was thrown over the saddle, so that two cantinas rested on either side of the horse. When the rider was in the saddle, his legs came between the front and the rear cantinas. At the way stations, with only two minutes allowed for changing horses, the mochila could be thrown quickly over the saddle of the fresh horse.

The cantinas were locked in St. Joseph. Three of them that held California mail could be opened only by the postmaster in Sacramento. The fourth contained mail for Salt Lake City and other towns along the way. Postmasters in these towns had keys for it.

Letters, which were written upon thin paper, were wrapped in oil silk before being placed in the cantinas. The charge for carrying a letter by pony express was at first five dollars for each half ounce. Later this price was reduced to one dollar per half ounce.

When the weather favored them, pony express riders took the mail from St. Joseph to Sacramento in ten days, but in bad weather a longer time was required. However, even when the snow lay deep in the mountain passes the men made splendid records for their speed.

No story in all our American history is more thrilling than the tale of the pony express. It was the "air mail" of 1860. Its fearless young riders, pounding across the continent, faced the dangers of the lonely trail with only courage and fast horses to bring them through.

If a rider met Indians who were not friendly, he had either to outshoot or to outride them. If he came to an overflowing river, he must swim the horse across. When snow and ice lay deep over the earth, he could either follow the old trail or make a new one. When

[185]

his horse gave out under him, he must quickly pull the mochila from the saddle and set out on the run for the next station. If the relief rider was not at the station when he came to the end of his own stretch of riding, the pony express rider had to mount a fresh horse and push on for another seventy-five or hundred miles. Always, under all conditions, the rider knew that "the mail must go through." In performing his duty the pony express rider gave America a record of courage that has not often been equaled.

The first pony express riders set out on April 3, 1860, one from Sacramento riding east, and the other from St. Joseph riding west. If you had been in the little Missouri city on that April day, you would have felt the excitement which stirred the people. Perhaps if you try to think that you are going in and out of the crowd listening to the eager talk, you too may catch the spirit of the occasion. Questions and answers fly back and forth.

"I hear that the train carrying the pony express mail was hours late in reaching Hannibal. That means she won't be here till night."

"You forget that Ad Clark's the engineer on the run from Hannibal. Ad'll be sure to make up any lost time."

"Did you hear who won when the men drew lots to choose the first rider?"

"Have you seen the bay mare that is to make the run?"

[186]

"Yes, they have her down at the Pikes Peak stables. I got some hairs from her tail to make into a watch chain."

So the talk goes as men and women walk up and down the streets or stand about in the Patee House, the splendid hotel that offers the last bit of luxury to be had before the raw life of the West begins. The half-dozen riders who will cover the eastern end of the trail are now gathered in the Patee House, where they are the center of interest. Men crowd eagerly about them, proud to be seen in company with these daring young fellows.

Outside, a brass band plays between speeches. The men who control the pony express tell of the benefits which it will bring to the country. Last of all comes the mayor of St. Joseph, who says of the present and the future:

"Hardly will the cloud of dust which envelops the rider die away before the puff of steam will be seen on the horizon. Citizens of St. Joseph, I bid you give three cheers for the pony express, three cheers for the first overland passage of the United States mail!"

A whistle cuts the air. The train rolls into the station only two and a quarter hours late. Ad Clark has indeed made a record run, crossing the entire state, a distance of two hundred six miles, in four hours and fifty-one minutes. Quickly the forty-nine letters, the five telegrams, and the several newspapers are put into the cantinas.

The mayor throws the mochila over the saddle. The young rider leaps upon the back of the bay mare. In front of the Patee House a cannon booms the signal which tells the captain of the ferryboat to stand by ready to take horse and rider across the Missouri River.

Cheer upon cheer rises as the people go wild with excitement. The prancing horse is edged through the crowd. At last they are off! Like a streak they flash north along Eighth Street to Jule, then west toward the ferry which lies at the foot of Jule Street. Onto the boat, across the river, through the cheering crowds in Elwood, out on the winding trail toward Troy races the bay mare. The pony express is heading for California tonight.

Ten days of being changed from horse to horse brought the mud-spattered mochila into Sacramento on the thirteenth of April. There the last rider on the

western end of the trail was met by cheering crowds, pealing bells, parades, and bonfires.

For nineteen months the pony express riders kept the great relay race moving. Except for four weeks when an Indian war stopped the service, mail went through either once or twice each week. When horses fell under the strain, new horses were bought. When men gave out, new riders were ready to take their places. Over two hundred thousand dollars was lost by the men who set up the pony express. In spite of all these difficulties the mail went through, until one day the last wire was strung and a telegraph line reached from St. Joseph to Sacramento. This spelled the end of the pony express, for horseflesh was not as fast as electricity.

The pony express was, for its owners, a failure. But what a glorious failure that was, which gave America a picture of daring and courage that will never fade!

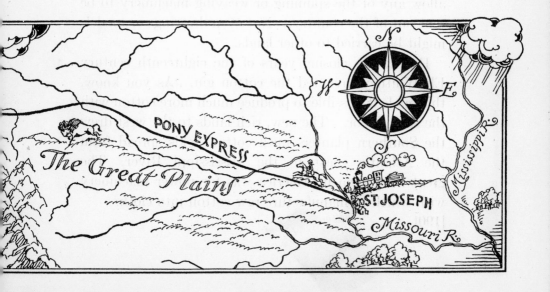

## New Inventions Bring Greater Riches and More Comforts

**From hand to machine labor in making clothing.** — For hundreds of years thread was spun and cloth was woven by hand labor. Colonists coming to America brought their spinning wheels and looms in order that they might provide themselves with clothing.

In England certain cities gradually became centers where thread was spun or cloth was woven, but even in such centers the work was done by hand. During the eighteenth century, however, great changes took place in the business of making cloth. Power machines were invented not only for spinning thread but also for weaving the thread into cloth. With such machines working in its factories, Great Britain saw a chance to control the manufacture of cloth for the whole world. In order to keep this control, the British refused to allow any of the spinning or weaving machinery to be sent out of the country. Not even drawings or models might be carried to other lands.

During the closing years of the eighteenth century Eli Whitney invented the cotton gin. As you know, this made it possible to produce much more cotton with the same labor. The new, rich lands to the west drew the Southern planters until cotton fields spread from the Atlantic coast to the Mississippi River. The great need then in America was for power machinery with which to manufacture raw cotton into cloth.

[190]

Several men attempted to set up factories, only to find that their machines failed to work well; but in 1790 there came to America a young Englishman named Samuel Slater, who said that he could build a spinning machine. With only his memory of the machines he had used in England to guide him Slater built the machine, and ran it with power furnished by a water wheel. This first power spinning in America was done at Pawtucket, Rhode Island, in 1793.

Other mills were built in the eastern part of the country. The thread manufactured in them was sold to weavers and sometimes to housewives. It soon became clear, however, that power looms were badly needed, since spinning could now be done so much more rapidly than weaving.

Francis C. Lowell, a Boston merchant, decided to build a mill where not only spinning but weaving could be carried on by machine labor. He visited the mills of England but was not able to obtain drawings or models. Again workmen had to build from memory, but this they did so successfully that by 1814 the new mill at Waltham, Massachusetts, was turning out well-made cotton cloth.

So great was the demand for their products that other mills were soon humming along the rivers of New England, where numerous falls furnished water power. Woolen as well as cotton cloth was made. Many of the present-day manufacturing cities of that region had their beginnings during these early years of the

nineteenth century, when for the first time in America it was possible to manufacture cloth by machine labor.

When pioneers moved west the spinning wheel and the hand loom were among their most prized possessions. On every frontier there was a time during which the settlers had to depend almost altogether upon their own work to provide clothing. These were the years when pioneer women spun thread and wove it into cloth, and sometimes even tanned deerskins from which they made hunting shirts and moccasins. As ways of travel and trade improved between the frontier and the older parts of the country, more and more factory-made cloth was shipped west. The power machinery in mills and factories thus came to do work which had once been done in the homes, and the busy housewives were relieved of part of their tasks.

For many years after machine labor was used in making cloth, garments were nearly all made in the homes. Since all the sewing had to be done by hand,

this was slow, tiring work. One day as Elias Howe, a young machine-shop worker, watched his wife stitching away on a garment, it occurred to him that he might be able to make a sewing machine.

At first Howe worked at his invention only in his spare time, but as he became more deeply interested he wanted to give all his time to the matter. Since he was very poor, this did not seem possible until a friend offered to support his family and advance him the money that he needed to buy materials. The friend was to have a share of the money which Howe expected to receive for his invention. The help this man gave made it possible for Howe to continue his work until he had a machine that sewed successfully. This was in the year 1846.

In spite of this success, Howe had to face many difficulties. He had a sewing machine that sewed a firm lock stitch, yet he could find no one who would buy. The tailors feared to have the new machine used lest

[193]

they lose their jobs. The housewives were so in the habit of sewing by hand that they did not realize at first how much labor and time a sewing machine could save.

The inventor went to England in the hope that he might sell his product there. After meeting difficulties which left him poorer than ever, Howe finally returned to America. Upon landing with only a few pennies in his pocket he received the news that his wife was dying. Her sickness had been brought on by the hardships which she had suffered during their years of poverty.

Soon after his wife's death Howe learned that certain men had used his idea to build machines of their own which they were now selling. A friend helped him with money so that he could bring suit against these men and at the same time could begin manufacturing his own machines. If the country was now ready to buy sewing machines, Elias Howe wanted to be in a position to sell them.

In 1854 the courts decided the suits in Howe's favor. Every other person who had manufactured and sold sewing machines was required to pay the inventor twenty-five dollars for each machine sold. Almost at once Elias Howe found himself rich.

More than one man before Howe had tried to invent a sewing machine. Many who came after him made improvements, but to this man alone belongs the honor due the inventor of a great labor-saving machine. With this invention the last step was complete
[194]

in the change from hand to machine labor for the making of clothing. Spinning, weaving, and stitching were no longer tasks that must be performed by the hands of the busy housewife.

**From hand to machine labor on the farm.** — Just as women had for centuries labored with their hands in order that their families might have clothing, so men had also labored with their hands in order that there might be food. The tools used on the farms when the United States was a new nation were little better than those employed by the farmers of old Rome. A rude wooden plow with only a small iron point did little more than scratch the surface of the field. Grain was sown by hand and cut with sickle or scythe.

As farmers cultivated larger farms in the West, where labor was scarce, they felt a need for more and better tools. This need was gradually met by the invention of machines which did much of the work that had been performed by hand.

One of the first tools to be improved was the plow. As change after change was made, the wooden plow of early times gave place to one whose curved steel plowshare turned a deep furrow. Without such a plow as this it would have been almost impossible to turn over the tough sod of the prairies.

Machines for sowing wheat were first made in England, but after 1840 they were manufactured and sold in the United States. Other machines, used for

[195]

planting corn, were invented at about the same time.

Many men helped to give the world better farm machinery, but no other one became so well known as Cyrus Hall McCormick. This man was not only an inventor, but a splendid businessman and a citizen who did his country a great service.

Several men before McCormick had attempted to make machines which would cut grain. At least one man made a very successful reaper before McCormick did, yet McCormick is usually called the inventor

[196]

of the reaper.  This honor belongs to him not because his was the first machine ever made but because it was the one that came into general use.

While he was a boy, Cyrus McCormick watched his father try to make a machine that would cut wheat and the father's efforts set the son to thinking along the same lines.  By the time he was twenty-two, he had a machine ready to try in his father's wheat field.  Can you imagine how young McCormick felt as he drove his machine into the field that July day?

The whole family has gathered near the little patch of grain which has been left standing so that Cyrus may test his reaper. Everyone watches eagerly as the machine slowly moves into the wheat. The grain is swept down upon the knife; the shining blade moves back and forth; the cut grain tumbles over on the little platform. A sigh of relief rises from the anxious watchers. The new reaper moves with jolts and jerks, but it does cut the grain.

The harvest season is so nearly over that the young inventor must wait another year to make a test before a larger crowd. He uses the time to make further improvements in his machine. Now, in the following year, we find him ready to try the machine in a wheat field a few miles away from his home.

Over a hundred people are here to see the test. In the crowd are a number of men who each year hire themselves out to work in the harvest fields. They do not feel very friendly toward this new machine which threatens to take away their jobs. As they wait for the test to begin they make fun of the rude object.

The field is hilly and rough. As the reaper moves along, it jolts up and down and rocks from side to side. The wheat does not fall under the blade as smoothly as the young inventor had hoped that it would. The men in the crowd laugh and call out joking remarks. Now the owner of the field rushes up and orders McCormick to stop before his grain is all ruined.

Things look dark for the success of the machine, but there is one farmer in the crowd who believes in this new reaper. He steps forward to say that he owns the field across the road. Since this is a level piece of ground, he invites McCormick to take the reaper there for a test. At once the young man accepts, and drives into the other field while the crowd follows.

Here the machine moves easily over the level ground, cutting the grain smoothly as it goes. Back and forth, back and forth the horses go, while the jokes grow fewer and fewer. At sunset six acres of grain are cut.

That day in the Virginia wheat field proved that the reaper could do its work, yet eight years were to pass before McCormick sold a single machine. In 1834 his invention was completed, but not until 1840 was he able to find a buyer. That year he sold two machines. Four years later he sold fifty.

McCormick realized by this time that a workshop in Virginia was a poor place in which to manufacture reapers. Materials had to be brought great distances, and the reapers, which were nearly all sold to farmers in the Mississippi Valley, had to be shipped even farther. The inventor decided to build a factory nearer the wheat fields. He moved to Chicago and within a year had five hundred machines ready for the harvest.

Cyrus Hall McCormick went on from this beginning to larger and larger successes. He constantly improved

[199]

his reapers. He sold machines to farmers who needed them even though he sometimes had to wait for the payment.

The invention of the reaper was an important event in America. The principle used in cutting grain was followed in other machines used for cutting hay. More important than this, however, was the effect of the invention upon America's moving frontier. When farmers could harvest grain quickly and cheaply, they wanted larger farms. This growing demand for more land caused settlers to push farther west. It has been said that the reaper moved the American frontier west at the rate of thirty miles each year.

During the first half of the nineteenth century the United States pushed its boundaries to the Pacific coast. At the same time the American people greatly improved their manner of living. For half a century the country had turned its face toward the West, yet all the while a quarrel had been growing between the North and the South, which finally engaged the nation in a struggle for its very life. By 1861 this quarrel had become so bitter that the people of America plunged into a bloody war in which neighbor fought against neighbor, and sometimes even brother against brother.

## A Word Game

Here are some words which you should look up in the word list in the back of the book. Be able to use each word in a sentence of your own.

| | | |
|---|---|---|
| toll | steersman | steamboat |
| vehicle | towpath | packet |
| landlord | keelboat | electricity |
| roustabout | mochila | cantina |

## A Map Study

On a wall map of the United States trace the several routes mentioned in this chapter. Among these were the Lancaster Pike, the National Road, the route of the Clermont's first trip, the Erie Canal, the Mohawk and Hudson Railroad, the first telegraph line, the routes of the overland mail and pony express.

If your home is east of the Mississippi River and north of the Ohio, it is likely that a canal may have been built somewhere in your state during the first half of the nineteenth century. Inquire as to whether or not this is true. If there is a canal, learn what its route is and any facts you can about its early history.

Learn what highway today follows the route of the old National Road. Studying a road map of the United States will help you answer this question.

## Finding Answers

### Part I

Below are some questions which you should be able to answer when you finish this story. If you do not know the answers after the first reading, read again more carefully

[201]

until you find them.   You may want to use the questions in a match or race.

1. Why did the westward movement of the pioneers cause a need for better ways of living in America?
2. Where was the first paved road in the United States built?   When?
3. Why did Congress provide for building the National or Cumberland Road?   Where was this road?
4. For what was a Conestoga wagon used?   How did it look?   How did it receive its name?
5. What new improvement did John Fitch make in transportation?
6. What did Robert Fulton show by his trip in the *Clermont?*
7. Why did canal building become popular in the United States during the early part of the nineteenth century?
8. What was the effect upon New York City of the building of the Erie Canal?
9. What was a line boat?   A packet boat?
10. When was the first railroad built in the United States? How does this compare with the time of building the Erie Canal?   With the trip of the *Clermont?*
11. What were some of the difficulties and dangers which passengers on the first trains met?

## PART II

Here are some more questions.   Do you know all the answers?

1. What hardships did Morse have to meet while working out his plans for a telegraph?

2. By what routes could mail be sent to California in the fifties?

3. How was mail carried by the Butterfield Overland Mail Service?

4. What was the route of the pony express? How was the mail carried? Why was this service not continued longer?

5. Who built the first power spinning machines in America?

6. Why were spinning and weaving mills often located in the Northeastern states?

7. What difficulties did Elias Howe meet when he decided to make women's work easier?

8. Why is Cyrus Hall McCormick better known than any other man who invented a reaping machine?

### Some Things to Do

1. Look in the library for other stories about how men traveled, carried news, and found better ways to live. Tell your classmates some of the new facts that you learn.

2. Study pictures which show early trains, flatboats, keelboats, steamboats, canalboats, Conestoga wagons, and stagecoaches. Make models of these various boats and vehicles.

3. Pantomime scenes described in this story. Some good ones for this purpose would be the arrival of a stagecoach at a tavern, the first trip of the *Clermont* up the Hudson, the first trip of the *De Witt Clinton*, the loading of a steamboat, the testing of McCormick's reaper.

4. Write riddles about some of the inventions which are mentioned in this story. Here is a sample of such a riddle:

This machine was small but very strong. It did the work for which it was built, but did not win an important race. What was it?

5. Imagine that you have had one of the experiences described in this story. Tell this experience, trying to make your listeners know how you felt about it. You might pretend that you have stopped at a Western tavern, ridden in a stagecoach, made a trip on a canalboat, seen a train for the first time, or made a dress on the newly invented sewing machine.

6. Make a set of panel pictures to fit spaces on doors or between windows in your schoolroom. In these pictures tell the story of how news was carried in America before 1861. Cut paper can be used very nicely for such work.

### Some Books to Read

*Give Me a River,* by Elizabeth Palmer tells a part the river played in the lives of one settlement.

*Pony Express Goes Through,* by H. R. Driggs is the story of a boy who became an express rider.

*Smoke Blows West,* by Helen C. Fernald is a tale of railroad building and frontier life in Kansas.

Clara I. Judson tells the life of Robert Fulton in *Boat Builder,* and of George Stephenson in *Railway Engineer.*

Clara Lambert writes of the telegraph in *Talking Wires.*

Canalboat stories are:

*Dick and the Canal Boat,* by Sanford Tousey

*Jon of the Albany Belle,* by Hazel R. Langdale

If you read very well, you will want to try *Ox-team Miracle: the Story of Alexander Majors,* by Hildegarde Hawthorne.

The story of clothmaking is told in *Spin, Weave, and Wear,* by Irmengarde Eberle and Phyllis A. Carter.

# DIVISION THREE

*The Nation Struggles for its Life*

Robert E. Lee leads his men under the Stars and Bars.

# A BITTER QUARREL IS SETTLED

## The Background of the Quarrel

**Slavery gains a foothold in America.** — If you are to understand why a terrible war was fought between the people of the North and the people of the South, you must turn your thoughts back to colonial times, and from that early day watch the growth of the quarrel which was settled only on the fields of battle.

Because there was much to be done in the new country, the early setttlers in America felt a great need for workers. One way in which they met this need was by purchasing Negro slaves from sea captains who brought the black men from Africa. The first Negro slaves to be brought to the English colonies of America were landed in Virginia in 1619.

Although the Spanish had sometimes made slaves of the Indians, the red men did not make good workers. On the other hand the Negroes from Africa proved to be quite useful. When the word *slave* is used to refer to a worker in America, it may usually be supposed that a Negro slave is meant.

It seems strange today to think that less than a hundred years ago there were men, women, and children here in America who were the property of other people. These slaves were owned just as horses or cattle were. They were expected to work, and if they refused they could be punished. They might be bought or sold as their owners wished.

The use of slaves soon spread from Virginia to the other English colonies. At the time of the Revolutionary War slaves were held in each of the colonies, although there were many people who did not own any.

Slaveowners soon found that the Negroes were well suited to certain kinds of work. They were useful on the farms. The men did well when working as carpenters or blacksmiths or at other trades that were easy to learn. The women could be trained to do housework of all sorts and they made most faithful nurses for children.

[208]

The Southern colonists had found it hard to work in the heat of their long summers. The Negroes, coming from the hot regions of Africa, did not suffer in the Southern heat. Since they were useful on farms and could endure the climate of the region, Negro slaves were suited to life in the Southern colonies.

You will recall that while the United States was yet a very young nation the cotton gin and power machinery for spinning and weaving were invented. The gin made it possible to prepare cotton at a much smaller cost, while the machines for spinning and weaving created a greatly increased demand for raw cotton. Naturally, the Southern people who had the right soil and climate for growing cotton planted larger and larger areas to the crop. This brought a great need for more workers in the cotton fields — a need which the planters met by purchasing more slaves.

Cotton was not the only crop grown in the South although it was the most important one. Rice was well suited to the lowlands of Georgia and South Carolina, while Louisiana grew sugar cane. In Virginia and neighboring states splendid crops of tobacco were raised. Everywhere there were cornfields and gardens. All through the long hot summer days slaves labored in the fields of the South plowing, planting, hoeing, and picking.

During these years when slavery was gaining a strong foothold in the Southern States, quite a different thing was happening in the North. The farmers there grew corn too, but they also grew great fields of wheat, oats, rye, and barley. These grains did not require as much hard labor as did the crops grown in the South. In the North the factories were bringing thousands of people to live in cities and towns, but slave labor was not found to be useful in these factories.

[210]

Thus it happened that as slavery became more firmly fixed in the South it died out in the North. This made the United States a nation composed partly of slave and partly of free states.

As the years passed, the question began to be raised by a few people as to whether or not it was right to hold human beings as slaves. It was very easy for the Northern people who did not use slaves anyway to decide that slavery was wrong. On the other hand, it was just as easy for Southern people who depended upon slave labor to feel that slavery was right. This does not mean that all the people in the North objected to slavery, nor that everyone in the South believed in it, but only that the largest part of the people in each section decided the question in the light of their own need for slave labor.

However, the feeling against slavery grew stronger as the years passed, not only in America but in other parts of the world. The English, for example, did away with slavery in their island colonies and paid the owners a hundred million dollars for the loss of their slaves. This movement against slavery placed the South in a difficult position, since it was holding on to a custom which was passing away in other parts of the world.

## The Everyday Life of the People before the War

Just as the North and the South differed in their use of slave labor, so they also differed in their ways of living. As the people of a section developed certain customs of their own, they tended less and less to understand and like the customs of people who lived in other parts of the country.

Even within one region the people did not all live in the same way. In the South there were planters who owned great plantations and many slaves, but there were also farmers who owned few or no slaves and who did much of the work of their small farms with their own hands. There were some free Negroes, and a large number of very poor white people sometimes scornfully called "poor white trash" by their more fortunate neighbors. In the mountains the people were poor too, but they were also very proud. Southern towns and cities had their merchants, doctors, lawyers, and other workers just as Northern towns and cities had. Some of these people owned slaves, while others did not.

[212]

In the North many people lived on farms, but the cities were growing rapidly. The building of factories, canals, and railroads helped to cause this rapid growth. Much of the need for workers had been met in the North by using laborers from European countries. These people, called *immigrants* because they came to a new country to live, helped to build railroads, dig canals, work in factories, and cultivate new farms.

It will help you to understand the bitter quarrel which broke out between the North and the South if you will try to catch some glimpses of America as it was in the years just before the war began. Can you, first of all, imagine that you are visiting on a cotton plantation in Alabama in 1858?

**Glimpses of country life in the South. — When** we reach the plantation on a pleasant summer morning, we find everyone bustling about the place. A barbecue is to be given that day, and the preparations for this gay event keep both the slaves and their owners busy. In the great pits fires which have burned all night are now a mass of glowing red coals. Over these hang the joints of meat, browning slowly as the slaves turn

[213]

them back and forth. The dripping juice falls on the
hot coals with a great hissing, while delicious odors
rise to greet the eager noses of the workers.

The planter directs his men as they turn the meat,
for it is his boast that nowhere else can guests find
such perfectly cooked pork and beef as are served at
his barbecues. His wife directs the slaves who are
putting up tables under the trees and laying them with
dishes, silver, and linen.

Toward noon carriages roll into the driveway. Out
of these pour people of all ages — old gentlemen leaning
on their canes, pretty girls in hoop skirts, older women,
fat black "mammies," and children. Nearly all of the
men who are young enough to ride arrive on horseback.
The slaves lead the horses away to the barns, where
they will be fed and cared for during the day.

Soon the great white house and the shaded grounds around it are filled with groups of gay, laughing people. Young men flock around the prettiest of the girls, the older men stand about in small groups talking, while the women sit in the parlor where drawn shades keep out the light of the midday sun.   As we pass from group to group we hear talk of balls, politics, and babies.

The slaves are as happy as their master and mistress at thus entertaining company.   Not only does a barbecue mean a change from the usual daily work, but it brings their black friends from all the neighboring plantations.   They too exchange news with old friends. Especially happy today is Mose, the coachman, for his broad wife, Nancy (a wife living on another plantation), has come with her mistress to the barbecue. When Mose took a wife on a neighboring plantation, he knew that he could see her only now and then, but his master has promised that if cotton·brings a good price this year he will purchase Nancy.   Mose has this good news to tell his broad wife today.

Best of all for the slaves, however, is the prospect of their own barbecue.   Back of the carriage house is a second pit over which meat is also roasting.   Here the Negroes of the plantation and their friends from the neighborhood will feast.

Throughout the day the merrymaking continues among both whites and blacks.   When evening comes, good-byes are said with regret, for everyone is sorry to end such a pleasant day.   We are glad that we may remain for a few days longer in the great white house. In the true Southern manner our host has invited us to stay as long as we like.   Guests often remain for weeks and sometimes for months.

The day after the barbecue we are surprised to find

[216]

our hostess still busy. Instead of having nothing to do because there are nearly a hundred slaves on the plantation, the mistress finds that each new slave adds something to her cares.

We see her going about, followed by a small black girl who carries a basket of keys. In the kitchen the mistress plans with the cook for the day's meals. Calling for her key basket, she opens the cupboard and gives the cook the necessary food supplies. Then follows a talk with Mammy about the little lad who yesterday ate too much at the barbecue. As she feels his hot little head, she once more calls for her keys. This time it is the medicine chest which is opened. Here on this great plantation far from a doctor the mistress must care for all small sicknesses, whether they be of black or of white people.

We follow this busy woman as she goes out to the "quarters" where the slaves live in little cabins. She has a sharp eye for dirt, for one of the first rules of the plantation is that the cabins must be kept clean. In one she visits an old Negro who is too lame to leave his chair. His old black face lights up with joy when he sees "Missus."

In another cabin she looks in on a mother and a tiny new baby. Passing on from the cabins to a long building near by, she inspects the work of the women who are weaving. Part of the coarse cloth which is used for the slaves' clothing is made here on the plantation, but the mistress must see that the work is well done.

[217]

As noon approaches, the Negroes begin to come in from the fields where they have been at work. Once more the mistress calls for her keys, this time to open the storehouse. As she directs the work a big black man passes out the food for the day: a quart of corn meal, half a pound of salt pork, two or three big yams, and a small jug of molasses for each slave. Besides this food each Negro has vegetables in the little garden which he is required to grow beside his cabin. Many also have a few chickens and a pig or two of their own.

We return to the big white house, and find its wide verandas and long central hall cool and comfortable after the outdoor heat. When we have made ourselves tidy in one of the big bedrooms on the second floor, we come down the great curved staircase and enter the dining room. Such a feast as we find awaiting us! A platter of ham is at one end and a plate of fried chicken at the other, while between are dishes of yams, hominy, and string beans. All through the meal small black slaves run back and forth between dining room and kitchen bringing in plates of biscuits and corn bread, so hot that they turn the butter into a golden pool upon our plates. When we have eaten the first course, the slaves clear the table and bring us each a helping of blackberry dumpling covered with cream. All during the meal a half-grown Negro girl waves a long-handled brush made of peacock feathers over the table to keep the flies away.

[218]

During dinner we ask our host about his work. He tells us that he has spent part of the morning with his overseer. This is the white man who directs the field work. With him the planter has gone out to examine the quality of the cotton crop. Later he worked in his office on the accounts of the plantation.

Yesterday, as we watched the gay crowd at the barbecue, we thought that plantation life was happy and carefree. Today, as we see the planter and his wife going from one task to another, we realize that like other kinds of business a plantation must be carefully managed if it is to make money for its owner.

Following dinner comes an hour of rest, which is very welcome in this warm climate. As we talk to the family during the afternoon, we learn more about plantation life. We find that the house servants feel themselves better than the slaves who work in the yards, gardens, barns, carriage house, blacksmith and carpenter shops, or weaving house. These Negroes, however, in their turn hold themselves much above the field hands.

We find that on this plantation any slave who cares to is allowed to grow a little patch of cotton. When this is sent to market the money from its sale belongs to the Negro. Not all planters permit their slaves this privilege, but it is common on many plantations.

As evening comes the "quarters" take on new life. Over the supper fires Negro women call back and forth to each other. We catch some talking of the baptizing to be held on Sunday, when a number will be received as members of the church; we see men working on their

[220]

own little patches of ground; a boy picks on a banjo while bare black feet begin to slap the ground in a clog dance; as the dance ends, the banjo player swings into a low, wailing song which is soon caught up by voices from all over the "quarters." To the white family sitting on the veranda of the "big house" comes this sound of the singing voices. The planter and his wife

smile at each other when they hear the sound, for to them it is the sign of happy, well-cared-for slaves.

We shall not see the whole South by visiting on this great plantation. If we journey only a few miles from the planter's beautiful white house, we come to a small tumble-down dwelling where dirty-faced children and lean, hungry-looking dogs watch our approach.

Here a few acres of land so poor that it is of little worth are farmed by the tall, bony man who now appears in the door. He watches us with dull eyes which show little interest in anything around him. His skin is dry and yellow-looking, his manner lazy and careless. Faded cotton trousers and a torn shirt are his only garments, for he is barefooted and bareheaded. Surely this man who looks so sick and beaten down by hardships cannot be a neighbor of our planter friend!

Yet it is true that within a few miles of each other dwell these two men with such different ways of living. The children of one will be taught by private teachers, while the children of the other must learn all that they know in this tumble-down house and the poor fields around it. One man grows rich by using slave labor and managing his plantation well. The other tends a few acres of cotton, raises a pig or two, and depends for part of his living upon help from his richer neighbors. The planter, respected by both blacks and whites, is one of the South's leading citizens. The other man, dull, lazy, and half sick, is looked down upon, not only by the well-to-do whites but by the well-cared-for blacks as well, who speak of him in scorn as "poor white trash."

But still we have not seen all of the South. Let us go next to a farm in southwestern Kentucky. Here, as in many other places in the South, lives a farmer who is neither "white trash" nor planter. He owns his land and cultivates it with the help of his sons and one slave family.

The house which he built when he brought his bride to this farm was a one-room log cabin. When he grew more prosperous he added another cabin beside the first, and covered the passage between them. As his family grew larger he raised the roof of the cabins to form a second story, so that now he has a four-room house.

In the big kitchen his wife cooks on a huge fireplace. In this same room the table is spread for dinner, with a red checked tablecloth and dishes well heaped with bacon, corn bread, mush, and cabbage. A pitcher of molasses, a plate of butter, and glasses of milk complete the simple dinner.

The room across the passage serves as a bedroom for the farmer and his wife, and as a sitting room when the family want something better than the kitchen where they usually sit. Upstairs are two small bedrooms for the children and any guests who may come.

The Negro family lives in a cabin in the back yard. Sometimes the slave mother helps the farmer's wife, but at the seasons when the corn must be hoed or the tobacco wormed, she leaves her black babies to play with the smaller white children and works in the field. At such times the farmer's wife goes about her household tasks with an eye on all the children, white and black alike.

This farmer, although working his own fields and living in a simple log house, is also a slaveowner in a small way. His children will receive some education and will go out into the world to be farmers, merchants, and perhaps even doctors, lawyers, or preachers. This hard-working farmer is a respected even if not a rich citizen.

One more glimpse we must have of country life in the South. This time we look in upon a family that lives high up in the mountains of eastern Tennessee. Here, too, we find a log cabin, but this one contains but a single room and a loft.

Outside the door the man of the family stands. His hand rests upon the barrel of his gun, for he has just returned from squirrel hunting. Half a dozen dogs lie about his feet, their tongues lolling out as they pant. The man's eyes are steady and straight as he watches our approach, and his head is held high. Although he is dressed in homespun trousers and cotton shirt, this mountain man has dignity.

We know as we watch him that he is proud and with-

out fear.   He will share his corn pone and bacon with us because we are his guests, but he will not talk to us about his business.   Here is a man living much as other people in the mountains have lived for many years past, and loving freedom even as they loved it.   In the mountains of Virginia, Kentucky, the Carolinas, and Georgia we could find thousands of other men who are very much like this Tennessee mountaineer.

**Glimpses of life in the North.** — People of the North did not all live in the same way any more than did the people of the South. There were farms both in the long-settled regions of northeastern United States and in the newer lands farther west. Seaport cities had grown rich on the profits of trade. Mill towns drew workers from all the country round and held them to hours of labor that were longer than those usually in force among slaves on the plantations. Here and there a man grew rich in a few years, his profits made from some business that had prospered as the country developed. Fortunes were made in Western fur trade. Others had their beginning in profits from railroad building. Owners of mills where cotton and wool were turned into cloth became wealthy. There were of course merchants, doctors, lawyers, teachers, and many other workers who supplied the everyday needs of the people.

To picture all of these types of life is not possible, but we may catch glimpses of a few. Let us look first at New York City in the years which followed the great fire of 1835.

The city which has grown up after this terrible accident has more than a quarter of a million people, a larger number than have ever before lived together in one city in America. Building is going forward on every side. The Astor House, which promises to give the world a new standard of luxury in hotels; bridges to connect the city on the island with its neighbors on the mainland; great water systems to carry pure water for the use of the citizens; these and many other improvements tell us of a growing city.

What may we see as we walk through the streets? Everywhere there is color, movement, noise. Carriages move along the streets beside heavy wagons and carts. Boxes and barrels, recently arrived by ship, joggle along on the loaded wagons as they are carried to the merchants' warehouses. Carts loaded with fruit stand waiting for a passing buyer. Barrels filled with lemonade offer a drink to any thirsty person who has a few pennies. The baker boy rings his bell and cries, "Hot bread, who buys?" Ladies in rustling silks drive slowly along in their carriages, taking the air and exchanging greetings with friends. This jumble of sights and sounds gives us some key to the nature of this pushing city that has gone ahead of all its sister cities in the race for wealth and size.

Let us pass over a few years of time and travel to Lowell, Massachusetts. Here is a city whose whole business life is concerned with the manufacture of cotton. It depends for workers almost entirely upon the women from the country and smaller towns, for about seven eighths of the factory workers are women.

[227]

The rich millowners know that it is important to keep conditions such that parents will be willing for their daughters to enter the mills. They have met this need by building company boardinghouses where the girls live.

Hours are just as long here as in all the other cotton mills where men, women, and little children labor for twelve hours or more a day. However, in Lowell the workers are still looked after when they return to their boardinghouses, for even the times when they get up and go to bed are fixed by rule. If we want to know how mill hands work, let us follow some of these girls through one day.

It is the middle of the winter and cold, but the rising bell rings at five in the morning. Shivering, the girls quickly dress, eat breakfast, and are off for the mills. Lamps burn for several hours after the workers are in their places.

[228]

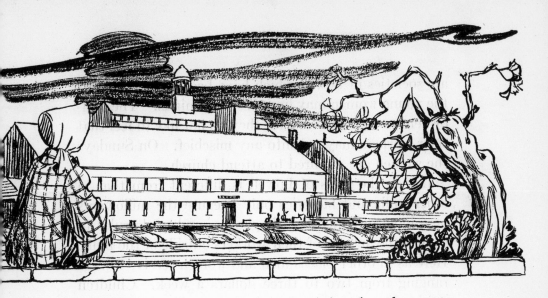

All morning the women stand, performing the same act over and over thousands of times as they tend the machines. Noon whistles bring a brief change, for a half hour is allowed for lunch. In that time the workers must walk to their boardinghouses, eat, and return to the mill.

The afternoon is spent as was the morning, standing before whirring machines. The air is thick with the lint from the cotton, and not a window is open. Factory owners cannot be expected to waste heat, and in any case opinion in 1850 holds that fresh air is dangerous. As evening comes the lamps are again lighted, and their odor makes the already foul air a bit worse. However, seven o'clock finally arrives and factory workers are free for the rest of the day.

They eat supper in their boardinghouses and have the time from then until ten o'clock for sewing, washing, ironing, reading, visiting, shopping, and the like. There

[229]

are societies in Lowell which have been formed so that the young women may improve their minds. The millowners encourage these, for they do not like to feel that their workers may get into any mischief. On Sundays the women are required to attend church.

Life in the mills of Lowell is different from that in other mills and factories only because the millowners here have provided boardinghouses and made rules to govern the actions of their workers outside of the mills. Here as in other places men and women receive a wage ranging from two to three dollars a week. Children receive less.

Many people in the North had more interesting lives than the poor millworkers. Perhaps we can see some of them if we imagine ourselves traveling across the rolling prairies of Illinois in 1850. It is autumn and everywhere the cornstalks stand row upon row, their leaves turning from green to brown. Great ears of the ripening grain hang heavy on every stalk. Already the farmers are in the fields with their wagons, tearing the ears from the plants, stripping off the husks, and tossing the ears into their wagon beds. Now a loaded wagon starts toward a corncrib which stands near a farmhouse.

Not only corn but pigs are to be seen on every hand. The two go together in Illinois, where the rich black soil gives the farmer great harvests and where much of the corn in its turn becomes food for hogs. If we stop at a railroad station, we are almost sure to see a load of these squealing animals starting their journey for Chicago, where packing houses are growing larger each year.

If we pay a visit to a farmhouse after freezing weather has come, we may find butchering day in full swing there. What a hurrying and scurrying! What a bustle of preparations as the farmer makes ready his outdoor fires, scalds the freshly killed animals, and scrapes off the bristles! Indoors the housewife is only waiting for her husband to finish dressing the animal so that she may begin grinding sausage, making head cheese, and rendering lard. Tonight the kitchen will be filled with the delicious odor of fresh pork frying over a wood fire.

Corn harvest! Butchering time! What else can Illinois show us in the autumn? There are schoolhouses along these roads, and red-cheeked boys and girls swinging along toward them, each with a dinner pail in hand.

We meet a lawyer riding his circuit in a rattling old buggy drawn by a big, rawboned horse. Over fourteen counties he rides, trying law cases in the courts of each. When night comes, he stops in a tavern if one is near. If not, a farmhouse will be equally welcome, and for the shelter and food received by him and his horse the farmer will probably accept no money. A visitor means news of the towns, a pleasant change for a farm family.

Another traveler who also rides his circuit over these

Illinois prairies is a Methodist preacher. Mounted on a horse, with his Bible and a clean shirt in his saddle-bags, he goes up and down the country preaching to the people of the rewards and punishments of a future life.

A strange little figure comes tramping along. It is a short, squarely built man with a great pack on his back. His dark face has a foreign look, and his speech when he greets us shows that he is indeed the son of another land. The dark little man is a peddler, and in the pack on his back he carries goods to sell to the farmers' wives.

[232]

What a happy day it is when he opens his pack and takes out dress lengths of bright calico and good stout woolens, packages of needles, bolts of braid, and dozens of other articles dear to the hearts of women!

Past farmhouses and through villages we travel until we come at last to Springfield. This little capital town is rapidly taking on city ways. In the pages of the *Journal* and the *Register* its merchants announce all manner of articles for sale. Telegraph wires bring news from many other parts of the country.

The public square and the main streets in the business district are paved with boards. Some citizens are insisting that waste should no longer be thrown in the alleys. The town council has passed a law which states that no hog shall be allowed to run at large in the streets unless it has a ring in its nose. Pretty frame houses and larger ones of brick and stone make comfortable dwelling places.

As in Illinois, so in many other parts of the North, men and women are happy and contented as they see their farms grow richer and their towns become larger year by year. In a region where every man is a free man, people learn to respect each other and to have little feeling that one man is better than another.

## The Growth of the Quarrel

**Slavery extends to the territories.** — Even though one part of the country was slave and one part free, that in itself did not cause the quarrel. This came about over the question of whether states formed in new territory should become free or slave states. The Ordinance of 1787 had stated that slaves should never be held in the Northwest Territory, but when the lands lying west of the Mississippi River were added to the United States a policy about slaveholding in these regions had to be determined.

It seemed very important to the South that there should always be as many slave as free states. Since each state had two Senators, the South could protect its own interests as long as there were as many Senators from slave as from free states. Naturally, whenever new territory was to be made into states, a struggle followed between the two sections, because each was trying to gain its own ends.

The first of these struggles came when Missouri asked to become a state. After long debate, the question was settled in 1820 by a law known as the Missouri Compromise. This law permitted Missouri to become a slave state but stated that no other slave states could be created north of a line extending along the southern boundary of Missouri.

This compromise settled the struggle for a time, but in 1850, when the new territory gained in the Mexican War had to be made into states, feeling ran high again. It seemed for a time that the nation would break apart over the question, but once more the quarrel was quieted by a famous compromise. Henry Clay proposed this new compromise, which made it possible for each side to have some things which it wanted and required it to give up other things.

Tempers were white hot, and no man in Congress wanted to yield an inch. When Clay saw that his bill would not pass unless he had help, he went one night through a snowstorm to ask Daniel Webster, of Massachusetts, to aid him. A few weeks later, this great Senator made a speech which probably saved the Union, for it secured the passage of Clay's compromise. This delayed the final struggle for another ten years.

**The North and South do not think alike.** — Each time that the question of extending slavery came up, feeling between the North and the South grew more bitter. Some of the Southern leaders began to say that it would be better for their states to leave the Union and to form a new nation of their own. South Carolina, in particular, felt that it must withdraw from the Union if things continued as they were. A great leader from this state who had long held this belief was John C. Calhoun.

During these troubled years the United States Congress had three members who had great influence. Calhoun, the Southerner, believed in the right of each state to leave the Union if it desired to do so. Webster and Clay, on the other hand, felt that nothing was so important as preserving the Union. In the years since the Constitution was written, love of the Union had greatly increased. More than anyone else Daniel Webster had been the cause of this new feeling. In all his speeches he talked of the necessity for building a strong Union.

The quarrel between North and South would never have grown so bitter had people in these different sections known and understood each other better. People did not travel as much or receive news of each other as easily as we do today. Since they were not well acquainted, people did not learn to like and trust one another.

In both North and South there were people of extreme ideas. In the South such people constantly talked of how much more capable Southern people were than their Northern neighbors. In the North certain extreme groups were always trying to have all slaves freed. Naturally, such ideas on either side only stirred up more bitter feelings and drove the two sections further apart.

The South insisted that if slaves ran away to the North they should be captured and returned to their owners by Northern officers. Many people in the

North objected to this and some even helped slaves to escape to Canada. Of course this dispute made even wider the difference between the two sections.

**The Southern states leave the Union.** — By 1860 feeling had become so bitter that leaders in South Carolina and certain other states said that they would take their states out of the Union if Abraham Lincoln were elected President of the United States. This man, little known until a short time before 1860, was an Illinois lawyer who loved the Union. Southern people felt that he would favor the North, and perhaps free their slaves.

With Lincoln's election in November, 1860, the Southern leaders began to make good their threat. On December 20 South Carolina seceded, which means that the state announced that it was no longer a part of the Union. The people of Charleston were wild with excitement. Church bells rang, cannon were fired, and the state flag was hung in every doorway while crowds cheered. "Thank God they have put her out at last!" cried one man. His friend replied, "I breathe free at last."

By the end of February Georgia, Florida, Alabama, Mississippi, Louisiana, and Texas had followed South Carolina. A new government was set up for these "Confederate States of America," as the seceding states chose to call themselves. Jefferson Davis of Mississippi was elected President.

When Abraham Lincoln was inaugurated as President of the United States on March 4, 1861, he faced a hard task. Seven states had seceded. Other Southern states were debating the question of whether to stay or to secede. Northern people were divided. Some believed that the seceding states should be allowed to go in peace, while others held that the United States should go to war if necessary in order to force the seceded states to return to the Union.

Conditions remained about the same for a month
[238]

after Lincoln took office. Then came an event which decided the course of action for both North and South.

The Confederate States expected to take over property owned by the United States within their territory. Near Charleston, South Carolina, were three forts which the Government was asked to surrender to the Confederates. When the officer in command refused to surrender, the Confederates opened fire upon Fort Sumter. Can you imagine that you are in Charleston on that April day long ago?

Gray dawn has begun to streak the sky, while a light rain falls over the city as the first boom of a cannon is heard. Almost before the sound dies away a door is jerked open, then another, and another. People are streaming out of the houses. With no thought of the rain, they pour through the streets toward the harbor. The docks, streets, and yards along the ocean front are soon crowded.

Like a group watching a play, these people watch the shelling of Fort Sumter. Each shot which reaches its mark brings a round of clapping from the men of Charleston while the women wave their handkerchiefs in delight.

The guns from the fort reply, and as the hours pass the firing continues. The rain ceases and pale sunshine dries the clothing of the watching people, but still they hold their places along the ocean front. Now a vessel bearing supplies appears outside the harbor, but having no guns it dares not go to the help of the fort.

[239]

Night brings a storm, but even this does not drive back the eager watchers. When morning of the second day dawns, they see that the walls of the fort are giving way. Now a part of the building is burning! The Confederate commander again calls upon the fort to surrender. Again the officer refuses. The flagstaff is shot down, but the soldiers nail it back in place. The guns on shore still boom and the guns in the fort reply. Flames burst out in new spots. At last, on the afternoon of the second day, a white flag is run up on the fort. The officer and his men can do no more.

It is arranged that on the next day, April 14, 1861, the men are to march out of Fort Sumter. All of Charleston seems to be crowding the water front to see the surrender. The sea is a deep, rich blue under the spring sunshine. At two o'clock the officer in command fires a last salute of fifty guns and marches his men out. The Confederates march in; a new flag is run up; and the crowds cheer.

Swift as lightning the news travels over the telegraph

wires, "Fort Sumter has surrendered." Southerners are delighted. Not only have they won their first fight, but this victory has brought in other states. Virginia, North Carolina, Arkansas, and Tennessee soon join the Confederacy.

In the North, President Lincoln calls for seventy-five thousand men to serve as soldiers, that the Union may be saved. With the flag fired upon, Northerners are no longer divided in their thinking. A united North faces a united South. The long, bitter quarrel has at last become an open war.

## The Leaders in the Conflict

Before we read the story of the war years that followed Fort Sumter, we must learn somthing of the men who were leaders in this conflict. Among these leaders were many army officers who fought with courage.

Respect is due such an officer in the Northern army as Ulysses S. Grant, under whose command the Union forces finally won the war. Another Northerner was William T. Sherman, who from the beginning saw clearly the steps that must be taken to end the war. George H. Thomas was a Union officer who won for himself the nickname "the Rock of Chickamauga" when he held his men to their positions while all around them Northern soldiers retreated. In the Southern army the great leader was General Robert E. Lee, but among the other men whose fame has lived was "Stonewall" Jackson, whose death was one of the greatest losses that the Confederates suffered. Joseph E. Johnston was a careful and able general, while one of the most daring was Nathan B. Forrest, who, when asked by a woman the secret of his success, replied, "Ma'am, I got thar fust with the most men."

[242]

Not only army officers but men who served their governments in other ways should be counted among the leaders. In the South, Jefferson Davis was called to be President of the Confederate States. He would rather have served as an officer in the army, but he accepted the work that he was called to do and held the office of President until the close of the war. After the conflict had ended in defeat for the Confederate States, Jefferson Davis showed himself to be unusually fair and open-minded. In those bitter years which followed the war, while hate still burned white-hot, he was a big enough man to say to his neighbors in Mississippi, "The past is dead, let it bury its dead — before you lies the future. Let me beseech you to lay aside all bitter, sectional feeling, and to make your places in the ranks of those who will bring about a reunited country."

In the North one great leader appeared to stand head and shoulders above all other leaders in the conflict. This man was Abraham Lincoln, the President of the United States. In the South the great hero of the Confederates was their commanding officer, General Robert E. Lee. Of these two men we shall hear more.

[243]

**The man who saved the Union.** — Probably no other man who has been President of the United States has been so much scorned during his life and praised after his death as has Abraham Lincoln. Who was this stranger who came almost unknown from the prairies of Illinois to lead the nation in a time of great trouble? Why was he hated by some of the very men who had helped elect him to office?

The long quarrel over the matter of extending slavery into the new territories had helped to bring about changes in the political parties in the United States. The group founded by Thomas Jefferson had become known as the Democratic party. Opposing it was another group whose members called themselves Whigs. Each party had members in both the North and the South. When the feeling over slavery became very bitter, there naturally came to be divisions of opinion within each party. As a result of these political difficulties a new party, which took the name Republican, was formed in 1854. Its chief purpose was to prevent the spread of slavery to territory north of the line that had been established by the Missouri Compromise.

Abraham Lincoln, who had been a Whig, joined the newly formed Republican party and soon became one of its leaders in Illinois. In 1858 he ran for the United States Senate against Stephen A. Douglas, a Democrat who had served Illinois in that office for some years. The two men held debates at many places in the state, and it was the speeches which he made on these occa-

[244]

sions which first caused people in other states to take notice of Abraham Lincoln. Stephen A. Douglas won the race for Senator, but the tall Illinois lawyer had made himself known throughout the country.

Two years later the Republican party chose Abraham Lincoln as its candidate for President of the United States. The Democratic party was in a difficult position because its members had split over the question of slavery. The Northern Democrats, who were opposed to extending slavery, named Stephen A. Douglas as their candidate, while Southern Democrats named John C. Breckinridge. Another group put a fourth candidate into the race, but he had no chance to be elected. With the Democratic vote split, the new Republican party had a splendid opportunity for success. Thus it was that Abraham Lincoln, a man with small experience in affairs of government and little known beyond his own state, became President of the United States in 1861.

True to their threat made before the election, certain of the Southern states seceded. Fort Sumter was forced to surrender. What would the tall, lank lawyer in the White House do in such a time?

Many of the leading Republicans doubted whether Lincoln was an able man. They did not expect him to take an active part in governing the country, but rather to turn over many of his duties to them. Never did men make a worse mistake. The big, quiet President had little experience in matters of government,

but he had something more important — a great love for the Union. He had taken an oath to support the Constitution of the United States of America. He believed that that oath meant that he should save the Union which he loved. That thing he meant to do, and he did it.

To understand the man, Lincoln, we need to look back across the years and know the boy, Abraham. In a tiny, one-room log cabin near Hodgenville, Kentucky, Abraham Lincoln was born on the 12th of February, 1809. This cabin was a poor little house, with a dirt floor, a fireplace of logs lined with mud, and a single window without any glass in it. The rough farm with its red clay soil yielded a poor living for Thomas Lincoln and his family, so three years after little Abraham was born the father took his wife, Nancy Hanks Lincoln, little Sarah, who was then five, and the small boy to another Kentucky farm a few miles away.

There on the Knob Creek Farm, as it was called,
the boy lived until he was past seven. He grew old
enough to attend the pioneer school, and twice a day
walked the four miles which lay between his father's
cabin and the log schoolhouse. He learned his letters,
and a little of reading, and how to write his name.

[247]

With his sister, Sarah, he picked wild berries, grapes, and fruit. He helped to shell the corn and grind it between two rocks into coarse corn meal. He gathered walnuts in the fall and had hands stained brown with the walnut juice. When planting time came, he dropped corn, beans, and potatoes for his father. Everyone must work on a pioneer farm, and small Abe had to do his share.

Thomas Lincoln had heard of the rich, black soil of Indiana. It was hard for a poor man to make a living in Kentucky; so he decided to move to Indiana. In 1816 he and his family reached the farm which he had taken up on Little Pigeon Creek in the southern part of the state. They had not even a horse or a cow. Around them stood the trees of the wilderness. Above their heads was a winter sky.

For shelter the family built an "open-faced camp" — a three-sided cabin open to the south. On this side a log fire was kept burning day and night. Inside the cabin were beds of dry leaves covered with home-spun blankets and bearskins.

In this poor shelter the Lincolns lived for a year while the father cleared the land, planted a bit of corn between the stumps, and prepared logs for a real cabin. The children carried water from a spring a mile away. For food they had wild game that their father killed, wild berries and fruits from the forest, fish from the creek, and the little corn that they raised.

Only a little while after the family had moved into

the new cabin Nancy Hanks Lincoln became sick. The nearest doctor was thirty-five miles away; so the pioneer mother died without a doctor's care. She was buried under a tree not far from the cabin, in a coffin that Thomas Lincoln made for her. Abe and Sarah were left to keep house for their father as best they could.

Some two years later the children stayed alone while Thomas Lincoln made a trip back to Kentucky. What a pleasant surprise they had one day when a wagon pulled by four horses appeared at their door! As they stared in wonder, their father climbed down and helped a woman to the ground. Out of the back of the wagon rolled a boy and two girls. Thomas Lincoln led the woman toward the staring children and said, "Here's your new Mammy." Thus it was that Sarah Bush Lincoln, who had been the Widow Johnston, came to her new home with the three Johnston children.

Out of that wagon came also feather beds and pillows, a walnut bureau, a chest, some chairs, and many small household articles. Sarah Lincoln brought comfort never before known in the cabin on Pigeon Creek, but to the growing boy she brought something more precious than the soft feather beds. She gave him love, sympathy, and understanding. When his father objected to the boy's wasting his time over the few books that he could get, the new mother said that Abe should study as much as he liked. She saw that he attended school whenever there was one at the log schoolhouse, though all the terms together did not give the boy more than four months of schooling.

During the years on Pigeon Creek Abe grew taller and taller. When he was seventeen he stood six feet four inches. This young giant had learned to do the work of a pioneer. He could chop trees, split rails, cut logs, drive a plow, husk corn, and do a hundred other things required of a pioneer boy. Because he was long-legged, he could run faster than the other lads, and his strength made it easy for him to win in wrestling matches. Although he could do what other boys and young men of the frontier were doing, Abe Lincoln was different. He wanted more than anything else to get on in the world — to have an education, to be a man of importance.

Young Lincoln worked as a farm hand, ran a ferry-boat, and helped to take goods down the Ohio and Mississippi Rivers on flatboats, but all the time he was eagerly reading every book that he could borrow.

He seldom had money enough to buy one and books were scarce on the frontier. Even so the young backwoodsman managed to find some to read. When he was twenty-one, he went with his family to Illinois, which he was always, after that, to call home. Not long after, he left his father's house for New Salem, where he intended to work in a store.

During the next few years Abraham Lincoln worked as a storekeeper; served as a captain in the war against Black Hawk, an Indian chief; acted as a surveyor; sat as a member of the state legislature; and studied law. One March day in 1837 he rode into Springfield, the new capital of Illinois, on a borrowed horse. He had seven dollars in his pockets and he was more than a thousand dollars in debt. The poor struggling young lawyer was coming to the new capital to begin his practice.

The next twenty years brought some of the things that the boy Abe had so much wanted. The young lawyer began to win cases. His gift of storytelling and speechmaking brought him success. He rode the circuit and tried cases in many towns. His funny stories and kind acts brought him friends. He made money, paid his debts, and lived in a comfortable house.

As he grew older and thought more about matters of government, Abraham Lincoln came to believe that in the growing quarrel between North and South the one important thing was to save the Union. He
[252]

did not want to see slavery extended, but it was not what happened to slavery but what happened to the Union that concerned him.

When the South seceded, the newly made President called for men to fight to save the Union. When the border states, Maryland, Kentucky, and Missouri, found it hard to decide whether or not to follow the example of the Southern states, he set out to hold them in the Union, and he succeeded. For four years he directed the war, sometimes having the support of the Northern people and sometimes hearing them cry, "Down with Lincoln!" Even important Republicans treated him with scorn, saying that he did not have fine manners, that he was a nobody risen to power. The strong face took on deep lines, the broad shoulders stooped, but the man who had set out to save the Union never turned back.

He lived to see victory come to the Northern army, to know that, at last, the nation was saved. Then, as he sat watching a play in Ford's Theater in Washington, D. C., he was shot by a half-crazy man named John Wilkes Booth. His wife and friends carried him to a house across the street. Men in high offices came and stood around his bed, but the Great Leader never knew that men who for four years had scorned him were now ready to pay him honor. As morning broke over Washington, the telegraph wires carried to Americans, both North and South, the terrible words, "Lincoln is dead!"

The man who grew up on Pigeon Creek lies under a marble tomb in Springfield, the town where he first found success. In Washington, where he faced laughter and scorn, a grateful nation has built a beautiful white marble monument to his memory. But neither tomb nor monument is needed, for the Union which he saved is the only monument to this man's greatness that is needed.

**The best-loved Southerner.** — When the leaders of the Confederate cause were looking about for a commander of the army, their choice fell upon a tall, handsome Virginian named Robert Edward Lee. That this choice was a popular one with the Southern people there can be no doubt. "Marse Robert," as his soldiers called him, became the best-loved man in the South. In victory he showed himself to be a wise and able general, but in defeat his real greatness shone forth like a lighted candle glowing in a dark room.

Robert E. Lee came of a very old and famous family. His father, nicknamed "Light Horse Harry" Lee, was a dashing young officer of the American Army during the Revolution. For his bravery in this war he won high praise.

The boy Robert grew up in Alexandria, Virginia, the little town which stands only a few miles from Mount Vernon, the home of George Washington. Although that great American was dead before Robert E. Lee was born, the child was much influenced by the memories of Washington that lived on in the little

[254]

town. He went every Sunday to Christ Church, where the first President had worshiped. He played with little Mary Custis, a great-granddaughter of Martha Washington. Often the two children listened to stories told by Mary's father, George Washington Parke Custis, who was proud of the fact that he had been loved and treated as a son by the great hero.

It is small wonder that the black-eyed, black-haired little boy came to have a great love and respect for George Washington. Small wonder, too, that he learned to love the two things which Washington had loved best — Virginia and the Union. When as a young man he made Mary Custis his wife, he had set still another link between his life and that of the First American.

In 1825, when he was eighteen years old, young Robert E. Lee went to West Point, the school where American army officers are trained. Here he studied to be an engineer and finished his course with honors. The tall Virginian was so handsome that his friends called him a "marble model." They liked him, and voted him the most popular man in his class. This was perhaps a little surprising, since he did not do many things that were considered correct for a young gentleman of that day. When his friends drank liquor, young Lee took ice water. When others smoked, played cards, or attended the theater, he quietly refused to join them. Though they did not always understand such actions, Lee's classmates respected him for doing what he believed to be right.

It was during the Mexican War that Robert E. Lee first had opportunity to show his skill as an army officer. He was one of the engineers who planned and carried out the siege of Veracruz and the storming of Chapultepec. General Winfield Scott, the American commander in the Mexican War, said of the younger man, "He was the very best soldier that I ever saw in the field."

In the quarrel which was growing between North and South Robert E. Lee did not find himself in entire sympathy with the Southern position. He loved the Union, and any idea of breaking it apart seemed wrong to him. He had long hated slavery and had already given his own slaves their freedom. Because of his years at West Point and in the army, he knew Northern men and he did not for a moment share the view held by most Southerners that the Northerners were cowards who could easily be defeated.

As state after state seceded, Lee looked on with a troubled mind. In 1861 he wrote a letter in which he told how he felt about the matter. He said in part, "I wish to live under no other government, and there is no sacrifice I am not ready to make for the preservation of the Union, save that of honor. If a disruption takes place, I shall go back in sorrow to my people and share the misery of my native state, and save in her defense there will be one less soldier in the world than now."

Fort Sumter was fired upon. Virginia seceded. What would Robert E. Lee do? This soldier was a deeply religious man. Every day of his life he prayed that God would guide him to do the right thing. Can you understand how terrible was the problem which this man faced? He was an officer in the army of the United States. He loved the Union which his father had helped to found. On the other hand, he was a son of Virginia, and deeply devoted to his native state. For three days after Virginia seceded Lee struggled with this problem of where his duty lay. Then he resigned from the army of the United States and accepted the position of commander of the Virginia forces.

Robert E. Lee still hoped that he could fight only in defense of Virginia, and not against the Union. Time was to prove that this was not possible, and General Lee was finally to think of the cause of the Confederate States as his cause. However, to the end of the war he remained directly in command of the army of Virginia and left to other officers the fighting which had to be done in other parts of the country. Once, when President Davis suggested that it might be wise for him to go to Tennessee, General Lee said, "My heart and thoughts will always be with this army," meaning the army of Virginia.

For four years this gentle man led his boys in gray, fighting bravely a fight which at last ended in defeat. Riding on his big gray horse Traveler, he was a well-known and well-loved figure.

Although he was always reserved, he had a friendly understanding for his soldiers. Himself a deeply religious man, he was glad when he found his men in prayer. One story is told of a soldier who approached the general and asked for "a chaw of tobacco." Without any reproach for the man's boldness in making such a request to his commander, General Lee, who never

[258]

used tobacco, quietly sent the man to get the tobacco from another officer who had some.

When the war ended, there were men in the Southern army who would have been glad to continue the fighting alone or in small bands after they returned home. General Lee put an end to any such ideas when he said, "All you boys who fought for me go home and help build up the shattered fortunes of our old state."

Robert E. Lee was a great man in the war years, but a greater one in the troubled years which followed. While many men, both North and South, were still filled with hatred and bitterness, he talked of the need for peace and friendship. He appealed to the people of the South to join hands with their neighbors of the North in order that the United States might once more become a great country. So we honor "Marse Robert," a loyal Virginian, a brave Southerner, and a great American who at all times did his duty as he saw it.

[259]

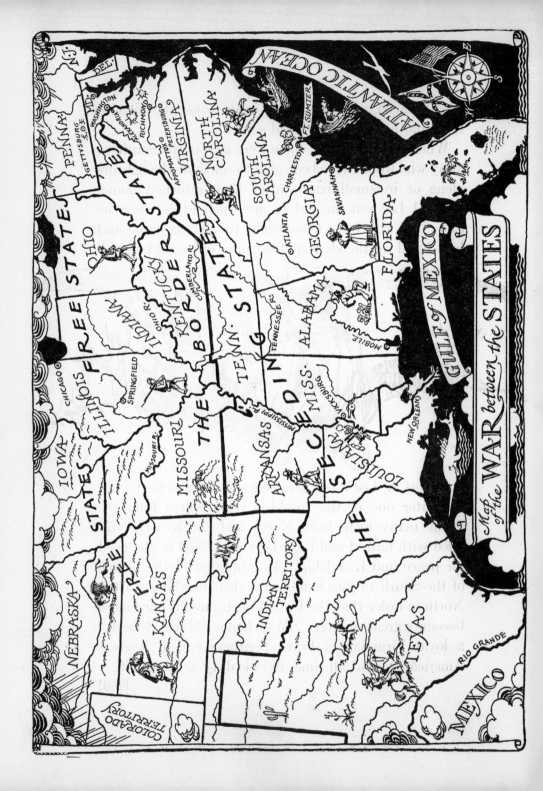

**The plan which won the war.** — When the War between the States began, leaders in the North had no clear plan for fighting it, but they finally came to see that there were four steps which must be taken to conquer the South. To General Grant and General Sherman belongs much of the credit for making and carrying out this plan.

First of all, the North must close the sea to Southern shipping. This was called putting a blockade around the South. This was important because the South had much cotton and tobacco but few factories. As long as the Southern people could ship their cotton and tobacco to Europe they could buy the guns, bullets, powder, shoes, clothing, and other articles that they needed to fight a war. President Lincoln established a blockade soon after Fort Sumter surrendered. Of course some ships, called blockade runners, did get through to Southern ports, but on the whole the blockade was one of the strongest weapons that the North used in the war.

The second important thing for the North to do was to seize control of the Mississippi River, for this would cut the Confederacy into two parts. Much of the meat used by the Southern soldiers came from Texas. With the North holding the Mississippi, supplies could not be shipped to the Confederate armies east of the river.

The third step in the plan called for Northern troops

[261]

to make a drive through the heart of the Confederacy. They were to take over the Tennessee and Cumberland Rivers and to sweep across Georgia from the mountains to the sea. Such a drive as this would destroy much of the food that was being grown to feed the Confederate army. It would also make it possible to destroy the railroad lines which ran out of Atlanta, one of the best railroad centers of the South.

The last step needed to overcome the South was a drive against Lee's splendid army of Virginia, which guarded the Confederate capital at Richmond. For a long time the Northern leaders saw this as the only really important step, and they lost thousands of soldiers in battles fought in northern Virginia. However, it was not until after the Mississippi had been taken and the central part of the Confederacy entered that Richmond finally fell.

**Carrying out the plan.** — During 1862 and the early
months of 1863 General Grant labored in the West to
get control of the Mississippi.   Admiral Farragut of the
United States Navy had sailed past two forts and
captured New Orleans, but the Confederates had a
strong position at Vicksburg, Mississippi.   During a
very wet winter Grant moved his men into position
around Vicksburg.   Since he could not take the city in
battle, he sat down before it for the slow business of
starving the Confederates into surrender.

For six weeks this condition continued, with the two
lines so close together that Northern "Yanks" and
Southern "Johnnies" called greetings to each other
and traded supplies.   A "Yank" usually had bread,
and a "Johnnie" tobacco.   Many a package was
tossed from one line to another or passed across on the
point of a bayonet.   Paper became so scarce in Vicksburg that newspapers were printed on the back of wall-
paper.   The Northern men liked to get copies of them.

There came a day, however, when the Confederate commander met General Grant under an oak tree and arranged the conditions of surrender. On July 4, 1863, the Union army entered Vicksburg and the entire Mississippi was in the hands of the North.

That week was a time of rejoicing for Northern people, for on the third of July General Lee's army had been defeated at Gettysburg, Pennsylvania. The Southern commander had led an army into the North to threaten Pennsylvania and perhaps New York. He met the Northern army under General Meade, and after three days of fighting around the little Pennsylvania town was forced to retreat into Virginia. The combined effect of winning the Battle of Gettysburg in the East and capturing Vicksburg in the West greatly encouraged the Northern people.

This news of victory in 1863 was more than usually welcome in the North because during the first two years of the war the South had won the larger part of the battles fought. President Lincoln appointed one general after another to command the Northern forces, but they all seemed equally weak. While this was happening in the North, General Lee and General "Stonewall" Jackson were winning some great victories for the South.

The drive into the heart of the Confederacy was the combined work of several Union generals, but it was General Sherman who was called upon to lead his men across Georgia. With that able Confederate, General

Joseph E. Johnston, hindering him at every turn, he made his way to Atlanta, which he captured and held as his headquarters. The citizens of Atlanta were sent out of the city and it was turned into an army camp. The loss of this city was a great blow to the South because of its importance as a railroad center.

After some two months, the Northern general set out on what has become known in history as Sherman's march to the sea. In a little less than a month the Union army marched from Atlanta to Savannah, destroying supplies, railroad lines, roads, bridges, and many buildings. A path sixty miles wide was left bare and ruined — silent witness to the cruelty and terror of war.

All the Georgia men who could carry guns had long since gone to the front, leaving only the slaves, women, children, and very old men at home. It was not a part of General Sherman's plan to injure or kill any of these people, and for the most part they were not harmed. But it was part of the plan to destroy everything which could be used to help the Confederate soldiers. Cotton that might be sold to bring money was burned. Food that might feed the army was destroyed or seized. Roads and bridges over which troops might march were torn up. Rails over which goods could be shipped were pulled up and twisted out of shape.

To the people of Georgia who had to stand by and watch their property destroyed, this seemed a wicked waste. Some of the bitterest memories left by the war

[265]

were caused by this march to the sea, yet it certainly did much to make the war shorter and thus to save lives that would have been lost in battle. At its best, war is a cruel business.

On Christmas Eve, 1864, President Lincoln received from General Sherman a telegram which said, "I beg to present you as a Christmas gift the city of Savannah, with one hundred and fifty heavy guns and plenty of ammunition, also about twenty-five thousand bales of cotton."

[266]

When 1865 opened, the Southern cause seemed lost.
The blockade had cut off supplies from other countries.
It was clear by that time that neither England nor
France was going to give help to the Confederacy as
Southern leaders had so long hoped that they would.
The states west of the Mississippi could no longer give

aid. A strong Union army was camped in Georgia, ready to march north across the Carolinas.

Yet, bad as things were, the South would not yield. President Jefferson Davis felt that while there was a Confederate to bear arms the fight must go on. General Lee and the other army leaders would not surrender as long as their President called upon them to fight. So the weary struggle continued into the spring months. The Confederate soldiers were ragged and hungry, often without bullets for their guns, and almost never having medicines or bandages to care for their wounds; yet they stood by their leaders to the bitter end. Northern soldiers might feel that the principles for which the Confederates fought were wrong, but they never questioned the courage with which they carried on that fight.

Grant, who after his success in the West had been made commander of all the Union forces, now took the last step in the great plan. He gathered all his strength for a drive against Lee in Virginia. With Sherman pushing north from Georgia, Grant closed in on Lee, who held Petersburg and Richmond. There was hard fighting at a number of points, but it could only be a losing fight for the Confederates, who were far outnumbered by the Union forces. On the second of April, Petersburg fell and Jefferson Davis, together with other officers of the Confederate government, fled from Richmond. On the ninth, as a battle was about to begin, an officer rode out from the Confederate lines

[268]

waving a white flag. He carried a note from General Lee asking that fighting cease while terms of surrender were agreed upon.

At a private home near Appomattox Court House, Virginia, there occurred, a few hours later, one of the most famous scenes in American history. Can you see the two generals as they meet to end this cruel, bloody war?

Grant, squarely built, looking a little short because of his slight stoop, wears the dusty, wrinkled uniform of a private soldier. Only his shoulder straps on which three stars gleam tell that this shabby-looking man is the general who has won the war. Lee, when forced a few days before to leave all baggage behind, had put on his one good uniform; so today as he stands straight

and tall, with snow-white hair and beard, he makes a gallant figure. At his side swings the jeweled sword which was Virginia's gift to him.

The two generals shake hands and talk of the days when they both fought in the Mexican War. Now the Southern leader raises the question which is close to his heart. What are the terms of surrender? General Grant replies that the Confederate soldiers are not to serve again against the Government and that supplies are to be treated as captured stores. Then, glancing down at Lee's shining sword, he adds that officers shall be allowed to keep their own arms and baggage. Upon learning that the Southern soldiers own their own horses, he says, "Let the men keep their horses; they will need them for the spring plowing."

General Lee expresses his thanks for these very generous terms. He adds that he would like to return Northern soldiers held as prisoners, for he has nothing but dried corn either for his own men or for the prisoners. Grant quickly agrees to this, and arranges at the same time to send food for the use of the Confederate troops.

Once more the two men shake hands. As the tall Virginian passes out of the room, every Union officer stands at salute. The white-haired general slowly mounts Traveler. As he rides away, the Northern men follow General Grant's example and stand with bared heads until he has passed from view. Thus they pay honor to a brave foe.

[270]

The surrender at Appomattox is often spoken of as the end of the War between the States, although the other Confederate armies in the field had still to be surrendered. The chief one of these was the force commanded by General Joseph E. Johnston, which that general surrendered on April 26th to General Sherman. Once more generous terms were offered and accepted. It is interesting to know that these two men, who for so long had been fighting each other, became warm friends. One of the last acts of Joseph E. Johnston's life was to help carry to its grave the coffin of his one-time enemy, William T. Sherman.

**The effect of the war upon slavery.** — When we remember that slavery had been one of the chief causes of the quarrel between the North and South, we want to know what effect the war had upon the lives of the slaves. Many of the slaves were loyal and remained with their owners until the close of the war, giving much aid to the Southern cause by helping to raise food for the army. Some slaves ran away after the war began.

Before his election President Lincoln had never suggested freeing the slaves in the South, but only preventing the spread of slavery to other states. He had also held that if slaves were to be freed their owners should be paid for them. But, as you know, President Lincoln felt that his first duty was to win the war and thus save the Union. There came a time when he felt that this end could be more quickly reached by declaring

[271]

the slaves in all the seceding states to be free. On January 1, 1863, he issued the Emancipation Proclamation, which emancipated, or freed, the slaves in the Confederate States. This Proclamation helped the Northern cause, although little change was made in the lives of the slaves until after the war closed.

The slaves in the border states which did not secede were not freed until the war was over. Then the Constitution had added to it a part which stated that never again could any people in the United States be held as slaves.

## The Years That Followed the War

**The South is punished.** — The years that followed the War between the States were years of which every American should feel ashamed. Then it was that the Government, controlled by a group of men who were filled with deep hatred of the South, set out to punish the states that had seceded. President Lincoln had only the kindest feeling toward the Southern states, and before his death he had expressed the hope that they might quickly and quietly take their old places in the Union. Had he lived, he might have been able to do something to stay the tide of hatred which welled up against the South.

Andrew Johnson became the President when Lincoln was killed. He would gladly have carried out Lincoln's plans, but he was not strong enough to control the men who were determined to punish the South.

[272]

What conditions did the Southern soldiers find when they returned to their homes? They had land but little else. For four years they had used Confederate money, and this now had no value. Much of the wealth of the planters had been in the form of slaves. When these were freed, the owners lost all that the slaves had cost.

The Negroes were still in the South, but no one had any money with which to pay them for their work. They had had no training to take care of themselves; so many of them had a hard time.

In those parts of the South where the armies had fought, conditions were even worse. There the returned soldier often found that he did not even have a house or barn left on his land.

Even without slaves, money, or houses the white people of the South would not have suffered so bitterly had it not been for their loss of political rights. The men who were elected to Congress from the former Confederate states were not allowed to take their seats. Most of the men who had fought in the Confederate army were not allowed to vote, but at the same time the right to vote was given to Negro men. Since these former slaves had had no experience in matters of government, they could not be expected to vote wisely. Often their votes were controlled by white men of very low morals.

There were many men from the North who flocked to the South to make their fortunes by buying land cheaply or by taking advantage of the poor, ignorant

[273]

Negroes, whose votes they used. The white Southerners nicknamed such people "Carpetbaggers" because they usually arrived with all that they owned in a small traveling bag made of carpet. There were some low-class Southerners also who were glad of an opportunity to make money at the expense of their own state. These people received the name "Scalawags." For some years the state governments in the South were largely controlled by Carpetbaggers, Scalawags, and Negroes. This was a time of great hardship for most of the white people.

Soldiers were kept in the South until 1877. Their presence made for more bad feeling between the Southern states and the United States Government. When the Carpetbag rule ended and the soldie s were removed, the South entered upon a new period of growth.

So it was that the long, bitter quarrel was finally settled. The war, with its terrible waste of men and property and the years that followed in which hatred burned white-hot were at last ended. Out of this great struggle came two facts that from that time forward have been accepted by all Americans: there shall be no more slavery in the United States; this nation shall for all time remain one Union.

## A Word Game

Try to use each of the words below in a sentence of your own.

| | | |
|---|---|---|
| hoop skirt | plantation | barbecue |
| veranda | yam | molasses |
| circuit | overseer | corn pone |

Some words that you should add to your list of history terms are *slavery, secede, conflict, immigrant, candidate, blockade, surrender,* and *emancipate.* Of course you should be able to pronounce and use each word before you write it in your notebook.

## A Map Study

On p. 260 is a map which shows the states that seceded from the Union, the so-called border states, and the free states. The border states remained in the Union, but in most of them there were many people who favored the Southern cause. Can you see a reason why this would have been true?

Use this map to locate the battle areas mentioned in this chapter. A favorite plan of generals in time of war is to split an enemy's forces. Why did Grant take Vicksburg even at the cost of a long wait? What did Sherman gain by marching from Atlanta to Savannah?

Using a blank outline map of the United States, show the country as it was divided during the War between the States.

[275]

Make the Confederate states one color and those that remained in the Union another color. Regions that are today states but that were then territories should be marked in a third color. By adding small drawings that fit each region you can make this a picture map.

## MAKING LISTS

One way to remember important facts is to list them and then to study your list. On a sheet of paper write these headings: Union Generals, Confederate Generals, Battles. Under each heading list the names called for. Read the chapter again as often as you need to find them. Only the most important of the generals and battles are mentioned in this book. As you read stories of the war in other books, you may find others mentioned. If you care to, you may add these to your lists.

Use at least one class period to talk over the things that you have learned. It may help you to remember these if, with the help of your teacher, you will make blackboard lists to show:

The Conditions That Caused the Quarrel to Grow
The Steps by Which the War Was Won
The Ways in Which the South Suffered after the War.

[276]

## Some Things to Do

1. Collect pictures that will help you to understand how people lived at the time of the War between the States. You can probably find pictures of houses, furniture, and clothing used during this period. You may be able to find pictures of Union and Confederate soldiers.

2. Look in the library for longer articles about the people mentioned in this story. You may like to choose one person and prepare to tell your classmates a great deal about him.

3. There are people still living who were boys and girls during the years of the War between the States. Ask such a person to tell you what he (or she) remembers about that long-ago time.

4. Learn from your parents whether or not your grandfathers or great-grandfathers served in the war. If they did, on which side did they fight?

5. If there is a battlefield of this war in the part of the country where you live, make a trip to see it and learn the story of the battle that was fought there.

6. Plan to show how people lived in various parts of the United States in the years just before the war. You might do this by acting scenes, by drawing pictures, by making dioramas, or by building scenes on the sand table. No matter what means you choose, you will need to read carefully pages 212 to 233, and to study the pictures in this and other books.

7. Imagine that you are a child in 1860. You may pretend to be the child of a rich planter, of a poor farmer, of a factory worker, or of any other person whom you choose. Write a letter to a friend in another part of the United States telling her of your life and of how it is affected by the war which threatens.

[277]

Remember to tell only the facts that a child in your condition would have known.

8. Sing some of the songs that were popular at the time of the war. Among these are "Dixie," "Battle Hymn of the Republic," "Maryland, My Maryland." Among the songs that the Negroes loved are "Swing Low, Sweet Chariot" and "Ain't Gwine to Study War No More." Ask your teacher to help you find other songs of this period.

9. Ask your teacher or some other older person to read to you some of the poems that have been written about Abraham Lincoln. One of these is "O Captain, My Captain," by Walt Whitman. An easy poem that you can read and understand for yourself is "Lincoln," by Nancy Byrd Turner.

### SOME BOOKS TO READ

Two stories that show life in the South are *You Shall Have a Carriage*, by Elizabeth Coatsworth and *No Surrender*, by Emma Gelders.

Life in the North may be glimpsed through:

*Hannah Courageous*, by Laura Long
*College in Crinoline*, by Marjorie Medary
*Invincible Louisa*, by Cornelia Meigs
*The Cowhide Trunk*, by Eleanor W. Nolen
*A Recruit for Abe Lincoln*, by Maribelle Cormack

Three stories of Abraham Lincoln, the first of which is very easy, are:

*Abe Lincoln, Frontier Boy*, by Augusta Stevenson
*Abraham Lincoln*, by James Daugherty
*Abe Lincoln Grows Up*, by Carl Sandburg

If you read well, you will enjoy *The Little Giant*, by Jeanette C. Nolen.

[278]

# DIVISION FOUR

*The Nation Becomes Full Grown*

☆

The dream of a waterway across America comes true.

## NEW FRONTIERS AND NEW LANDS
## BECOME AMERICAN

### AMERICA'S LAST FRONTIER

As you know, the frontier, which had moved step by step to the prairies west of the Mississippi River, leaped across the plains and mountains to the Pacific coast. This sudden movement toward the West was made in answer to the call of gold in California and of furs and rich soil in Oregon. After this far-western coast was well filled with people, the line of settlers began to turn back toward the dry plains over which earlier pioneers had passed.

Thus it happened that America's last frontier lay in that great area between the Middle Western prairies and the settled region along the Pacific coast. In this vast territory were included both the Rocky Mountains and the dry, flat region known as the Great Plains.

There were several reasons why people were slow to settle this last frontier. The plains were so dry that it was hard for a settler to make a living. The high mountains made travel difficult. The constant danger of Indian attacks threatened all who came into the region.

Settlement would not be made in the face of these difficulties until the country held promise of rich rewards for those who dared its hardships. When gold and silver were discovered in the mountains, when cattle raising became established on the plains, and last of all when the homesteader was given free land, then the last frontier offered rewards to those who would claim them. At the same time the United States Army was slowly overcoming the Indians, so that this danger was removed.

**The cattle kingdom.** — For many years the Spaniards of the Southwest had great herds of cattle. These animals fed upon the native grass, drank at watering holes along the rivers, and increased rapidly in numbers. Because there were so many of them, cattle had no great value. If a man wanted beef, he killed a cow and took the meat. If he wanted leather, he killed a cow and took the hide.

These animals ran on the range, as the open grass lands were called, for there were no fences. It was probably the Mexican ranchers who first used brands to mark their cattle. When a brand was burned into the animal's hide, nothing could ever remove it. Since calves always ran with their mothers for a year, the owner could keep his herd marked by branding the calves each spring.

From the Spanish lands cattle raising spread into American territory. Even before the War between the States some cattle from Texas had been driven North to market. The war put a stop to this business, but, when the conflict ended, the plains of Texas were covered with cattle for which a market was needed. The next few years saw the trails filled every summer with great herds of the animals, moving slowly north.

At first the markets were usually found in Missouri,

but, as the railroads pushed farther west, cattle towns sprang up in Kansas. In 1871 over six hundred thousand cattle crossed the Red River headed for Northern markets.

Not all the animals from Texas went to the packers, however, for now the cattle kingdom began to spread. As the danger from Indian attacks was gradually removed, ranchmen started new herds on the plains. They bought cattle from Texas, but usually improved these "longhorns" so that a better grade of beef could be produced.

The important event for the cattleman was the round-up. On the plains north of Texas there were usually two roundups each year. The one in the spring was for the purpose of branding calves, and that in the fall for selecting the animals that were to go to market. In the early years of ranching on these plains there were no fences; so all the cattle ran on the range. Because of this the ranchers had to work together in the roundup, each man choosing his own cattle by their brand.

There came a time when fences began to be used. This change caused trouble. Some ranchers fenced in not only their own land but free range that was still owned by the Government. Other difficulties were caused by men fencing water holes so that the cattle belonging to other ranchers could not get water. Sometimes barbed-wire fences were run across the old trails so that men and animals could not travel in the paths that they had always followed.

[284]

Fences were often cut. Guns were sometimes used to back angry words. But as with every other great change, the new way won in the end. The days of free range passed, and the ranches of the plains were fenced. Deep wells were sunk and windmills pumped water for the thirsty animals so that water holes on the rivers were no longer important. Barbed wire was invented in 1874. By 1885 ranchmen had accepted the fact that the old free range was gone, and fences had come to stay.

The best-known person in the cattle kingdom was the cowboy. Whether his work required him to drive the cattle over the long trail from Texas, to ride the range, or to "cut out" the cattle in a roundup, the cowboy had to be strong, quick, and daring. His work often kept him in the saddle for twelve hours a day, and it was not unknown in periods of heavy work for a cowboy to ride for eighteen hours out of the twenty-four, getting such sleep as he had on the ground. Only young men who were hard as iron could stand such a life.

The cowboys lived together, sleeping in the "bunkhouse." A cook was with each outfit, and when work took them far from the home ranch the cook went along in the "chuck wagon." Jokes were common in the bunkhouse, but no joke was made at the cook's expense. He had too many ways of getting even. Flapjacks might be heavy, bacon burned, or beans half-done, but the cowboys held their tongues and hoped for better meals.

Each outfit had a large herd of horses which were in

charge of a man or boy known as the *horse wrangler*, a fellow who commanded no one's respect. A cowboy was very proud of his skill in riding and throwing a rope, or *lariat* as it was called, but he looked down upon the man who merely took care of the horses.

Had you lived during the seventies when ranching was at its highest point in America, you would have wanted to visit the West where both cattle and sheep ranches were common. Perhaps you can catch something of the spirit of that long-ago time if you will suppose that you are at a spring roundup on the range in the days before fences had come into use.

Roundup districts have been laid off and every cattleman within the district is sending cowboys to a point where it has been arranged that all are to meet. We arrive at the gathering place for our district two days before the roundup is to begin, but many men and horses are already there. Each outfit has its own chuck wagon and cook, and its own horse wrangler with his string of horses.

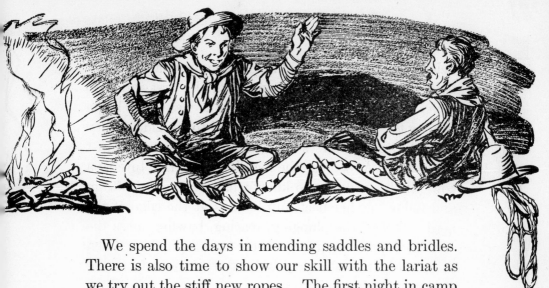

We spend the days in mending saddles and bridles. There is also time to show our skill with the lariat as we try out the stiff new ropes. The first night in camp we have a merry time around the campfires, singing and recalling stories of other roundups. The second night, however, the order is "Early to bed"; so almost as soon as we have put away the bacon and beans we roll up in our blankets and stretch out on the ground.

Long before day we awake with a start at the sound of our cook beating a spoon on a tin pan. Breakfast is quickly eaten, horses bridled and saddled, and we are riding away in small groups to form a huge circle around the district. All morning we ride, keeping sharp eyes for stray animals. By noon we are closing in near the camp with more than a thousand head of cattle in the center of the great circle. We ride closer, pushing the frightened animals into a solid herd. Everywhere there is dust, noise, movement!

Now comes the work of "cutting out" the cattle that

[287]

belong to each ranchman. Certain men are told to hold the herd. The cowboys from the first ranch to have its cattle cut out ride into the herd and begin driving the cattle bearing their brand to one side. They are mounted on horses that have been trained for just this work. As soon as the man begins to ride toward a cow, the horse seems to know what is expected of him and follows at her heels until she is at the edge of the herd. Out of the plunging, rearing, bawling mass the men again and again cut their own animals. When these are gathered at one side, the cowboys from the next ranch take their turn.

When the cattle from the various ranches are collected in separate groups, the work is not yet finished, for the calves must still be branded. Now a cowboy rides into his own herd and cuts out a cow that has a calf beside her. When, with the calf at her heels, she is a little away from the other animals, there is a whir of rope and the calf falls, held by the lariat.

Some of the men have been busy at one side heating their branding iron over a fire. At once we drag the kicking calf toward the fire, where several men grab and hold it. We hear the sizzle of the hot iron on the calf's hide and catch the smell of burning hair. Then the rope is taken off and a branded calf runs bawling to its mother.

Dust! Sweat! Shouting, swearing men! Swinging ropes! Panting horses! Bellowing cattle! This is the spring roundup.

[288]

**The mining towns.** — When the placer miners working the streams of California began to find less and less gold, they set off to look for the precious metal in other places. Passing north into Oregon, Washington, Idaho, and Montana, they found gold at a number of points. While some men went north, others were exploring Colorado and Nevada. Here again success rewarded their efforts.

As gold was discovered in a new place, the events which had marked the days of '49 in California were repeated. A town sprang up almost in a night. Where wood could not be secured for houses, canvas tents were made to do instead. Prices went sky-high. The men and women who made it their business to entertain men in such camps flocked into town. Dance halls, saloons, and gambling houses lined the main streets.

A few men made rich finds and spent their money like water. Most of the men worked long and hard and made only enough to buy food. "Bad men" formed gangs which robbed and killed miners who had got their gold by honest work. Sometimes when one of these gangs had seized so much power that it was in complete

[290]

control of a town, honest men joined together in a secret group for the purpose of breaking up the gang. After such a group, usually called a Vigilance Committee, had captured and hanged a number of the best-known "bad men," there was likely to be peace in the town for some time.

Like the earlier gold fields in California, these later mining camps brought a rush of eager settlers. Not only old miners from other camps but men from the East who knew nothing about mining set out to seek their fortunes. Gold is a magic word. Always it has had that power to draw men even when common sense should tell them that there is little hope of finding riches.

That many gold seekers returned to their old homes poorer than when they left is well shown by the story of the man who set out in a covered wagon for Colorado, during the Pikes Peak rush in 1858. On his wagon cover he had painted in large letters, "Pikes Peak or Bust." A year or so later he returned, but this time his wagon cover carried the single word, "Busted."

Through the '50's and '60's mining towns continued to spring up in various parts of the West. Silver began to be mined, although it did not fill men with such a fever of desire as did gold. Some of these towns grew into cities, but in the larger number of them the boom died as suddenly as it had grown, leaving only a village to mark the place where once a city of huts or tents had carried on its busy life.

[291]

The last of the great mining rushes came in the middle seventies when gold was discovered in the Black Hills of South Dakota. The town of Deadwood sprang up as the result of this rush. Before we leave this last frontier, let us have a glimpse of a street in Deadwood as it probably looked one July day in 1877.

Located in the heart of the Indian country with the nearest railroad many miles away, Deadwood depends upon the stagecoach and the wagon train. To get the gold which is mined to some place for safekeeping is the great problem, for the "bad man's" gang already has a hold on the town. Wells, Fargo & Company have agreed to carry gold out twice a month.

Today we see the steel-lined coach that makes these journeys starting off down the narrow street. Into

this one coach has just been loaded $350,000 worth of
gold, the largest amount that has ever gone out of Deadwood at one time. We do not wonder that the man
on the seat beside the driver has a drawn six-shooter
in his hand, or that other men on horseback ride on all
sides of the coach, each man with his hand on his gun.

Wagons loaded with supplies come creaking along the
street, each one pulled by a team of ten oxen. Leather
whips crack and the air is filled with shouting as the
men guide the slow-moving animals. All kinds of
people crowd the narrow streets. Among them are
workmen from the mines; a Catholic priest; girls who
act in the Gem Theater each evening; well-dressed
gamblers; members of the brass band which plays in
front of the theater; an Indian squaw; and a Methodist

preacher.   Rich and poor, good and bad, wise and ignorant people are all here in this little mining town.

**A railroad across the continent.** — For years men
had dreamed of a railroad across the continent, but it
was not until 1869 that the band of steel which connected the East and the West was completed.   In that
year the last rail was laid and the last spike was driven.
If a traveler were willing to make all the changes required, he could go by train from the Atlantic to the
Pacific coast.

The plan of building provided that the Union Pacific
Company should begin at a certain point near the
middle of the country and lay track toward the west.
At the same time the Central Pacific Company began
in California and worked toward the east.   The companies received a great deal of aid from the Government.
Gifts of land lying along the railroad and loans of money
were both made.

The men who laid the tracks met many hardships and
dangers.   There was little food to be had on the plains
and almost none of the supplies that were needed
to build a railroad.   Food, tobacco, clothing, tools,
bullets, rails, and even much of the wood for ties had
to be carried from the East.   For the parties that
worked ahead, laying out the route, these supplies had
to be taken forward in wagons.   In addition to these
hardships there was constant danger from the Indians,
who strongly objected to the coming of the whites.

The men lived in tent cities which were moved from

time to time as the track was put down. These simple towns drew some of the same kind of people who always hung about mining camps. Saloonkeepers, gamblers, and dance-hall girls were there ready to help the worker spend his pay.

On May 10, 1869, the ceremony of connecting the rails took place at Promontory Point, Utah. What could we have seen that day?

Trains have come from both east and west bringing guests to the ceremony. Now the governor of California steps from the train which has arrived from the West and comes forward to shake hands with the president of the Union Pacific Company. A preacher raises his hand, the laughing crowd grows quiet, and the preacher offers a prayer of thanksgiving for this great dream that has at last been realized. Workmen step forward, and one who bears in his hand a golden spike kneels and puts it into place. Then the great sledge hammers are lifted by strong arms. The hammers fall, blow upon blow, until the spike is driven home. A railroad now crosses America from shore to shore.

The greetings of the guests, the words of the prayer, the blows of the hammers have all been carried to the rest of the country by the telegraph wires that stretch along the track. Almost as soon as the golden spike is in place in Utah, in many other parts of the country whistles blow, bells ring, banners fly, and men shout their joy over this new deed done.

[295]

**The Indians' last stand.** — The story of America's growth is a sad story for the red men who once held this whole vast continent as their own. From that day when John Smith first went to the Indians near Jamestown to get corn, until the last frontier was gone, white men were forever wanting something that the Indian had. Not only wanting, but more often taking as has been the way of white men everywhere. Sometimes as at Jamestown it was only food; now and then it was a bit of metal which a red man had found; more often it was furs; and most often of all it was land.

Americans have always been land-hungry people. A tale of rich, black soil lying somewhere to the west was enough to set thousands of pioneers moving. Even the dry dust of the last frontier called men who dreamed of a new chance in a new country. That all of this land belonged to Indians who had lived on it for years meant nothing at all to the American pioneer, or at most meant only that he might be in some danger from arrows and tomahawks.

Sometimes in the early settlements white men did buy the land from the Indians, but very often they simply

[296]

took it.   After the United States became a nation, our government tried to deal with the Indian tribes by making treaties.   You will remember that General Wayne made one of the earliest of these treaties at Greenville.   Usually such treaties arranged that if the Indians would give up their old lands now desired by white settlers they would be moved to new lands farther west.   Treaties were sometimes made in times of peace, but more often after the Indians had been defeated in war.   What could the red man do but accept the new land and leave forever the old home that he loved?

So the weary business of fighting, making treaties, and moving Indians went on for many years.   In the region of plains and mountains which we now call the last frontier, the Indians were allowed to live much as they pleased for many years.   This was, of course, only because at the time the land had little or no value to white men.

Here were the native homes of all those tribes which we group together under the name Plains Indians. They had long ago learned to fit their manner of living to the country in which they lived.   Two animals of the plains made this life possible.   One was the horse; the other the buffalo.   Horses, first brought to America by the Spanish, had increased until they could be found in great herds.   They furnished the Indian a means of swift travel.   The buffalo, native of the plains, furnished the red man almost everything else that he needed. Meat from its flesh, clothing from its skins, tools from its bones, cords from its sinews — these and many other necessary articles came from this great beast.

When white men reached the plains, they not only took land, but they killed the buffaloes in great numbers. In many ways the loss of the buffaloes was a greater hardship than the loss of the land.

So it happened that the Indians hated the white men and fought them long and bitterly. Not only did the red men fight in open war, but they took every chance which they found to kill anyone who might be alone or in a small group. Cowboys, miners, stage drivers, farmers, railroad workers were all picked off by keen-eyed Indians who then galloped away.

In battle the Indians were always cruel enemies. They asked no mercy and showed none. There are many tales of American soldiers who went to their death fighting bravely, only to be scalped and cut to pieces where they had fallen by the savages against whom they had fought. Such events did not make white people any more ready to deal fairly or kindly with the Indians.

In the years which followed the close of the War between the States there was much difficulty with the Indians. Many of the officers of that war gave gallant service in these later Indian wars. The Indians were making their last stand for their lands and the right to live on them in the old way. It was only natural

[299]

under these circumstances that they should fight desperately. Some of the Indian chiefs were wise and able men who planned their battles in a way that would have been a credit to any general. But no matter whether they won or lost a particular battle, the Indians were fighting a losing fight. They could not stand forever against the white man's coming. As has been the way since time began, the weaker people had to submit to the stronger.

With thousands of their people killed, the tribes one by one surrendered. Most of them made treaties which required that they live on an area of government-owned land known as a *reservation*. Here they were taught by white teachers and trained to work. The members of some tribes received land of their own. Usually such land was not considered to be of great value when it was granted, but in certain places oil was afterwards discovered on it. Thus in recent years we have had some wealthy Indians in the United States.

The words with which Chief Joseph, one of the ablest of the old fighters, surrendered, tells you much of the sad story of the Indian. He said, "I am tired of fighting. Our chiefs are killed. It is cold and we have no blankets. The little children are freezing to death. My people, some of them, have run away to the hills, and have no blankets, no food. I want to have time to look for my children. Hear me, my chiefs. I am tired. My heart is sick and sad. From where the sun now stands I will fight no more forever."

[300]

**The homesteader.** — The last settler who came to the plains was the farmer. His coming was in part due to a law passed in 1862, known as the Homestead Act. This provided that any settler might receive one hundred sixty acres of free land if he would live on it and cultivate it for five years. Such a piece of land was called a *homestead*.

Thousands of people accepted this offer from the Government. Many Northern soldiers who returned from the war to find their old jobs gone set out for homesteads. Immigrants from European countries flocked to America in great numbers to take up new land. At first homesteaders took farms in places where the climate favored farming, but as this land became settled they pushed on into the dry plains. So the last pioneer of the last frontier was the man who attempted to farm the plains which before had known only the Indian, the cowboy, and the sheep herder. In order to grow crops on this dry land the farmer had either to irrigate or to use new methods of cultivating the soil. Where water was to be had men irrigated, but in large areas "dry farming" was used. It is interesting to know that in recent years there has been much trouble in the dry-farming areas with dust storms. Some wise men say

[301]

that it is best to seed these plains to grass again as they once were.

America had land rushes as well as gold rushes. Sometimes a whole area was opened for settlement on a certain day. When word went out that this was to happen, people went to the border of the new territory and camped to wait for the day when they could move into the new land. The region now included in the state of Oklahoma received a huge land rush in 1889 when Indian lands were thrown open to white settlers.

What a sight you might have seen had you been among the people camped along the border that April day when the rush began! Here are people in wagons, in carriages, on horseback, and on foot. Everyone is wildly excited. There is much pushing and stirring, for each person wants the best possible position. Up and down the border the guards walk, keeping the anxious people back. As the hour of twelve draws near the strain becomes terrible.

Now an officer rides to the highest point of ground in

the neighborhood. At exactly noon he blows a blast on a bugle and at the same time drops a flag.

Like bullets shot from guns the people leap over the line and are away on the great race for homes. Some will farm the land which they claim. Others will start towns where goods can be bought and sold. Many intend to take up land now and sell it later for a large price. All are alike in one way — they hope to make themselves better off than they are at present.

America's last frontier in the main body of the country is settled. No longer do covered wagons cross the continent, nor Indians ride the trail in war paint and feathers. The old pioneer way of life is gone, never to return. Boys and girls growing up today will eagerly read the tales of those daring men and brave women who made this land what it was in frontier days, but they must prepare to live in a new and different America. What some of the conditions of life may be in the nation of the future will be suggested in later stories in this book.

## AMERICA'S NEW TERRITORIES

The United States holds some territories in parts of the world that are far away from this country. How these distant lands became American is part of the story of how the United States became a full-grown nation.

**Alaska is purchased.** — Alaska, in the northwestern corner of North America, was explored and settled by the Russians during the early part of the eighteenth century. It remained a Russian colony for more than a hundred years, but in 1867 the Russian government offered to sell it to the United States.

Many people were opposed to the purchase, saying that the bare, cold northland was of no worth, but the Secretary of State believed it was a good bargain. He got the Russians to set the price at $7,200,000, a sum that was less than they first asked. Even so, people still showed their scorn by calling Alaska an "icebox." However, because of the friendly feeling

[304]

which there was between the United States and Russia the purchase was completed.

Thus it happened that in the little Alaskan town of Sitka, on the 18th of October, 1867, Russian and American soldiers marched side by side through the streets. When they were ranged before the house where the chief Russian officer lived, each party of troops fired a salute. Then the Russian flag was slowly lowered and the Stars and Stripes began to climb up the tall flagstaff. A cannon boomed. The Russian officer spoke the words of transfer. The American officer replied. Alaska became a part of the United States.

This new territory proved to be much more than an icebox. Its rich products have been worth many times the purchase price. Gold was discovered, and Alaska had a gold rush much like those that the United States had known in earlier years. Silver, lead, copper, and coal were also found. Great quantities of lumber have been taken from the forests of Alaska. In its waters live millions of salmon. The furs secured from Alaska have been worth enough to pay the purchase price several times over. In very recent years American farmers have gone to Alaska. Several new farming regions have been developed. There seems reason to believe that in the future farming will be even more important in Alaska than was once thought possible. The coast is popular as a vacation land, many Americans going each year to enjoy its beauty.

When the United States and Japan went to war in

[305]

1941 Alaska at once became important as a center for
defense. American forces moved into Alaska and the
Aleutian Islands that extend southwest from the mainland. Up to this time transportation between the
United States and Alaska had been possible only by
water or air. The need for a road to connect the two
was so great that plans were made for one. The road
began at Dawson Creek in Alberta, Canada, a town
already connected by railroad and road with points in
the United States. The road extended to Fairbanks,
Alaska. The route lay through country so wild that
some people said a road could not be built across it.
Nevertheless Americans did it in record time, in 1942,
building the sixteen hundred miles in seven months and
seventeen days.

[306]

This road promises to be of great importance in peace as well as in war. It is quite likely that pioneers of the future will travel the Alaskan Highway to the northern territory, which may prove to be a land of promise.

**Hawaii is added.** — In the days when explorers were sailing the seas, an English captain on an exploring trip in the Pacific discovered what we know today as the Hawaiian Islands. This little group was more than two thousand miles from North America, yet this continent was its nearest large neighbor. Perhaps for that reason the islands were visited by Americans more often than by other people.

American sea captains found the islands a convenient stopping place when they made their long journeys to China. Whaling ships put in there for water and fresh food. American missionaries who went to the islands taught the natives to read and write and led many of them to accept the Christian religion. Hawaii was ruled by a native king who often asked for advice from the missionaries. When gold drew men to California in '49, many of the brown-skinned Hawaiians went there to seek their fortunes.

People from various lands settled in the islands, drawn there by their pleasant climate and rich soil. Among them were many Americans, most of whom raised sugar cane and pineapples.

In 1891 there came to the throne of Hawaii a queen who took away from the people many of the rights that had been granted to them by earlier rulers. A few years later, a group of citizens refused any longer to accept the rule of the queen, and set up a new government. American troops from a battleship which was in the harbor helped to keep order during this period of change. The officers of the new government asked the United States to annex Hawaii. This request was not granted at once, but in 1898 Congress voted in favor of the measure, and the Hawaiian Islands became American territory.

These Pacific islands have proved to be of a great deal of value. They produce fruit and sugar cane. Ships making the long journey across the ocean put

in at Hawaii for supplies, and the Government developed a great naval base at Pearl Harbor. It was the Japanese attack on Pearl Harbor which brought the United States into the Second World War. The islands have become so well known for their beauty that many have visited them on pleasure trips.

**A war adds new territory.** — Directly south of Florida and only ninety miles away lies Cuba. In 1896 this island and a few smaller ones near by were all that was left in the Western world of the Spanish empire which had once spread over much of North and South America. For many years the Cubans had been trying to win their freedom from Spain, but they had never been strong enough to do so. Fighting was more or less constant in the island.

The ruler of Spain, determined to put an end to the difficulty, sent a general to Cuba whose methods of war were so cruel that he won the nickname "The Butcher." Reports of the terrible things that were being done reached America, where people were filled

[309]

with anger and horror. American newspapers sent men to Cuba to learn more about the matter and printed stories of cruel acts performed by the Spanish general and his soldiers. Americans became thoroughly aroused and demanded that something be done to help.

Spain had lost much of its former power but none of its pride. In answer to American demands for peace and freedom in Cuba, Spain at first did nothing.

However, upon finding how deeply angry the Americans were, the Spanish ruler called the cruel general home and offered to take other steps advised by Americans. In all of these acts Spain moved slowly because its pride would not permit it to seem to yield to America.

At the same time that these things were happening certain Americans were talking of the need for sending troops into Cuba to secure the freedom of that island. Probably a part of these people hoped that the United States could get Cuba for an American colony. It seems likely that some newspapers tried to bring about a war because they wanted to see America get more territory. Other people did not believe that Spain could be trusted to do the things that were promised. So, for one reason or another, there was talk of war.

Then in February, 1898, came an event that did much to change this talk into action. The American battleship *Maine* was blown up in the harbor of Havana, the principal city of Cuba. Two hundred sixty of the crew were killed. It was not known for certain what caused this accident, nor has anyone ever been able to find out since. Because their feelings were already aroused, many Americans believed that the ship had been blown up by the Spanish. Probably the government of Spain had nothing to do with the matter, but the effect of the accident was to bring war still nearer.

President McKinley did not want war, but it seemed that Congress and many of the people did. On the twenty-fifth of April, 1898, war was declared.

[311]

Strangely enough, the first blow was not struck in Cuba but in the Philippine Islands. When war began, Admiral George Dewey of the United States Navy was near these islands, which were Spanish territory. Steaming straight to Manila, the chief city, he defeated a Spanish fleet and took control of Manila Bay.

The war against Spain was very brief, the fighting lasting only from April until July. In that time an American fleet won a smashing victory off the coast of Cuba, and American soldiers did some gallant fighting on land. The best-known of these land battles was the charge up San Juan Hill that was led by Theodore Roosevelt. This man, afterward President of the United States, had a company of soldiers who were known as the *Rough Riders*. On that day when they charged the Spanish guns and took the hill, the Rough Riders won fame that has lived on through the years.

[312]

The treaty of peace, signed in December, 1898, provided that Spain should grant freedom to Cuba. The Philippines and two other Spanish islands, Puerto Rico and Guam, were transferred to the United States. This country in turn agreed to pay Spain twenty million dollars.

The Spanish-American War was of small importance as a war, but few events in American history have been of more far-reaching importance in some other ways. Through all the early years of its history the United States had devoted itself to its own affairs in North

America. It had taken no interest in getting territory in other parts of the world, had seemed to have no thought of empire. Now, with the close of this war, the United States had suddenly gained an empire. People of many races were brought under the American flag. The interest of the nation was centered on the other side of the Pacific in a spot where other great world powers also had interests. In order to care for these territories the United States found that it must take a larger part in world affairs.

The first task which lay before the Americans was to establish peace and good government in the new territories. While Cuba was to be free, the United States had to advise the leaders of the new government. In the Philippines the natives who had been fighting the Spanish turned their war against the United States. It took three years to conquer them and many more to bring health, education, and self-government to the Filipinos. There as in all the territories the Government set up free schools, built water systems, opened hospitals, and did dozens of other things to teach the natives better ways of living.

For years it has been the hope of the Filipinos that they may become an independent people. In March, 1934, the Congress of the United States passed a law which set forth the steps by which this territory was to be changed into a free and independent nation to be known as the Commonwealth of the Philippines.

The Philippine legislature accepted the plan made by

[314]

Congress. A constitution for the new nation was written and accepted by the Filipino people. In 1935, the first president of the Commonwealth was elected. This man, Manuel Quezon, had been a leader in the fight for independence.

The plan provided for a ten-year period during which time it was thought the Filipinos would have a chance to get their new government working smoothly. July 4, 1945, was set as the date upon which the Commonwealth of the Philippines was expected to take its place in the family of independent nations. In 1941 the Japanese attacked the Philippines. Although bravely defended by native soldiers and American troops, the islands were taken by the Japanese in 1942. President Quezon and certain other officers of government escaped to the United States. There Quezon died in 1944, and the vice president took his place. The United States has pledged itself to free the Philippines from the Japanese and to grant the independence promised the people of these islands.

**The United States builds a canal.** — During the Spanish-American War a ship which was in the Pacific had been ordered to join the Atlantic fleet. The only way that it could reach the Atlantic Ocean was to go around South America. As the people of the United States followed the progress of this ship on its long voyage, they realized as never before the great need that there was for a canal to connect the two oceans. After the war closed and the Philippine Islands were left as American territory, it was clear to everyone that the United States must build such a canal.

There were two possible places where the canal might be built, but President Roosevelt and many other people favored the route through Panama. Some years before, a French company had started to build a canal over this same route but had given it up. The United States bought the interests of this company.

The next step was to secure from Colombia the right to build a canal across Panama, for this region belonged to the South American country. The United States made an offer which Colombia refused to accept. President Roosevelt became angry when he heard of Colombia's action. He had set his heart on getting the Panama route without delay. Instead of making another offer he got what he wanted in another way.

The people of Panama were anxious to have the canal built and so were angry at Colombia because it had refused the offer. They had often before rebelled against the government in power. What could be more
[316]

simple than to rise against Colombia, declare themselves independent, and make their own deal with the Americans? While President Roosevelt did not suggest this action, he was very prompt to take advantage of it when it came. Panama declared itself independent on the fourth of November, 1903. On November 6 the United States recognized the new republic, and on November 18 a treaty was made by which the United States received a strip of land ten miles wide and gave Panama ten million dollars and certain other benefits.

Since Colombia was a small, weak nation there was nothing that it could do about this loss of Panama except to hate the United States. That Colombia did very thoroughly for many years.

The building of the canal was a great benefit not only to the United States but to all nations. Certainly little Panama was much better off after the Americans taught its people how to be clean and healthy. The building of the canal was one of the most splendid pieces of work ever done by any nation. In view of all these good features it is a matter of regret to most Americans that this country used such hasty measures to secure the desired route.

Before any real work could be done on the canal, Panama had to be made a safe place for Americans to live. Because it is very close to the equator, Panama has a wet and a dry season and great heat at all times. In such a climate mosquitoes are sure to be found. These insects carry the germs of malaria and yellow

[317]

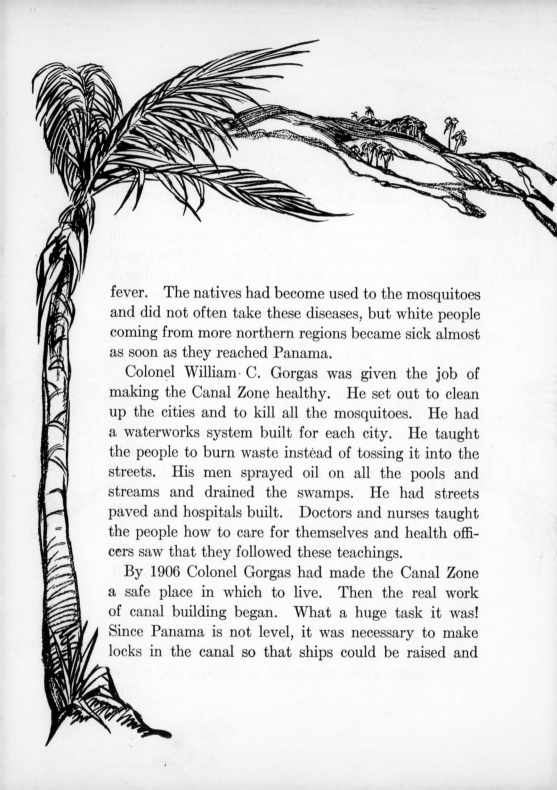

fever. The natives had become used to the mosquitoes and did not often take these diseases, but white people coming from more northern regions became sick almost as soon as they reached Panama.

Colonel William C. Gorgas was given the job of making the Canal Zone healthy. He set out to clean up the cities and to kill all the mosquitoes. He had a waterworks system built for each city. He taught the people to burn waste instead of tossing it into the streets. His men sprayed oil on all the pools and streams and drained the swamps. He had streets paved and hospitals built. Doctors and nurses taught the people how to care for themselves and health officers saw that they followed these teachings.

By 1906 Colonel Gorgas had made the Canal Zone a safe place in which to live. Then the real work of canal building began. What a huge task it was! Since Panama is not level, it was necessary to make locks in the canal so that ships could be raised and

lowered.   The finished canal has three pairs of locks at either end.   By using lakes and rivers on the route it was not necessary to dig all of the canal, but one part nine miles long was cut through solid rock.   At some points there was great difficulty with landslides which came down again and again to fill the huge ditch.

[319]

At last, eight years after the work began, there came a day when a ten-thousand-ton vessel entered the first lock on the Atlantic side. What fun it would have been to ride on that first boat which passed through the Panama Canal!

The electric engines quickly move the vessel into place in the first lock. The great gates swing to behind her, and the water begins to flow into the lock chamber. The little electric "mules" tow her slowly down the length of the lock; the vessel rises foot by foot. Through a second and a third lock in the same way, and then the boat floats out upon Gatun Lake, eighty-five feet above sea level.

Traveling now under its own power, the boat goes across this lake, through the great cut, into a second lake, and enters the locks on the Pacific end of the canal. Again small electric engines tow the vessel through the lock chambers. The water slowly drops lower, until once more the boat rides at sea level. The first vessel has passed through the Panama Canal. The old dream of a waterway across America has at last come true.

[320]

Except for a few small, scattered islands these territories of which you have read are all that belong to the United States. To the people in each of them our government has tried to bring better ways of living. Our service to these citizens of the territories is something of which Americans may for the most part well be proud. Free public schools are found wherever the Stars and Stripes fly. The brown- and yellow-skinned children of the Pacific islands; the squat little Eskimos of Alaska; the dark-eyed child of Puerto Rico; these and many other small people in American territories have learned, just as you have, to say, "I pledge allegiance to the flag of the United States of America."

## A Word Game

You can find the meaning of each word below by reading carefully the paragraph in which it is used in the text. For which words is the meaning explained exactly? For which do you have to get the meaning from the way in which it is used? Watch for other words, the meaning of which is suggested but not told exactly.

| | |
|---|---|
| range | placer miner |
| longhorns | homesteader |
| brand | roundup |
| chuck wagon | bunkhouse |

Make a list of the American territories and possessions mentioned in this chapter. Learn to pronounce and spell the name of each.

## A Map Study

In this chapter a series of small maps shows the principal territories and possessions of the United States. After you have looked carefully at these, locate them on a wall map of the world. Using the scale of miles given on the wall map find about how far each is from the United States.

[322]

Other small island possessions of the United States in the Pacific include Wake, Midway, Johnston, Palmyra, Howland, and Tutuila. Locate these on the world map. Of what use are these small possessions?

In the Caribbean the United States owns the Virgin Islands. These were purchased from Denmark in 1917. Why do you suppose this nation wanted them? Study your map to find the answer.

The map of Alaska also shows the part of western Canada through which the new Alaskan Highway runs. Trace the route of this highway.

## Reasoning from Cause to Effect

History usually happens as it does because certain conditions are present. It is important for you to be able to tell the effect which certain conditions have had.

At the beginning of this chapter you are told that the area between the middle-western prairies and the Pacific slope contained dry plains, high mountains, and savage Indians. As a result of these conditions settlers were slow to enter this region.

Below are listed certain statements, each of which mentions a fact or condition that had a result. If you do not know what this result was, read the chapter again. Number a paper from 1 to 8 and write the effects which followed each of these causes.

1. The plains of Texas were covered with cattle for which a market was needed.
2. Placer miners working the streams of California began to find less and less gold.
3. The horse and the buffalo were found in great numbers on the western plains.
4. White men took land and killed buffaloes.

[323]

5. In 1862 a Homestead Act was passed by Congress.
6. A highway was built connecting Alaska with the United States.
7. The United States defeated Spain in war.
8. The only way a ship could go from the Atlantic to the Pacific was around South America.

## Some Things to Do

1. Look among the geography reference books in the library for more facts about the territories of the United States. Prepare to tell your classmates some interesting facts about life in one of the territories.
2. Make a bulletin-board display of pictures which show scenes in the territories.
3. Ask a man who fought in the Spanish-American War to tell you of his experiences.
4. Write a paragraph using one of these sentences as your opening sentence: The spring roundup is an exciting event. A cowboy's clothing suited his work. Life was never dull in a mining town. A homesteader on the Great Plains had a hard life. The Indians fell back before the whites. A golden spike was the last link used to join two oceans.
5. Make a set of pictures to show life on the last American frontier. Here are some scenes that you might show: a cattle drive, a roundup, a scene in the "chuck wagon," the stagecoach leaving Deadwood, an Indian riding toward the setting sun, men driving the golden spike, the land rush into Oklahoma. These pictures

could be used in a frieze, as a movie reel, or as panel
pictures for your schoolroom.

6. Sing some of the songs that have been written about
   cowboys. One of these is "Home on the Range."

7. Act some of the scenes described in this story. Plan
   your action and try out various speeches before attempting to write any lines. Perhaps you can use
   some of the cowboy songs if you act a scene in the
   cattle country.

8. Read aloud to your classmates some of the most
   interesting events described in a life of Theodore
   Roosevelt.


### SOME BOOKS TO READ

Stories of the cattle country that you will enjoy include:

*Whitey's First Roundup*, by Glenn Rounds
*Cowhand Goes to Town*, by Phil Stong
*Cowboy Tommy's Roundup*, by Sanford Tousey
*Open Range*, by Hildegarde Hawthorne
Richard A. Summers tells in *The Battle for the Sierras* of
building a railroad across the mountains.

Life in various frontier communities is described in:

*A Bride Goes West*, by Nannie T. Alderson and Helena H.
Smith
*Lone Boy*, by Margaret A. Hubbard
*The Story of the Great Plains*, by May McNeer
*The Willow Whistle*, by Cornelia Meigs
*Sheep Wagon Family*, by Myra R. Richardson

Stories of life in various parts of the United States in the
years between frontier days and the present are told in:

*Trader's Children,* and *Waterless Mountain,* by **Laura A. Armer**

*All Over Town,* by Carol Brink
*Children of the Prairies,* by Alice B. Curtis
*The Middle Moffat,* by Eleanor Estes
*A Little Girl of Nineteen Hundred,* by Lois Lenski
*Roller Skates,* and *The Year of Jubilo,* by Ruth Sawyer
*The Middle Button,* by Kathryn Worth
*River Boy: The Story of Mark Twain,* by Isabel Proudfit

Two tales about the noted western frontiersman are *Buffalo Bill,* by Frank L. Beals, and *The Story of Buffalo Bill,* by Shannon Garst.

Two stories of the Canal Zone are:

*Soldier Doctor,* by Clara I. Judson
*Goethals and the Panama Canal,* by Howard M. Fast.

*Tired men leave the steel mill as the shift changes.*

# THE MACHINE AGE COMES IN AMERICA

A man walks toward the entrance of a large hotel. As he approaches the door, it swings open as if by magic for him to enter. The magic, however, is supplied by the electric eye which cannot only open doors but can count cars and perform a number of other useful services.

In a canning factory cans travel on a belt to a machine where they are counted and inspected. With no help from human hands the machine kicks out of line every can that lacks a paper label.

In the printing plant paper is fed from a roll into a giant press, where it is printed, cut, folded, and fastened together. Within a few minutes the paper is delivered from the press in the form of a magazine well filled with pictures.

A mechanical man sits in an electric station. As orders are spoken or whistled to him over the telephone by living men some miles away he moves levers, starts, and stops machines. He alone is in charge of this station.

These happenings cause us to exclaim with wonder. It is hard for us to believe that such remarkable acts can really be performed by machines. Yet they are only a few of the thousand surprises that have come with the use of machines. Some of these wonders no longer excite us because we have become used to them, but they are no less remarkable because we use them every day. If you will think of all the things you do in one day, it may surprise you to learn what a large place machines have in your work and play.

Because machines do greatly affect the life of people today, America is sometimes said to be living in the Machine Age. The machines are for the most part power-driven. Electricity, steam, and falling water are the most common kinds of power used to drive machines.

It is not possible in the limits of one book to tell about all the machines that now serve us, but in order to understand this time in which we live, we shall learn how a few of the more common ones came into use.

## IMPROVEMENTS IN TRANSPORTATION AND COMMUNICATION

**The automobile.** — Efforts to make a "horseless carriage" go back to 1765. In that year James Watt, an Englishman, made a successful steam engine. Almost at once men began to ask why a steam engine could not be used to drive a carriage. Although Watt was not interested in this use of his engine, other men were. Not only in England, but in France and Germany as well, steam-driven vehicles were built. In England a law was passed which required that when one of these steam carriages went along the road a man must walk ahead of it. During the day he was required to carry a red flag and at night a lantern. The owner of the carriage was also compelled to pay a high tax. These laws put a stop to the use of steam vehicles in England, but in France and Germany men still continued to build a few of them.

About the middle of the nineteenth century some men in the United States discovered how to refine crude oil. From this evil-smelling black oil came kerosene and gasoline. The next step was to make an engine which would burn these fuels. When that was done, a long step toward the modern automobile had been taken.

During the eighties French and German inventors began to produce vehicles driven by gasoline engines. The first one of these cars to be brought to America was shown at the World's Fair in Chicago in 1893.

[331]

In the meantime a number of Americans were also building gasoline-driven carriages. Newspapers had become interested, and one of them, the *Chicago Times-Herald*, offered a prize of $5000 to be given to the winner of a race which would be held in Chicago on Thanksgiving Day, 1895. Can you imagine what an exciting day this was for the men who had been making the new motor carriages? Two cars were sent from Europe to enter the contest, and there were several of American make. A few of these were driven by power from electric storage batteries. Suppose you try to imagine yourself in Chicago on that Thanksgiving Day.

A ninety-two mile course has been laid out. The start is to be made in Jackson Park, which lies along the lake front on the south side of the city. The finish will be at Waukegan, a town farther north on the lake.
[332]

The day is cold and a sharp wind is blowing. Snow covers the ground except in those streets where the horses' feet have trampled the surface into mud.

The cars are really only buggies with either engines or electric storage batteries mounted on them. Not one of the vehicles has a top. The drivers, sitting in the high seats bundled up in thick coats, shiver as they wait for the signal to start. This comes at last, and the queer little carriages begin to spit and chug down the street from the starting line.

The people who have gathered talk eagerly about the race. Each one tries to pick the winner. Some bets are laid as to the results. One man says that none of the cars can get to Waukegan through this snow and mud. It seems that the last remark may be correct, for already one vehicle is stuck. Men run for-

ward to help; the driver works with the engine; but the stubborn little machine sits right there until it is finally pushed off the street.

People are gathered along the course, eager to see such an amazing sight. They are rewarded now and then by seeing one of the little "horseless carriages" go put-put-ting along the street. They also see car after car fail, for the cold day, the muddy streets, and the long distance prove too much for most of them. One by one they drop out. All but one — for through that long, cold day young Charles Duryea keeps his gasoline engine working and his little car moving. Dark comes, and Waukegan is yet a long way off, but the wheels are still turning.

At last, ten hours after leaving Jackson Park, Charles Duryea drives into Waukegan. He has won the race and thus the $5000. More important still, he has proved that a gasoline-driven car is better than an "electric" and he has shown that an American automobile can beat machines made in Europe.

After this race Duryea and his brother who worked with him made and sold a number of cars. He won other races and thus proved again that he had a good automobile.

A question now arose that was of great importance not only to the men who were building cars but to other people as well. Should automobiles be so high-priced that only rich men could buy them, or should their cost be kept so low that many people could afford them? Two men at least believed that they should be made to sell as cheaply as possible. One was Ransom E. Olds, who was the first man to make a low-priced car. The other was Henry Ford, who also built light cars at a low price. Olds later changed to making larger and more costly cars, but Ford held to his first idea of building a car that could be bought by the average American family. How well Mr. Ford succeeded you may guess by looking at the large number of Ford cars to be seen everywhere.

In order to keep down the price it was necessary to buy materials very carefully and to find the best methods of work. Little by little Henry Ford bought iron mines, rubber plantations, forest lands, and other sources of raw materials that he needed for his automobiles. Today he owns or produces everything that goes into a Ford car. At the same time his factories constantly improved their methods of work so that cars could be produced rapidly.

The manufacture of automobiles has become America's leading industry. There seems every reason to believe that it will continue to be of great importance in the future. Cars change in appearance and design as new knowledge, needs, and style require, but the demand for automobiles continues.

When automobiles came into such general use, Americans found that they had many other problems to solve. Better roads were needed; so paved highways were built until now the United States has 1,373,000 miles of hard-surfaced roads. Travelers needed places to stop. Thousands of tourist camps, inns, and lunch stands sprang up along the highways. Gasoline was needed to run these cars. The oil fields were developed, pipe lines were built, and the oil was carried to great refineries to be made into gasoline and a number of other products. On every street and highway gaily painted filling stations were built, ready to supply the passing cars with gasoline.

Not all the problems created by the automobile have been so easily solved as these. Cities are still trying to find ways to prevent the slowing down of traffic which comes when many cars try to use the same street at the same time. Each year many thousands of people are hurt or killed in this country by automobiles. One of our greatest problems is how to direct and control this very useful product of the Machine Age so that people are not hurt or killed by it.

From a gasoline-driven carriage it was only a step to the building of a gasoline-driven wagon. In its simplest form this is all that a truck is. As time went on, trucks became larger and better suited to the different kinds of work required of them. You have only to stand on a busy street corner or to travel along a highway to learn the many uses which are now made of trucks.

The great buses which go speeding along our highways are the "stagecoaches" of today. Like those vehicles of an earlier day they follow the main roads, stopping at inns and rest stations along the way. They are somewhat like the long-ago stagecoaches, too, in the gay spirit which usually prevails on them. Passengers talk with their neighbors and ask the driver many questions. They pile merrily out at every rest station to stretch their legs and buy the great American sandwich — a "hot dog" in a bun. At the end of a journey fellow passengers may be friends — or enemies, but they are rarely strangers.

In a few of the large buses the seats are made into beds at night, but on most of them the passenger who travels through the night simply pulls up his coat collar and settles his head on the back of his seat. Lights are lowered; everyone grows quiet. At the wheel the broad-shouldered young driver sits with watchful eyes fixed on the road ahead. Passengers sleep, awake,

[337]

sleep again, but on through the dark the giant vehicle speeds.

**The airplane.** — It is three o'clock on the morning of April 17, 1944. Darkness still covers the earth but an airfield at Burbank, California, is stirring with life. Field lights send their beams over a giant airplane which is the center of interest at this early hour. A crew of men are busy checking the great humpback machine before it takes to the air. While they work, other men are arriving at the field and going aboard the plane. When the ground crew has finished and all the passengers are aboard, Howard Hughes climbs into the cockpit and takes his place behind the pilot's controls. Quickly the other members of the plane's crew — a copilot, a radioman, a flight engineer, and a navigator — move to their positions. The *Constellation* is ready to make a flight across the continent.

At exactly 3:57 A.M. (Pacific war time) the giant plane begins to roll down the runway. As its engines gather power, it starts to rise. Within a few seconds it is climbing smoothly and swiftly. Up, up it goes as the field lights fade below. At 15,000 feet Hughes levels off and sets his course toward the east for the *Constellation* is bound for Washington, D. C.

Within the plane the twelve passengers have abundant space for this sky giant is built to carry four or five times the number of passengers who ride it today. Indeed so huge is the plane that if there were need for it the inside could be arranged to carry one hundred soldiers. But on this first flight the *Constellation* has cushioned seats as well as bunks for those who wish to catch forty winks of sleep.

Through clear skies the plane races along. The towns of California are only winking lights in the dark below. As the *Constellation* wings over Arizona dawn breaks.

The passengers begin to think of breakfast. Two of the men go back to the galley at the rear of the plane and heat coffee. Boxes brought aboard at Burbank are passed. From them come orange juice, fruit, cereal, and rolls. With milk and hot coffee served from the galley a hearty breakfast is enjoyed.

Over southern Colorado clouds appear for the first time. Ice begins to form as the *Constellation* travels over Kansas. The pilot takes the plane above the clouds and it flies on under a dome of blue sky. At this height it is extremely cold outside but inside the plane the temperature is that of a pleasant summer day.

By the time Illinois is reached brisk tail winds are pushing the plane along even faster than before. The clouds are breaking. The pilot brings the *Constellation* down a few thousand feet but keeps it high enough to stay above thunder storms that are reported as likely. By the time the plane passes Cincinnati the passengers can see the ground again. It has not been in sight since the pilot took the *Constellation* to higher altitude over Kansas.

In the early afternoon as the plane nears Washington excitement mounts among the passengers. There are guesses as to the exact time when the pilot will reach the airport. There is talk of speed records broken by this day's flight.

At fifty-four minutes and fifty-one seconds past one o'clock (Eastern war time) the copilot, who is now at the controls, sets the *Constellation* down at the National Airport in Washington, D. C. The trip has required six hours, fifty-seven minutes, and fifty-one seconds and has set a new record for a flight across the continent. The crew has made no effort to break any speed record, but this four-engined giant with its wing spread of one hundred twenty-three feet and a weight of forty tons has averaged 355 miles per hour.

This flight of the *Constellation* is a striking example of the way distance has been conquered. But it is

[340]

only one of many such cases. During World War II the Army Air Transport Command set up a flying service that circled half the globe in less than three days. It had a chain of airfields on the route where fresh plane crews waited ready to take over the controls. Ground crews were on hand to put gasoline in the tanks and make repairs. Planes were serviced at top speed, for the one important thing was that the plane must go through in the shortest possible time. The demand for speed earned the name *Fireball* for this flying service of the Air Transport Command.

The cargo carried by the planes going out from the United States was bound for the fighting fronts in India, Burma, and China. On the return journey products of these countries made up the cargo. The planes carried as passengers only persons who had business that would in some way serve the war effort.

Suppose for a moment that we are among those passengers. We take off from Miami, Florida, on a run that leaves shortly after dawn. All is stir and hurry in those last minutes as the final check of the plane is made. When everything is in order, the plane roars down the runway, and we are off for Puerto Rico. There at Borinquen Field a few hours later a brief pause allows time to check the weather reports, eat a hasty lunch, and fill the gasoline tanks.

Then on the plane goes across the Caribbean Sea where once pirate ships roamed the blue waters to Georgetown, British Guiana, on the northeast coast of

[341]

South America. There are interesting things to see here, but a plane on the Fireball line can pause only for fuel and food.

Down the coast of Brazil and across the equator the plane wings its way, to Belem. Then on it goes over the green fields and forests of Brazil to Natal. The landing field here fairly simmers in the heat as we come down. The plane is serviced, a new crew takes over, and we are off for the Atlantic crossing.

Sailing through the sky above the Atlantic our pilot brings us some hours later to Ascension Island. This little point of land sticking up in the Atlantic Ocean between South America and Africa is a lonely spot. Its shores are so bare that they support but a single tree, a wind-blown palm. Nevertheless this rocky island is a welcome sight to all who ride the Fireball, for there the United States has built an air base where planes may find fuel and repairs.

From Ascension Island our plane flies on to Accra on the African Gold Coast. Here we see both mud huts and modern American-type houses; GI tanks and trains of native bearers, carrying in their loads of ivory.

Four hours of flying bring us to Maiduguri in Upper Nigeria, where black natives come with gas cans on their heads, from which they fill our tanks. The heat is so intense that we are glad to be on our way as soon as we have taken on fuel. We are off for Khartoum in the Ango-Egyptian Sudan. We fly over some of the finest game country in the world — a region often visited in earlier and more peaceful years by big-game hunters. Above the headwaters of the Nile and over a mountain range we fly to Khartoum where another brief pause is made.

Out over the Red Sea the plane roars, on its way to Aden. The heat fairly blisters as we come down in this city for a short stop. Then we are up again, following the Arabian Coast to Masirah Island, where our gasoline is pumped from underground tanks. The heat is so great that it might explode if stored in tanks on which the sun shines.

The jump across the Arabian Sea to Karachi in India is not long. From there we fly on to Agra, then to Gaya, and finally to Chabua. As the plane comes down at this last landing field on the Fireball run, we are at the foot of the Himalaya Mountains, halfway around the world from our starting point in Miami, Florida. We made this trip in about three days.

In 1945 the Army Air Transport Command set up a regular round-the-world air service. Planes traveling the route take off from Washington, D. C. They cross the Atlantic Ocean, North Africa, Asia, the Pacific Ocean, and the United States, making fifteen stops on the flight. Flying time for the trip is set at 151 hours, but flights are often completed in less time. The planes carry forty passengers. Today all the other people in the world are our neighbors. We no longer need to count distance in miles but only in hours of flying time—so much has flying shrunk the earth. It

[343]

has been said that "we are in sixty hours of anywhere." This means that with good flying conditions it is possible to fly to the farthest place on the globe in sixty hours. As planes are improved and airways made better we may expect that the sixty hours will be reduced to a smaller number. Whether we like it or not, we face a future in which it is very likely that airplanes will fly on regular routes over the whole earth. Probably no single invention has ever so completely changed the relations of nations as the airplane promises to change them.

It was not until the present century that men learned to fly but through the ages they longed to do so. Legends of several countries tell of men who are supposed to have flown. The great Italian artist, Leonardo da Vinci, drew plans for a wing-flapping machine in which he thought a man might be able to fly. In the nineteenth century men learned to make and fly gliders. While using these they discovered many facts that were of value later in flying planes.

Dr. Samuel Pierpont Langley believed that he could build a machine that would fly. He made a small model with a tiny steam engine to furnish power. This little machine flew successfully. He then received fifty thousand dollars from the Government to aid him in building a machine large enough to carry a man.

In October, 1903, Dr. Langley had his machine ready. He attempted to launch it from a boat on the Potomac River, but something went wrong with the

[344]

launching. A second attempt three months later also failed. With his money gone and people laughing at his efforts Dr. Langley was not able to go on with his work. He died not long afterward, a bitterly disappointed man. Later study of the Langley machine showed that it probably would have flown had he been able to get it launched.

Even while people were laughing over Langley's attempts to fly other men were doing it. Turn your thoughts toward the sand hills of Kitty Hawk, North Carolina, and try to see one of the famous scenes of history which occurred there on December 17, 1903.

Two young brothers from Dayton, Ohio, are here with a flying machine that they have built. For the past three years they have come each year to this wind-swept coast to practice with gliders. Now they believe that they can fly a machine that carries an engine to provide power. For several days the brothers have waited for the wind to be just right. But on this morning of the seventeenth they can endure waiting no longer. At ten o'clock they signal the men in a near-by life-saving station.

As the plane is put in place on a rail laid on the ground, a group of life guards arrive to watch. Orville Wright, the younger brother, climbs into the machine and lies down on the lower wing next to the motor. He releases the wire that holds the plane in place. The machine begins to move along the rail. Now it lifts slowly. Orville moves the controls and the machine

[345]

sails into the air. A sudden dart downward ends the flight, but for twelve seconds the plane has flown.

What joy! What new hope this brings! Wilbur takes his place in the machine. Again it slides down the track. Again it takes the air, this time for thirteen seconds. The brothers exchange places and Orville tries his skill another time. Once more success follows. A fourth flight, with Wilbur at the controls, proves the best of all. The plane stays in the air fifty-nine seconds and travels eight hundred fifty-two feet.

While the Wrights have been making history with these flights, the life guards have been watching. Now one of them turns and runs with all his might toward the little village of Kitty Hawk, where he cries out wildly, "They've done it! They've done it! Danged if they ain't flew!" Thus it was that the world learned that for the first time in history a man had flown in an airplane.

Strangely enough, however, people paid very little attention to the news of that great happening at Kitty

Hawk. They had just heard of Langley's failure. The Wrights were simply two young men who ran a bicycle shop in Dayton. Most people refused at first to believe that they had succeeded in doing something. that Langley, a noted man of science, had failed to do.

Several years of hard work followed for the Wrights and others who were working with airplanes. In the United States there was little interest in flying, but France and Germany showed more liking for it. However, in 1908, the Wrights built the first plane for the United States Army. This machine could fly more than forty miles an hour, which was at that time considered a great speed.

In 1914 the first World War began. Planes were used by each side to observe the action of the other. Then machine guns were mounted on the top wings (almost all planes at that time had two sets of wings), and the airplane had become a weapon of war. By the time the United States entered the World War in 1917 airplanes had proved their value. This country built up an air force.

When the war closed, several thousand American men knew how to fly. There were many planes on hand which the Government sold cheaply. Many of these young Americans bought planes and went about over the country doing stunt flying at fairs and selling rides. These "gypsy fliers" as they were sometimes called took many chances and had more than a few accidents. But they kept interest in flying alive in a period when few people were concerned about a greater use of the airplane.

The first air-mail route was established in 1918. It was between Washington, D. C. and New York City. Little by little new lines were opened until three years later mail planes were flying from San Francisco to New York City. This growth of air mail has continued until today a large part of the world enjoys air-mail service.

Air lines for carrying passengers were established. By 1926, 5782 passengers were carried. Air travel has grown greater year by year. In 1941 3,768,892 passengers were carried in the United States. Giant planes wing their way swiftly across the continent. Inside passengers sit in seats that are like easy chairs. They eat hot meals, listen to the radio, read, and talk. Soundproof walls shut out much of the roar of the engines. Floors have soft carpets; windows have curtains. Temperature is controlled so that passengers are always comfortable. In some planes, the sky sleepers, seats may be made into beds at night. Such planes usually carry twenty-eight passengers, fourteen in upper and fourteen in lower berths.

Meeting the needs caused by flying has brought many changes in America. Today an airport arranged to provide for the comfort of passengers is as necessary for a city as a railroad station. Beacon lights send their gleam to light the night skies. Information about the weather is sent regularly to the radio-communication stations that are at various points on the airways. This information is of great importance to fliers. So also are the several kinds of radio aid provided on many of the nation's airways. The best known aid is the radio-range beacon, often called the "beam." This serves to guide pilots over the airways and keep them on the proper course. As long as a pilot is "on the beam," he hears in his radio receiver a steady hum. If he drifts off the line of flight the hum changes to another signal. The pilot then knows that he needs to steer the plane back to the course where he receives a steady hum.

The Government of the United States has made laws about matters of flying. These laws have for the most part aided in developing a wider use of the airplane. They have also made flying safer than it might otherwise have been.

Air-express service has not been as widely used as either air-mail or air-passenger service. It seems likely, however, that both air express and air freight will be more fully used in the future. Because of the need to move goods quickly in war, cargo-carrying planes have been much improved in the last few years. One of the recent planes built to carry cargo has a wing spread of three hundred twenty feet, is two hundred eighteen feet long, and weighs 400,000 pounds. It is built entirely of plywood and is provided with eight engines. This giant of the sky can fly at one hundred seventy-four miles per hour and carry 120,000 pounds of goods.

[350]

Airplanes are used in many kinds of work. Farmers have found them of value in sowing seeds, for dusting and spraying crops, and in sending certain vegetables and fruits to market quickly. Planes are used in looking over forests to figure the amount of standing timber and also to watch for forest fires. Airplanes have proved useful to fishermen because schools of fish can be seen from them. The pilots who patrol the ocean watching for submarines are now trained to watch also for these schools of fish. Photographs taken from the air are of value in many ways, one of which is to plan the work of building such things as dams. Another use is in making maps. Mining in regions far away from other means of travel is made much easier because men and supplies can be flown in by plane. Even the matter of keeping order in the country is aided by the airplane, for it is used both to catch lawbreakers and to take them safely to prison.

Gliders are older than airplanes. However they have come into a new use when they are towed behind planes to carry men or cargo. Usually such trips are short hauls but in 1943 a glider was towed from America across the Atlantic Ocean and on to Russia. It made the trip in twenty-eight hours, in spite of bad weather, carrying a ton and a half of medicine and supplies.

The Second World War has very greatly increased the use of the airplane. Both Germany and Japan had large air forces when they began fighting, and both struck their best blows with the aid of their air power.

[351]

This made it necessary for the nations fighting against them to build huge air forces. Each nation did this to the best of its ability. Since the United States had more materials and factories than any other nation, it was natural that we should make more airplanes.

Larger and larger numbers of planes came from American factories each year. In 1943, 85,946 airplanes were built in the United States. In training centers all over the country young men were trained to man and care for these planes. All over the world, wherever American fighting forces went, men were making bases from which planes could fly. Directly behind invasion troops went the giant "bulldozers," machines that leveled ground and prepared landing strips. On the ocean enormous aircraft carriers served as movable bases. Thus the United States had the three things necessary to fight in the air. These are planes, trained men, and air bases.

Planes were used in many ways in the war. To meet these various needs different types of planes were built. Some were used to get information about the enemy. Others were sent on bombing missions to destroy the enemy's cities and fighting forces. Many served as fighters. Some of these went with bombers to protect them. Others went up to meet enemy attacks, and many were needed on patrol duty to keep watch for the enemy. Large numbers of troops were moved from one area to another in planes. Sometimes troops flew over enemy territory and then dropped by parachute.

[352]

The Northern Hemisphere

As you know much cargo was shipped by air. Wounded men were flown to hospitals.

As the lessons of war taught men new facts, American planes were improved. The speed and power of many of the models produced were almost beyond belief. Then in 1944 the Superfortress, commonly called the B-29, went into action. One general called it, "a dream with wings." This giant bomber is ninety-eight feet in length with a wing span slightly more than one hundred forty-one feet. Its propellers are each sixteen and a half feet across. The B-29 is at its best at a high altitude where it can fly over three hundred miles per hour. When it went into action, this plane carried a heavier load farther and faster than any other bomber. In 1945 four B-29's made the first non-stop flight from Japan to Washington, D. C. Flying by way of the Aleutian Islands, Alaska, and Canada, the planes covered the distance in 27 hours and 29 minutes.

In the world of tomorrow America will lie at the crossroads. Already air routes have been established across Arctic regions in which transportation has before been limited because of the extreme cold. Distances between many of the world's most important cities is much less as measured by air than by ship and railroad routes. This fact means that air lines linking these cities will certainly be established now that war is over. Such lines will cross this country both from north to south and from east to west. Over these airways American citizens will fly to other parts of the world. Over them
[354]

also will fly citizens of other nations to visit ours. This net of air lines will tie the nations of the earth together into one great neighborhood.

**The modern train.** — Railroads were common in the United States long before the Machine Age began, but they have made many changes in order to keep up with the new demands of that age. When automobiles, trucks, buses, and airplanes began to speed across the country, they took much business away from the railroads. In order to hold their own the railroads had to find ways to give greater service at less cost.

Railroads carry freight, express, mail, and passengers, but they make the most money from carrying freight. In order to extend and improve their shipping services railroad companies have greatly increased the speed of their freight trains. It is now very common for a freight train to average forty to forty-five miles an hour, sometimes traveling at a top speed of sixty to sixty-five miles an hour. Railroad companies have built many different kinds of freight cars. Among these are flatcars, open-top cars, boxcars, refrigerator cars, stock cars, and tank cars. Each one is suited to the kind of goods that it carries.

It was not until refrigerator cars came into use that fresh fruit, vegetables, meat, and dairy products could be shipped long distances. More recently tank cars have been built for carrying milk. These are lined with glass and so made that they will hold the milk at an even temperature throughout the trip.

[355]

Like the freight cars, passenger cars have also been built for many purposes. The most common passenger car is the day coach, which is provided with either seats or chairs. By paying an extra fare passengers may ride in the parlor car, which has better furnishings than the day coach. For those who want to travel in comfort at night the Pullman sleeping car offers single berths, drawing rooms, and sometimes bedrooms. A drawing room, also called a stateroom, is a small space shut off from the rest of the car and containing an upper and a lower berth as well as a couch. It has its own private washroom. A bedroom-car contains little private rooms each furnished with a bed (or seat by day) and washroom conveniences.

A modern train carries a dining car with a kitchen to serve it. There may also be other cars where passengers can sit in easy chairs while they read, write, listen to the radio, and look at the scenery. On some trains there are shower baths and maids and barbers to look after the needs of the passengers. An up-to-date train is a great deal like a hotel on wheels.

Many trains have air-conditioned coaches and Pullman cars. These make it possible for the traveler to keep cool no matter how hot the weather may be. All trains are heated to a comfortable temperature in cold weather.

To meet the demands of today, passenger trains need to travel at a very high speed. To reach this speed, engines have been greatly improved, and both cars and

[356]

engines have in many cases been streamlined. A few years ago the Union Pacific Railroad brought out a streamlined train run by Diesel-electric power. A Diesel engine burns a cheap grade of oil and produces electric power which moves the train. This first train proved so popular that other roads very soon had trains of the same type. These trains have reached speeds as high as one hundred twenty miles an hour, with an average speed on long trips of eighty miles an hour. Diesel-electric power also draws freight trains, and these have made long hauls at an average speed of thirty-three miles an hour, with top speed at about twice this figure.

The principle of streamlining has also been applied to trains drawn by coal-burning steam engines. Some of these reach a speed of one hundred miles an hour, with an average speed on long trips of sixty miles an hour which includes stops.

In crossing mountains electric locomotives have proved their value. These are also used to haul trains into and out of large cities. This use of electricity keeps the city cleaner than it would be if coal-burning engines were used.

Trains are not only much faster than they once were, but they are also much safer. Improved road beds, better types of cars, better-built locomotives, the use of signals, and many other changes that have come with the Machine Age have reduced the dangers of travel by rail.

**The telephone.** — A young Scotsman who was much interested in the problems of speech came to America in 1872 and began teaching deaf-mutes to speak. His great interest in sound led him to attempt an invention which he believed would improve the telegraph. While working on this one night, he made a discovery that set him off on a new track. He had had the idea for some time that it might be possible to send the sound of the human voice over wires, and now by accident he had discovered how it might be done.

On that night the young Scotsman gave directions for making an instrument which he hoped might do the work. The very next night the world's first telephone line was put in place. It ran from an attic where the inventor tried his plans to the workbench of Thomas A. Watson, who helped him. When it was in place, Watson, two floors below the attic, heard the voice of Alexander Graham Bell. He could not catch the words, but the fact that the sound of the voice could be heard was joy enough for the time.

[358]

Then began months of hard labor for the two young men. Over and over Bell made plans and Watson built instruments. Again and again they tried out their instruments. Bell hired two cheap rooms on the top floor of a Boston boardinghouse, and here they worked day and night. They had their reward on March 10, 1876, when Watson heard Bell's voice saying, "Mr. Watson, please come here. I want you." That was the first sentence ever spoken over the telephone.

After this success the men improved the instrument so much that, as Watson said, "one didn't have to ask the other man to say it over again more than three or four times, if the sentences were simple." Bell had plenty of troubles, however, even though the invention gave every promise of success. He had become so interested in his invention that he had given up most of his pupils. He had no money, and most people did not think that his invention could ever be important. Two men believed in him, however, and they furnished him with some money and helped him start the Bell Telephone Company.

During these years while he was very poor Bell gave lectures in which he explained how the telephone worked. Receiving instruments were placed in the hall where he lectured, and these were connected by wire with a sending instrument some miles away. Watson was stationed at this instrument to send messages that could be heard by the crowd. He talked,

played musical instruments, and sang. The people who listened were always greatly pleased even though his singing voice was very poor. These lectures not only gave Bell some money when he needed it very much, but they brought the telephone before people and made them realize that it had practical uses.

The telephone received much public attention at this time because of a happy accident which occurred during the summer of 1876. A World's Fair was in progress in Philadelphia and Bell was given the right to show his new invention. It received some attention,

[360]

but most people called it a "toy" and passed by.
At last came the day when the judges were to look
at all the exhibits.   Let us see what the happy accident
was.

It is late afternoon and the judges are already tired
when they reach the table where young Bell sits hoping

for a word of praise from them. The men of science glance at the instrument, ask a question or two, and are already starting away when a party of gaily dressed men sweep up to the table. The surprised judges stop in wonder, for the most gaily dressed of all the men has rushed up to the young inventor and grasped both of his hands. The stranger fairly pours out a stream of greetings. This is the Emperor of Brazil, who with his party is attending the fair. Some time before while visiting in the United States he had met Bell and become interested in his work of teaching deaf mutes. Now he is amazed but delighted to see his former friend. Hearing of the new invention, he lifts the receiver but drops it in surprise as a voice reaches his ear.

The judges, who have paused to watch this meeting, now come back to the table with new interest. Each one must try both talking and listening over the new instrument. Each is amazed at what he hears. On into the evening they stay playing with the new "toy." When at last they leave to eat their long-delayed dinners, the success of the telephone is assured. These men of science have called it a great invention.

The Bell Telephone Company had to fight many suits brought by people who claimed to have invented a telephone before Alexander Graham Bell made his. It took years to get all of these suits through the courts, but Bell won every one of them. No inventor was ever given a clearer claim to his invention.

The first crude little instrument had to be improved, and in doing this new features were invented and added. Thomas A. Watson made some of these. New needs arose as telephones began to be used in large numbers. For example, a central switchboard for transferring calls had to be invented. Men have been at work constantly since 1876 making the telephone better.

The Bell Telephone Company employed in its early days a young man named Theodore N. Vail. He later became the president of the company To this wise and able man belongs much of the success of the modern telephone system. He made telephoning a great American habit.

As the service improved, long-distance telephoning became more common. One day in 1915 Alexander Graham Bell in New York talked to Thomas A. Watson in San Francisco. He said, "Mr. Watson, please come here, I want you." To this Mr. Watson replied, "It would take me a week now." Thus the first telephone message across a continent was sent by the same man who spoke the first words ever heard over the wire.

It was only a little while after this that people were talking by wireless telephone across the ocean. Today in all large cities there are girls whose sole business it is to handle foreign calls. The wireless telephone and later the radio used many of the same principles that were employed by Bell.

[363]

At first telephone wires were all strung on poles which were set along streets and roads. Many country lines are still run in this way, but at present in large cities lines are usually laid in cables under the ground. Another feature of modern telephones is the dial system. By using dial phones a company needs only a few girls at the switchboard. The great machine installed in place of the switchboard is costly, but it pays for itself by saving the money that would be paid to the workers. You can see by this that sometimes the machines that serve us also take away our jobs.

There are more telephones in the United States than in any other country. At the beginning of 1942 there were over twenty-three and one half million telephones in this country. During 1941 more than thirty and one fourth billion telephone conversations were held in the United States alone. Do you agree that telephoning is indeed a great American habit?

**The radio.** — The radio is familiar to almost every boy and girl in America for there are fifty-seven million radio sets in the United States. About thirty million homes have radios. As you know you have only to turn a small knob, and sound fills the room. As if by magic there come to you music, stories, speeches, accounts of ball games, news of the world, and dozens of other programs. To the child who cannot remember a time when there was not a radio in his home this may all seem a matter of course. However, the radio is a product of the Machine Age and one of its wonders.

This "modern magic" was not the invention of any one man. For many years men studied about electricity, and bit by bit new truths were learned about this great force. Many of those truths are today applied in making radio sets.

After the telegraph came into general use, men began to dream of a time when messages might be sent through the air without wires. Although a number of men worked at this idea, it remained for a young Italian named Guglielmo Marconi to perfect a plan which was successful. In 1896 he was able to send messages across his father's garden. He used the Morse key already well known on the telegraph, but he had dis-

[365]

covered how to send and receive messages which traveled through the air without wires.

Marconi improved his instruments until he was able to send messages several miles. Still he worked to discover new principles, and in 1901 he had a reward for his years of patient effort. In that year a message was sent from England to Newfoundland, off the coast of North America.

The inventor called his new instrument the wireless telegraph, and we sometimes hear that name still used. However, men of science were already at work on another problem which when solved became even a greater wonder than the wireless telegraph. This was the wireless telephone, over which spoken messages were sent. Out of these two inventions, the wireless telegraph and the wireless telephone, have come the modern wonder that we call radio.

Many improved features were invented to make the radio better. Perhaps the most important of these was the vacuum tube, which was the invention of Lee De Forest, an American who was a pioneer in radio work. By means of the vacuum tube the electrical waves can be increased many times, thus making it possible to send messages over great distances.

MARCONI

The radio entertains millions of listeners every day, but it also helps with the serious work of the world.

Airplane pilots are guided by radio signals delivered by radio telephone. By means of this form of communication a pilot is always in touch with the airports along the route he is flying. Another form of the radio telephone, popularly called the "walkie-talkie" is used by soldiers in the field. Over it they talk to headquarters.

Pictures, maps, and charts are now sent by radio. It is very common to see in the newspaper a picture of an event which occurred the day before in some place on the other side of the world. Such pictures could not reach this country for several weeks were it not for radio.

Ships at sea receive weather maps by radio. Pictures and fingerprints of persons who have committed crimes are sometimes sent by radio. Ships suffering from fires, storms, and accidents call for help by radio. Messages may be sent to people traveling at sea. News of important happenings is sent all over the world by radio. Weather and market reports are broadcast at regular times from most radio stations. These are only a few of the many ways in which the radio serves us.

In 1943 there were nine hundred forty-seven broadcasting stations in the United States. Each had its own call made up of a group of letters. Some years ago it was agreed among the nations of the world that

[367]

each nation should use only certain letters with which to begin its calls. The United States was given the right to use K, N, and W.

When some program of great interest is to be broadcast, many of the stations can be linked together in one "hook-up." The broadcasting is all done at one station, but the program is carried to the other stations in the network and then out to the listeners.

A new feature of radio that has not yet been fully developed is television. By television it is possible to broadcast a picture at the same time that sound is being broadcast. A very recent development known as *radar* makes it possible to locate and take pictures of objects that are much too far away to be seen by the human eye.

Most of the programs now "on the air" are paid for by companies that have products to sell. It is a way of advertising their goods, and at some time during such a program there is usually a speech which tells the listener why the company thinks he should buy this particular article. Since companies want people to listen to their programs, they often secure the services of very able men and women.

Like the airplane the radio has given us a new set of neighbors. Today the people on the other side of the earth are our neighbors, for we can exchange messages with them more quickly than an early-day American could reach his neighbor on the next farm. Sometimes we say that radio has made the world grow smaller. Do you understand why this seems to be true?

**The postal system.** — The postal system is not a product of the Machine Age, for we have had such a system for many years; but the services of the post office have been improved since modern machines came into use. Most of the mail is carried across the country on fast trains. On each of these is a mail car, which is really a small post office on wheels. The mail clerks work with flying hands as the train speeds along. They sort the mail, putting that for each city and town along the route into a separate bag. As the train slows down at a station, the locked mail bags are tossed out upon the platform. From there trucks rush them to the post office, where the mail is again sorted for delivery in the city.

[369]

The fastest postal service in the United States is provided by air mail. To handle the large amount of mail for soldiers serving overseas a new form of postal service, called V-mail, is used. A picture of the letter is taken on a very small film. This film is then sent by airplane across the ocean, where a copy of the letter, exactly as it was written, is made.

There was a time when people living in the country had to go to the nearest town or village for their mail. Now the Rural Free Delivery takes letters, cards, papers, magazines, and packages to farmers all over the United States. When this service was started some years ago, the carriers had to ride or drive horses over dirt roads. Today nearly all the rural carriers use automobiles and have at least part of their routes paved or treated with some other kind of "all-weather" surface.

Fast trains, trucks, airplanes, automobiles, and paved roads have all helped to make mail service more rapid. All of these are products of the Machine Age.

**The modern newspaper.** — Like the postal system, the newspaper is much older than the twentieth century. There have always been newspapers in the United States and the printing press has always been used to

[370]

print them. However, in early-day America type was set and presses were operated by hand. During the nineteenth century a machine for setting type was invented. It was called a linotype machine. Can you guess why it received this name? For a time steam power was used to run the presses, but today electricity does this work.

The small hand press has given place to a huge machine with many parts. No one man brought about all these changes. They have resulted from the work of a number of inventors, each of whom improved the printing press of his day.

The plan of gathering the news is no less remarkable than the great modern presses that print the papers. Large city papers publishing several issues each day keep a group of men and women busy day and night gathering news. These people, called reporters, write news stories about matters in the city.

Reports of conditions in other parts of the United States and in foreign countries are received by telegraph from one or more of the large news services which supply American papers. These are the Associated Press, the United Press, and the International News Service. The larger papers also have special reporters who are sent to different parts of the country or to other countries where news is being made. A fire, a flood, an accident, a war, or any other serious happening will draw a crowd of American newspaper reporters. Sometimes papers keep persons in foreign countries regularly.

[371]

Reports from these persons are sent to their papers by cable or by radio.

A modern daily newspaper sells for from two to five cents a copy. Even when a half million or more copies are sold each day, such a small price will not cover the cost of gathering the news and printing the paper. The owner depends for his profits upon the money that he receives from advertising.

Each member of the family can find a part in the paper that fits his or her interests. "Funnies," sport news, fashions, ideas about cooking, stories, radio programs, news from foreign lands, articles about politics and leaders in government, these and a great

[372]

many more features are in almost any large daily newspaper.

If you were to visit a newspaper office or the room where the paper is being run through the presses, you would find people hurrying about like mad. Noise! Rush! Bustle! Get the very latest bit of news into the paper! Get the paper through the press and into the delivery trucks! Send the great trucks banging over crowded city streets to get the papers to news-stands! Send out shrill-voiced newsboys to call, "Get a paper, read all about the latest . . . !" Noise! Rush! Bustle! Here in the making of a modern newspaper we catch the real spirit of the Machine Age.

## IMPROVEMENTS THAT AFFECT OUR HOMES

**Our houses.** — Modern houses have been much affected by the wide use of machines. Trains and trucks carry building materials. Steam shovels sometimes dig away the earth where a building is to be placed. If it is a large city apartment house, the steel beams of the framework are lifted in place by traveling cranes and derricks, with the power furnished by a

[373]

steam engine. The steel framework is fastened together with rivets, tossed up red-hot to the man who drives them into place. The rat-a-tat-tat of the riveting hammers can be heard wherever a big modern building is being erected.

Many of the houses built in America today have some means of central heating. Coal, gas, and oil are commonly used as fuels, and sometimes a house is heated by electricity. Very often a furnace has a heat control which is connected with a thermometer. A little pointer is set at the temperature that is desired in the house, and the heat control so regulates the burning of the fuel that an even temperature is maintained. Sometimes furnaces that burn oil and gas are arranged in such a manner that a fire is lighted when it is needed, without the help of any person.

In those parts of the United States where the summers are hot, people give as much attention to keeping cool in the summer as they do to keeping warm in the winter. Electric fans have been in common use for some years, and now air-conditioned houses are being built. In these, the temperature is held at a point low enough for comfort. This modern feature, first tried in public buildings, has proved very popular.

Most houses built today are provided with plumbing. A kitchen with hot and cold water at the turn of a tap, and a bathroom where the owner may choose between a tub and a shower bath, are a long way from the pioneer cabin with a spring at the foot of the hill.

[375]

Electricity has become the servant of millions of housewives in America. Refrigerators, vacuum cleaners, washing machines, irons, toasters, and sewing machines operated by electric power are all in common use. Electric lights are used by nearly everyone whose home can be reached by a power line. Some housewives cook with electricity as well.

The features which make modern homes more convenient and comfortable than were those in early-day America are all the products of the machine. But the service of the machine goes even farther. New materials are being put to use in building houses. Glass has now been treated in such a manner that it can be used as a building material. Metal houses are not common but can be built. A composition material prepared in sheets may now be used for the walls of houses. These and other strange materials give promise that the houses of tomorrow will not always follow the styles of the past.

The home in which you live, whether it be in city, town, or country, has been influenced in many ways by machines. Can you find what those ways are?

**Our food and clothing.** — The Machine Age has also brought many changes in our food. In the first place rapid transportation has given us food products not only from all over the United States but from all over the world. You will better understand the truth of this if you will think of all the places that helped to provide the dinner that you ate yesterday.

[376]

Men of science have also added to our list of foods by developing new and improved plants. Luther Burbank was a leader in this work. Other men have discovered how to make many products from certain plants. George Washington Carver, a noted Negro, who worked in the field of science, found three hundred uses for the peanut and about one hundred for the sweet potato. Not all the articles made from peanuts and sweet potatoes were food products, but many of them were.

The manufacturing of tin cans made a marked change in the manner of handling food. So great is the demand for cans that one plant in this country can turn out seven million cans a day. When you realize that the company that owns this plant has thirty-one other plants like it in the United States and that there are still other companies, you get some idea of the large use of tin cans. Almost every kind of food can be bought in a can. The sizes range from tiny ones only an inch or two high to one-hundred-ten-pound coffee drums.

Food is offered for sale not only in tin cans but in glass jars and bottles, in boxes, in packages wrapped in cellophane or tin foil, and in cloth or waxed-paper

[377]

bags.  The modern grocery store has little of its food open to the dust in the air.

The colonial housewife had few ways to preserve food.  She might dry certain fruits and vegetables, smoke some meat, and cook apple butter or other sweets until they would not spoil.  Beyond the few kinds of food that could be preserved in this way she had to depend upon getting food only when it was in season. On the other hand, the modern housewife who is in reach of a market may have fresh fruits, vegetables, and meat at any season of the year.  When they cannot be secured close at hand, refrigerator cars on fast-moving trains bring them from distant places.  In many communities plants have been built where fresh foods may be frozen and kept in this state until they are needed.

Grocers are much more careful than they once were to keep food clean.  The use of cans has made this easy.  Articles of food that are not in cans, boxes, or bags are usually protected from flies and dust by glass showcases.

Pure-food laws require that when coloring matter is added to a product the fact shall be stated on a label. These laws also forbid the adding of cheaper materials to make a food product go farther.  However, there are still many ways in which the manufacturer can cheat the buyer if he wants to do so.  Better pure-food laws are needed in the United States.

Much of the preparation of food has been taken out of the home.  The colonial housewife cooked in her own kitchen everything that her family ate. Today's housewife buys much of her food cooked. Her bread and perhaps her pies and cakes come from a bakery. Canned vegetables and fruits require little or no cooking. Soup needs only to be heated. Jellies and other sweets are ready to serve. Desserts which require only that hot water or hot milk be added are on the market. If she desires to do so, a housewife can serve meals day after day that need little cooking in her own kitchen. Certainly the Machine Age has made the work of preparing food much easier.

Machines have made it possible for people of the present day to have more clothes than any earlier people have ever enjoyed. Great power spindles and looms quickly turn raw cotton, linen, silk, and wool into cloth. In large factories much of this cloth is soon made into garments. Because all the work of spinning, weaving, cutting, and sewing is done by machines, the dresses, suits, and other garments are cheaper than they would be if they had been made by hand labor.

Another effect of having clothes made in large quantities is that people wear about the same styles. The maid and her mistress often have dresses that are cut very much alike, although the maid's dress is probably made of cheaper cloth.

The Machine Age has found ways to make new clothing materials. The one in most general use at present is rayon. This product, which is used for almost every kind of garment, is made from the fiber of plants. Cottonseed hulls, cornstalks, and wood pulp all make cloth of this type. The fiber is ground and treated in such a way that a thick liquid is formed. This is forced through tiny holes. When these streams harden they become fine threads which can be spun and woven. Another new material is nylon which is made from coal, water, and air.

In this hurrying, noisy twentieth century people move about a great deal. It is only natural that they should want clothing which allows their bodies to move freely and quickly. Modern clothing weighs less and is more comfortable than that worn by people even as recently as fifty years ago. Women have done more than men to free themselves from tight, heavy garments.

One man who was writing about the effect of the Machine Age upon clothing said, "When we recall the colonial housewives, bending over spinning wheels or the back-breaking hand loom, we begin to perceive that in the matter of clothes the machine has done rather better by women than by men. In a very real sense the making of clothing by machines has brought her liberty and freedom."

## IMPROVEMENTS THAT AFFECT OUR WORK

**On the farms.** — Much farm machinery was in use in America long before the period that we call the Machine Age. However, there is certainly a greater use of machines today than at any earlier period. Plows and harrows of various sorts prepare the soil. Grain drills, corn planters, or other machines are used in the planting. One machine called the rotary plow can do all the work of plowing, harrowing, and planting wheat fields. Corn and other crops that must be cultivated bring more machinery into use.

Most of the crops grown on American farms can be harvested by machines. The reaper cuts and binds grain. The mowing machine cuts hay wh ch is later gathered together with a hay rake. Corn pickers are now used on many farms in the Corn Belt. Corn cutters and shredders prepare stalks to be put into silos, while corn shellers shell the grain from the cob. For years men have been trying to make a successful cotton picker. In 1931 two brothers, John and Mack Rust, tried out a new cotton-picking machine that they had invented. This machine is slowly coming into general use. Such a change from hand to machine labor will throw many of the Negroes and the poorer white people of the South out of work.

[381]

Grain is now threshed entirely by machinery. Farmers with many acres of wheat use a machine called a "combine" which cuts, threshes, cleans, and sacks the grain as it moves across the field. It required twenty to thirty horses to draw a "combine" when this machine first came into use, but now a tractor has taken the place of the horses.

Tractors which receive their power from gasoline motors are common in all parts of the country. They are used to draw plows, grain drills, reapers, and various other machines. Their power is also used to run corn shellers, wood saws, and other types of machinery that do not have to be moved from place to place. Many tractors now have lights which make it possible for farmers to work at night. Tractors have somewhat reduced the need for horses on farms.

The wide use of farm machinery has not only made the work of the farmer less difficult, but it has also reduced the labor cost necessary to produce farm products. One hundred years ago it required about three and a half hours of laboring time to produce a

[382]

bushel of wheat. This labor cost seventeen and three-quarters cents. Today the labor time is cut to ten minutes and the cost to three and one-third cents.

**In industry.** — "Not counting simple tools, it is probable that there are more machines in the United States than there are people." These modern servants are present in every industry. In factories, shops, mills, refineries, plants, everywhere men and women are tending, directing, or controlling machines. In order to make the best use of this vast amount of machinery two conditions are necessary. The first is that there must always be a source of power to run the machines, and the second is that the articles turned out by a machine from day to day must all be exactly alike.

For thousands of years the muscles of men and women furnished the power that did the work of the world. When James Watt built a steam engine, he provided a new source of power. Coal or wood was used to provide the heat necessary in forming steam. As the years went by, men learned how to use crude oil and its chief fuel products, gasoline and kerosene. These fuels took

a place with coal as sources of power. In this modern Machine Age the steam engine, the oil-burning Diesel engine, and the gasoline motor each has a place, but more important than anything else is electric power. Both coal and water power are used to produce electricity.

When the hand worker of long ago made an article in his little workshop, it was not necessary that the parts of the article be exactly like similar parts that he had made for other articles. If the pieces did not quite fit, the workman had only to file, or chip, or shave a bit off until they did come together perfectly. This can be well shown by considering the case of a gunsmith in early-day America. He made the entire gun, filing here, grinding there until the parts fitted together. No two guns were exactly alike; so if one were broken the only way to replace the broken part was for the gunsmith to make a new piece.

There came a day when an American inventor and manufacturer tried a better plan. Eli Whitney, whom you remember as the inventor of the cotton gin, was also

[384]

interested in other matters. During the War of 1812
the United States needed guns very badly. There
were not enough gunsmiths in America to make them
by the old slow hand method. Eli Whitney took a contract to supply guns to the Government. However,
he did not begin at once to make guns. Instead he
spent many months building machines and arranging
his factory. The officers of the Government grew
anxious as the time drew near when the first guns were
to be delivered, but Whitney was not disturbed.

One day the inventor appeared at the office of the
Secretary of War with what seemed to be an odd lot of
metal pieces. He sorted these into piles, ten pieces
exactly alike in each pile. While the Secretary looked
on amazed, he picked out pieces from the various piles,
fitted them together, and fastened them in place. This
done, he handed the astonished Secretary a completed
gun. Repeating the same process again and again, he
soon changed the piles of metal pieces into ten guns.

In thus making his parts exactly alike so that pieces
would fit as well in one gun as in another, Whitney had

[385]

hit upon the plan which has become the first principle of modern factory production. Under this system of manufacturing a worker learns to make but one part. By operating a single machine or performing the same act again and again, the worker learns to be very rapid. The completed parts made by many workers using many machines must then be put together. One good example of this process of putting together can be seen in the assembly line of an automobile factory. Each workman along the assembling track puts a single part in place; when the end of the line is reached a finished automobile is driven away to the loading platform.

The huge production of goods made possible by machine methods in industry now threatens to use up certain resources provided by nature. Oil, iron, natural gas, copper, lumber, and fish are some of the resources which the world may have do to without at a not far distant time, if we continue to use them as rapidly as at present.

**In offices.** — Someone has said "the typewriter is the great-grandfather of office machinery." If that is true it has many grandchildren, for the modern office uses not only typewriters but adding machines, calculating machines, mimeographs, cash registers, and many other machines.

As you would guess from its name, an adding machine adds a column of figures. A calculating machine not only adds but subtracts, multiplies, and divides as well.
[386]

A mimeograph makes many copies of a typed page. A cash register records the amount of money placed in it and thus protects the owner from being cheated by clerks who handle money. In offices where card files are kept sorting machines are often used to separate the cards.

For many years men had tried to make a "writing machine," but it was Christopher Sholes who in 1867 had an idea which gave promise of success. With the help of some other men he built machines for a number of years. The name *typewriter* was chosen by Sholes for his new invention.

These first machines worked rather poorly, but by 1886 the Remington Company had taken over the manufacture of the typewriter and was producing some that worked fairly well. The typewriter has been improved by many new features. Today there are bookkeeping machines that put down rows of figures, add, and subtract; in short, that "keep books." There are typewriters built especially for the blind. There are other machines that write shorthand notes. Small, light-weight typewriters are built to fit into cases so that they may be carried about without difficulty.

Office workers today are very often women. The shift from men to women workers began with the use of typewriters. The Machine Age has not only made it possible to do office work more quickly with fewer errors, but it has brought several million women into positions in the business world.

[387]

## IMPROVEMENTS THAT AFFECT OUR PLAY

**The effect of the machine on play.** — It has been said that most of the men and women of America take their play sitting down. This means that instead of taking part in active sports such as swimming, dancing, running, or playing tennis these people either find their fun by watching someone else play, as in a baseball game, or by themselves playing a quiet game such as bridge. One reason why Americans take their fun sitting down as often as they do is that the Machine Age has turned most of the sports and amusements of the country into great business undertakings. Baseball games, rodeos, boxing matches, motion-picture shows, and many other amusements are provided in order that the people who own or manage them may make money. These people use every means that they can to make other people want to buy tickets.

Theodore Roosevelt was a very active man all of his life. He always wanted to be doing things himself instead of watching other people do them. One day while he was President of the United States a friend invited him to attend a baseball game. "What!" the President exclaimed. "Do you expect me to sit still for two hours and watch somebody else doing things?"

[388]

America needs more people with Mr. Roosevelt's spirit about play. Boys and girls usually like active games better than quiet ones, but sometimes even children spend many hours beside the radio or at the movies. Can you think why it is better for you to run, jump, swim, skate, or play baseball than to read the "funnies," see a movie, or ride in an automobile? Which kind of fun gives you stronger muscles?

The Machine Age has given boys and girls the most perfect toys that any children have ever known. There are tiny electric trains that look exactly like real trains. There are dolls which speak, stand, and dance. The furnishings in the doll houses are copies of real furniture. These and hundreds of other articles are gifts which machines have made for modern children. Do you suppose that you have more fun with these beautiful toys than little pioneer Sally had with a corncob doll, or than her brother had with the boat that he whittled from a block of wood?

**The beginning of the movie.** — Going to the movies is one of the most popular amusements in America. Every night in the year several million people sit before screens and watch shadows move back and forth, while out of the darkness the voices of these shadows seem to speak. Have you ever wondered how this modern magic came to be?

During the last half of the nineteenth century Leland Stanford was a wealthy and important citizen of California. He owned some splendid race horses and was

[389]

much interested in them. One day he was talking with some other men about how a horse lifted his feet while racing. Mr. Stanford said that at times a horse had all four feet off the ground at one time. His friends said this was not possible. Mr. Sanford decided to have some pictures of horses taken while the animals were running. He hoped that these pictures would settle the dispute.

The camera had already been invented, although the one then in use has been greatly improved since that time. A man was hired to make the pictures. He worked for several years at the matter, getting help from a young engineer who showed him that by placing a number of cameras in a row he could take one picture after another as the animals raced past. Mr. Stanford was very proud of his pictures and showed them wherever he went, for they did indeed prove that he had been right in saying a horse might have all four feet off the ground at one time.

A Paris artist showed how these pictures could be shown in a little machine that had been made some time before for a somewhat different purpose. In this way he got a very crude sort of motion picture.

About this time Thomas A. Edison became interested in making what he called "eyes for the phonograph." Edison had already invented not only the phonograph but a number of other things. During his long life he did more than any other one man of recent years to give the world useful inventions. Because he had so
[390]

many ideas he had a number of men who helped him. One was a lad named Dickson, and to him Edison gave the task of making "eyes for the phonograph."

By 1890 Dickson, under Edison's direction, had made two sorts of moving pictures. In one case the picture was thrown on a screen somewhat as modern movies are, while in the other the picture was seen in a tiny peep show. Edison used celluloid for his moving-picture films, an idea which he got from George Eastman, who was using it for camera films.

For a few years the little peep shows proved popular, but more and more people were becoming interested in the idea of showing life-size motion pictures. In France, England, and the United States men were working hard to make a machine which would throw pictures on a large screen. In 1895 Thomas Armat succeeded in doing this. It was arranged that machines made after his model should be manufactured in Edison's factory. In this way the new invention received certain benefits from the use of Edison's name.

The next step was to show these new life-size motion pictures to the public. Plans were made to do this in Koster & Bial's Music Hall at Broadway and Thirty-fourth Street, New York City. There on the night of April 23, 1896, occurred the first public motion-picture show in America. That is a date of importance in the amusement world. What would you have seen at that first "movie"?

On the stage a twenty-foot screen has been set in

an enormous gilded frame. Thomas Armat is at the
machine; Thomas A. Edison is in a box in the theater.

It is a pleasant spring evening and the house is
crowded with people eager to see this new wonder.
Tall silk hats, bare shoulders, gleaming jewels, and
gay silks tell that ladies and gentlemen of fashion have
bought tickets for this show.

All is ready! Armat turns on his machine. Pictures
fall upon the screen. There is a scene from a stage
show called "The Milk White Flag," a bit of a boxing
match, a famous dancer in action, and most exciting of
all a scene with the waves of the ocean rolling in and
breaking on the beach.

The people in the theater have watched the play, the

dancing, and the boxing in wonder, but those waves are too much. As they appear on the screen, seeming to roll straight toward the crowd, people on the front seats jump quickly from their places and rush down the aisles. They do not want to receive a wetting from those waves rolling up on the screen.

The show is a complete success. People can talk of little else. Newspapers write columns about the new invention. The "movie" has come to stay in America.

The next thirty years saw a great industry grow. Better and better pictures were made. Motion-picture theaters sprang up in every city and town in the United States. Americans became "movie-minded."

In 1927 the motion-picture industry took another

great forward step with the beginning of talking pictures. Edison's idea of "eyes for the phonograph" had in a way been realized, because what he really hoped for was the putting together of pictures and spoken words.

The "talkie" has reached a high level of success. Both voices and music have been successfully produced many times. Another forward step was taken when pictures were produced in colors. This new form of motion pictures is known as *technicolor*. Pictures made of drawings which seem to be in motion are very popular. Nearly every child in America knows Mickey Mouse, Donald Duck, and other movie characters that have been made in this way. The best actors from the stage are glad to appear in motion pictures. Splendid pictures are made in which no expense is spared to have setting and costumes perfect in every detail. Who can say what this modern wonder may do in the future?

**Good and bad effects of machines.** — Whether an American citizen stays at home or travels, whether he works or plays, machines serve him and at the same time influence his manner of living. Many of the changes caused by machines have been good ones.

Among the changes for the better may be counted the new ways of thinking that people have learned. Some of these changes for the better have been brought about by our use of machines. Some would have come anyhow. Better books, new methods of work, new subjects, and better buildings have made schools more

[394]

interesting for boys and girls. People who are compelled to live in prisons or in hospitals for the insane have been treated more kindly and wisely. The right of working people to form trade and labor unions has been widely recognized. Through the efforts of their unions the workers have often secured higher pay, shorter hours, and better working conditions. Machines have made it possible for people to travel rapidly, to send messages quickly, to live with less hard work, to have more leisure time in which to enjoy pleasures, to have many more goods to use.

By doing the work once done by human labor, machines have often caused people to lose their jobs. Because many workers are needed in a small area, people have been compelled to live crowded together in places where they do not have fresh air, sunshine, and space to move about freely. Since machine workers in manufacturing plants make only small parts of a product, they sometimes fail to find the joy in their work that was one reward of the old-time worker who made the whole article himself. Machines have made noise, dust, and smoke. Everywhere there is rush and hurry. These are evils of the Machine Age.

Whether or not you like this busy, bustling twentieth century, you must live in it. Very soon you will become the workers of tomorrow. You must learn to take your place in a world filled with machines. You must be wise enough to make those machines your servants, never to let them become your masters.

[395]

## A Word Game

Here are words that may be new to you. Be certain that you understand how to use them. It may be fun to see how many you can use in one sentence, but be sure that the sentence makes a sensible statement.

| | | |
|---|---|---|
| mechanical | glider | technicolor |
| lever | airport | cable |
| copilot | cargo | dial telephone |
| navigator | bulldozer | nylon |
| galley | airplane carrier | rayon |
| altitude | Diesel engine | vacuum tube |
| derrick | television | air base |
| pilot | radar | crane |

## A Map Study

On a wall map of the world trace the route of the Fireball. Mark the route on a blank map of the world. Be sure that you can spell the name of each place where a stop is made. It would be interesting to draw small figures around each stopping point and along the route to suggest the nature of the country over which the route extends.

Using the scale of miles on the wall map find about how long this Fireball run is.

On page 353 of this book is a map of the world with the North Pole as its center. As you can see, air distances measured across the North Pole between cities in Asia and Europe and cities in North America are often much less than the distance between these same points by rail and ship routes. In order to set up passenger and cargo service by plane between North American and European and Asiatic cities what problems would have to be solved? What steps have already been taken toward solving these problems?

Airplanes for Russia's use in the war are being flown from the United States by way of Alaska and Siberia. Trace on the map the route such planes probably follow. Might it sometime be possible to fly planes to Russia by an even more direct route?

With a piece of string and a globe compare the distance by rail and ship with the air distance between the following cities: Chicago and Leningrad, Russia; New York and Tokyo, Japan; Minneapolis and Berlin, Germany. Choose other cities and compare distances between them by air and earth routes.

## FINDING KEY THOUGHTS AND EXAMINING STATEMENTS

When we write or talk, we may use two kinds of statements. One kind tells about a single event or condition. The other kind is a general statement that describes a group of events or conditions or things that are alike. A general statement is often the key thought of a paragraph. Finding it helps you to unlock the meaning of the whole paragraph.

Turn to the section of this chapter on houses and let us examine some statements. In the first paragraph the sentence, *Modern houses have been much affected by the wide use of machines,* is a general statement. It also is a key to the meaning of the paragraph. The sentences that follow tell of the various machines that do affect houses, for example, trains, trucks, steam shovels, cranes, derricks, and riveting hammers.

In each of the five paragraphs that follow there is a key sentence that gives the principal thought of the paragraph. This key thought is in each case a general statement. There are also in each paragraph other statements that give facts which when put together make the general statement true.

Read each paragraph carefully. Choose the key thought or general statement. Then find all the sentences that support the general statement by giving single facts.

### Some Things to Do

1. Make a list of all the labor-saving machines that are used in your own home; in your school.
2. Make a list of the amusements in your neighborhood that have been made possible through the use of machines. In how many of these do you take an active part? In how many do you watch other people?
3. If you live near a factory, make a trip to see it. Notice how the machines make all the articles alike.
4. Look for pictures of machines used today. These may be displayed on a bulletin board, or you could make a scrapbook to give to the library for the use of future classes.

5. Look in the library for longer stories about the invention of various modern machines. Prepare to tell some interesting new facts to the members of the class.
6. Ask someone who has traveled by airplane or in a streamlined train to tell you how he enjoyed the experience.
7. If you live near an airport, make a trip to see it. Notice what has been done to make flying safe and comfortable.
8. Visit the post office and find the part that machines play in handling the mail.
9. Visit a telephone exchange and learn how calls are handled.
10. Build models of some machines now in use. Airplanes, streamlined trains, and trucks should be easy. Can you think of others to build?
11. Write riddles about machines, for your classmates to guess. Here is one to show you how to do it:

    I am a small machine. I am used in homes but in other places as well. Electricity makes me run. I help to get rid of something that is dangerous to health. What am I?
12. Ask your teacher to help you find some songs that tell of the work of machines.
13. Act some of the scenes described in this story. Remember that it is better to try out your speeches rather than to write them first.
14. Perhaps you can make a pageant to show how machines help us today. You might have a child go from the modern world of Work Together into a land called Live Alone where no machines are used, and where no one helps his neighbor.

Stories of the telephone are, *Talking Round the Earth*, by Francis E. Benz, and *The History of the Telephone*, by Herbert N. Casson.

*The Mail Comes Through*, by Charles G. Hall tells of the delivery of mail from the beginning till now.

Stories of railroads are found in *Through by Rail*, by Charles G. Hall, and *Clear Tracks Ahead*, by Henry B. Lent.

Airplane descriptions and adventures are in:

*The Flight of the Silver Bird*, by Ruth and Latrobe Carroll
*Skyways*, by Charles G. Hall
*Flying the States*, by Lt. Col. George R. Hutchinson
*Timmy Rides the China Clipper*, by Carol Nay
*The Airplane Book*, by William C. and Helen S. Pryor
*Riding the Air*, by Dorothy J. Sickels
*Air Patrol, Aviation Cadet, Bombardier*, and *Flight 17*, by Henry B. Lent
*Sky Hostess*, by Betty Peckham

The way modern newspapers are made is told in *Nose for News*, by Elliott Arnold, and *Your Daily Paper*, by John J. Floherty.

*Diggers and Builders*, by Henry B. Lent is an easy book that shows how large buildings are erected.

Two easy stories about automobiles are *Automobiles from Start to Finish*, by Franklin M. Reck, and *Wide Road Ahead*, by Henry B. Lent.

If you like science and read well, try *The Wonders of To-morrow; Chemurgy*, by Victor Schoffelmayer.

[400]

*American soldiers give aid in war-torn France.*

# THE UNITED STATES TAKES A PLACE IN WORLD AFFAIRS

## A World War Is Fought

**Europe goes to war.** — In America, July, 1914, was much like any other summer month. Farmers cared for their growing crops. City people talked of how to keep cool and made plans for vacation trips. In Europe, July of the year 1914 was a month of the greatest excitement. On the twenty-eighth of June the prince who was to be the emperor of Austria-Hungary had been killed by a citizen of Serbia. This act was like a spark dropped into a barrel of gunpowder. For years European countries had been arming, each with jealous eyes on its neighbors. This royal murder was the spark that set off the gunpowder of armed forces.

Austria-Hungary claimed the right to punish Serbia because of this act of a Serb citizen. Russia took Serbia's part. Germany, knowing that its old enemy,

[403]

France, would side with Russia, quickly invaded France, going through tiny Belgium. By crossing this small country Germany broke a treaty made many years before in which it had promised to respect the rights of Belgium. Great Britain, greatly aroused by this act, declared war against Germany.

During July events were moving so rapidly toward these ends that the early days of August, 1914, found a war beginning in Europe. On the one side Germany and Austria-Hungary were joined by two less important nations, Turkey and Bulgaria. On the other side were Great Britain, France, Belgium, Serbia, and Russia. This group of nations was known as the Allies. Before long Italy joined the Allies and other nations did the same, even faraway Japan finally coming into the fight. You can easily see why this great conflict became known as the World War.

**The United States remains neutral.** — To the people of the United States this war in Europe at first seemed much like the many other wars that that troubled continent had known. It did not seem to be any of America's concern. On August 4, 1914, President Woodrow Wilson proclaimed the neutrality of the United States. This means that he stated that the United States would not take sides in the war; would, in other words, remain a neutral country.

Even so, the war did influence American life. The fighting nations had to buy food, guns, and all sorts of other goods. As the profits from the sale of these ar-

[404]

ticles reached America, the daily wages of the working-man increased, but so did the cost of living. For the first time in its history the United States sold more goods than it bought. This meant, of course, that more money flowed into this country from trade than flowed out again.

It was one thing to proclaim that the United States was neutral, but quite another thing to have its rights as a neutral nation respected. Because Great Britain for many years had had a splendid navy, it at first controlled the seas. During this period of control it stopped American ships carrying cotton, meats, and other goods and seized the contents. Although it promised to pay for these articles later, American shippers were, of course, very angry at such high-handed treatment.

Germany, in turn, interfered with our neutral rights by using its submarines to destroy shipping. A submarine is a boat which can travel under water. Germany had a number of these boats, and they played an important part in the World War. When a vessel was bombed by a submarine, not only goods were lost but very often lives as well. In the first two and a half months of submarine warfare over sixty vessels were destroyed and two hundred fifty persons were killed. Among the vessels was one American boat.

In May, 1915, Americans were shocked to learn that the *Lusitania*, the fastest and most splendid passenger vessel on the Atlantic Ocean, had been sunk by a submarine. It carried a crew of over six hundred, and more than twelve hundred passengers, many of whom were Americans.

For six pleasant, sunny days the great vessel had sailed across the North Atlantic. Just as the green shores of southern Ireland came into view, there was a roaring sound and the boat trembled and began to dip. Life boats were lowered, but so many excited people crowded into them that they could not be properly launched and many sank with their loads. Horror, terror, and confusion filled the next few minutes. The

*Lusitania* sank rapidly. Out of the 1924 people on board, 1198 were lost. Among this number were 114 Americans. As the citizens of the United States read of this terrible event, they realized that even neutrals could be touched by war.

There were Americans who felt that this country should go to war with Germany over the sinking of the *Lusitania,* but President Wilson was determined to keep the peace if possible. After some effort he was able to make Germany agree to pay damages and to sink no more vessels in this manner.

[407]

In November, 1916, Wilson was again elected President of the United States. The slogan "He kept us out of war" helped to win votes for him.

The Germans, watching the election in America, had concluded that Americans were cowards who would stand any amount of bad treatment in order to keep peace. Acting on that idea, the German government on January 31, 1917, sent a note to the government of the United States in which it was stated that thereafter German submarines would sink at sight every vessel found in the Mediterranean Sea or in waters around Great Britain. More insulting than this, however, were the added lines which said that the United States might send one vessel per week to England provided it arrived on a certain day, followed a certain course, was painted with red and white stripes, and flew a red and white checked flag.

There seemed only one answer to make to such a note. President Wilson made it by sending all representatives of the German government home at once. In the meantime Germany had begun the promised submarine warfare. In February alone these boats sank about two hundred vessels. Then early in March, at almost the same time, three American vessels were sunk. President Wilson called Congress to meet in an extra session.

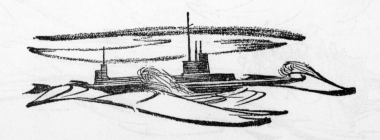

**The United States goes to war.** — It is the evening
of April 2, 1917. In Washington, D. C., a spring rain
is falling. The lighted dome of the Capitol stands out
against the dark, wet sky. Into the great white building under the dome men and women are hurrying, for
tonight the Congress of the United States sits in special
session to hear a speech from the President. On
Pennsylvania Avenue the tramp of horses' hoofs may
be heard, as a group of mounted soldiers ride with the
President to the Capitol.

The joint meeting of the two houses of Congress is
to be held in the hall of the House of Representatives.
Extra chairs have been placed in the front of the hall.
In the first of these sit the nine Justices of the Supreme
Court. Just back of them are the members of the
President's Cabinet, and behind these men the rep-
resentatives of foreign countries. The members of
Congress fill the other seats on the main floor. The
visitors' gallery is crowded with people.

[409]

At last the President enters and takes his place before the gathering. Probably no man in the world has a more able mind than this tall, slender schoolmaster who now serves his country as President. All his life he has dealt with ideas and has used words to tell others what those ideas were. For some months he has been dreaming of a world in which there would be no more wars. He has decided that the present war must be used to end all wars. He has come at last to believe that his own nation must fight, but he feels that this fight can be worth while only if it makes the world a place in which people may make their own laws. A government which gives its citizens this right is called a democracy.

Tonight Woodrow Wilson puts his dream into words, so that not only America but the world may know the ends toward which he is moving. He says in part, "We have no quarrel with the German people. We have no feeling towards them but one of sympathy and friendship. It was not upon their impulse that their government acted in entering this war. . . . We seek no indemnities [money for damages]. . . . We desire no conquest, no dominion [land]. We have no selfish ends to serve. . . . The world must be made safe for democracy. . . . It is a fearful thing to lead this great and peaceful people into war. . . . But the right is more precious than peace, and we shall fight for the things which we have always carried nearest to our hearts. . . . The day has come when America is

[410]

privileged to spend her blood and might for the principles that gave her birth and happiness and the peace which she has treasured. God helping her, she can do no other."

That night each of the two houses of Congress took up the matter of declaring war on Germany. On April 6, 1917, President Wilson signed the Declaration of War. America had entered the world conflict.

**The young men are called to the colors.** — If the United States intended to fight a war, there must be soldiers. The standing army was small. It would be necessary to make soldiers of the young men of the country. In earlier wars the Government had usually depended upon men offering their services, but it was feared that not enough men would quickly offer themselves to provide the many soldiers needed.

Did America dare to force its young men to go as soldiers? That question was asked often and anxiously during those spring months after war was declared. The answer was given on June 5, 1917, when every American man between the ages of 21 and 31 went peacefully to his voting place and registered his name. Nowhere was there the bloodshed that some had expected. Quietly these ten million young men performed this act which really said to the Government, "Here is my body, to be used as you need it in this war."

Not all the men were needed at once; so each was given a number. These numbers were then drawn by lot, and the men who had the first numbers drawn were the first to be called. In time all of this first ten million who were able to be soldiers were called, and other men were required to register.

The young men called to be soldiers found themselves made heroes overnight. They were praised in speeches made by important people. Their names were listed on honor rolls which were printed in newspapers and

[412]

placed in churches, schools, and clubs. The kind-hearted women of the neighborhood baked cakes, knitted sweaters, and packed boxes for them. The young girls spoke of how proud they would be to receive letters from heroes at the front. In that short time which lay between the day when he was called and the day when he left for camp, the young soldier-to-be was, perhaps for the first time in his life, the center of attention.

Perhaps you can feel the excitement and the sorrow which combined to make the day of leaving for camp a never-to-be-forgotten time, if you will try to imagine yourself at a railway station as a group of young men from the surrounding country board the train on an autumn day in 1917.

The little Missouri village where our eyes are turned stands almost on the spot where the prairies meet the foothills of the Ozarks. To the north stretch flat fields, rich now in the golden Indian summer with their harvest of corn. To the south are the hills, where people help out a poor living by a bit of trapping in winter or fishing in summer.

To this little village come the boys from both these regions, to take the train for camp. Most of them are big, husky fellows whose broad shoulders and tanned skins tell of their outdoor lives. Some are a bit uncomfortable in the "store clothes" which they have put on for this great occasion. A few have come in well-washed overalls.

[413]

The boys from the little town join them on the station platform. There is a young druggist; a bank clerk with his "war bride" holding to his arm; a carpenter; a lad just out of law school; the son of the town's ne'er-do-well family that has long lived on charity; a delivery boy; a grocery clerk. Well-to-do or poor, educated or ignorant, industrious or lazy, they are all heroes today.

Everyone in the village who can walk is at the station. Two old men lean on their canes and talk of the days of '61 when they were leaving home for the war. The school children arrive in charge of their teachers. Not knowing quite why they have received this holiday, they are nevertheless very merry over it. They skip about, getting in everybody's way and causing trouble for the young teachers, whose thoughts are more with the men who are leaving than they are with the children. Women of the Red Cross arrive, their arms loaded with boxes. Each young soldier-to-be receives one, to add to the already awkward load that he carries. Cakes,

candy, socks, cigarettes, and a dozen other gifts have
been pressed upon each young man until his bulging
suitcase will no longer hold them all.

The red, white, and blue bunting waves; mothers,
fathers, sisters, and wives crowd a little nearer their
loved boys; the teachers lead the school children in
singing "America" and "There's a Long, Long Trail."
From far down the tracks comes a whistle; a sudden
silence falls on the crowd broken by a sharp cry from
the bank clerk's bride and a sob from the mother of a
lad in overalls. Almost every eye is wet.

[415]

With a roar the train comes to a stop. The boys quickly gather together bags, bundles, and boxes. Their arms piled high with these, and their women-folk hanging on to their coat sleeves, they begin to move toward the steps of the train. There is a great stirring and moving back and forth as people crowd close for a last word.

The men are finally aboard, and almost at once their heads and arms appear at the open windows. As they wave, the air is filled with cries of "Now do write," "Be careful," "Remember me to the Kaiser," "Good luck," and "God bless you, my boy." The whistle blows; the train rolls down the track; waving arms grow smaller and soon disappear.

On the platform women weep and men stand with bowed heads, while the school children, awed by this queer conduct, stare at their elders. The day is no longer exciting — only terribly lonely. War did not seem very close to this little village when President Wilson stood before Congress and spoke of making the world safe for democracy, but on this Indian-summer day when the boys have gone, war has come home to the Missouri village standing where prairies and hills meet.

Not only did the Government have to call men to the colors, but it had to provide camps in which they could be trained. These were built during the summer of 1917, men working at top speed on them. In sixteen camps the buildings were made of lumber, while in the

Southern states sixteen others were set up with tents instead of wooden buildings. It was a huge undertaking for the Government, second only to the building of the Panama Canal. However, constructing the canal had required ten years, while these thirty-two camps were ready for use at the end of three months.

**Americans at home help to win the war.** — No matter how brave they might be nor how well trained they were, the soldiers alone could not win the war. The people at home must also do their part. Americans very quickly came to understand this and by their efforts helped to bring victory.

The industries of the country were put under the direction of one man. It was his job to see that all the factories and plants worked smoothly to provide needed supplies. The railroads also were placed under one-man control. Many of the country's ablest business-

[417]

men gave their full time to the service of the government. They were often called *dollar-a-year men* because they each received one dollar a year as their pay.

Ships and yet more ships were needed, for there were two million soldiers and billions of pounds of goods to be carried to Europe. Submarines continued to sink ships whenever they could, thus adding to the need. A great shipbuilding program was launched. Vessels already built were made fit for the service required of them. Men working in shipyards were excused from serving as soldiers. The result of this effort was shown on July 4, 1918, when the day was celebrated by the launching of about ninety ships.

One of the most serious problems that the country faced was the matter of making America's food go round. Our citizens at home, our soldiers, and our Allies all needed food. Herbert Hoover, who had already directed the work of feeding people in Belgium who were starving because of war conditions, was put in charge of the food problems of the United States.

Mr. Hoover asked Americans to grow more food, to eat the foods that were hardest to ship, to waste no food, and to save certain foods, for example, meat and wheat. People did the things asked of them, and there was enough food for all needs.

President Wilson created a Committee on Public Information. The work of this committee was described as "a fight for the minds of men." Directed by this committee artists made posters asking people to

buy bonds, save food, give money, and do other things
to help win the war. Motion pictures carrying messages about the war were made and shown. Speakers
were sent to talk at all sorts of gatherings. Singers
prepared songs for use in camps. Writers wrote
stories. Actors gave plays. Through these and other
ways the meaning of the war and its needs were carried
to all the people.

From Red Cross rooms set up in every community
came bandages, sweaters, socks, and many articles of
clothing. Not only the men in service but the people
in war-torn areas of Europe were supplied with needed
articles.

The Red Cross, the Y. M. C. A., the Knights of
Columbus, and the Salvation Army all followed the
men to the fighting fronts. Their work there was paid
for by money given by American citizens.

The Government raised money to carry on the war
by selling Liberty Bonds. Special drives were made

from time to time as it was found necessary to sell new groups of bonds. Each of these drives succeeded, with the result that huge sums of money were lent by American citizens to their government.

In the same spirit in which they bought bonds Americans faced the other problems growing out of the war. For the most part the people of the United States were proud to give their service, their money, and their sons for what they believed was a fight to save the liberty of the world.

**General Pershing takes command.** — In May, 1917, General John J. Pershing was given the command of American forces in Europe. He sailed at once to arrange for the care and training of the men who were to be sent abroad. From the first, General Pershing was determined that the American soldiers should form an army and fight as one group in France. English and French generals did not at first favor this plan, feeling that it would be better to scatter the American troops along the battle fronts in places where their lines were weakest.

The first American soldiers reached France late in June. Can you imagine how delighted the French people were after three years of fighting to see these husky young Americans? Wishing to honor them, the French arranged a ceremony to be held in Paris on the Fourth of July. Upon this occasion the President of France and several of the high officers of the French army extended a welcome to the American soldiers.

The troops then marched to the tomb of Lafayette, the Frenchman who had helped the Americans during the Revolutionary War. Here there were several speeches, including a short one by General Pershing. It was on this occasion that the General is reported to have said, "Lafayette, we are here!" General Pershing himself does not take credit for saying this. Instead, he reports that these words were used by another officer of the United States Army, Colonel Stanton. Whether spoken by General Pershing or by Colonel Stanton, those were fitting words with which to close this ceremony.

The Americans were first trained by French and British officers in camps back of the lines. After a time

they were sent to some quiet part of the battle front for experience. While serving in what was thought to be a quiet section, some of the Americans suffered a raid from the Germans. On the morning of November third three men were killed — the first Americans to lose their lives in the World War. They were buried

with honors by the French.  Before the war was over more than fifty-five thousand other American soldiers lay in graves in France.

**The Americans go into battle.** — Before the period of training was finished, the Germans began a great drive along the battle front.  Although he wanted later to form an American Army, General Pershing now offered the use of the soldiers already in France to Marshal Foch, who was in command of all Allied armies.

Thus it happened that the Americans received their first real experience in battle fighting beside other Allied troops.  At Château-Thierry on the Marne

[423]

River, American and French soldiers turned back the enemy after hard fighting.

In Belleau Wood a division of American troops faced the Germans. For the entire month of June, 1918, the battle raged fiercely. Fighting was from tree to tree and from rock to rock. German machine guns were planted in every possible spot where they could be hidden. Again and again officers sent word to their commander that their men were exhausted. The answer that came back was always the same, "The line must be held." With very little food, water, or sleep those American troops not only held the line but actually pushed it forward.

The Germans started a new drive on the entire front on June 13. Again our soldiers stood firm against the advancing enemy. On July 1 the Americans launched a drive of their own, pushing their battle front a thousand yards into German territory and capturing prisoners and guns. General Pershing later stated that over 1600 prisoners were captured during the month of fighting.

By their conduct at Château-Thierry and Belleau Wood American soldiers had proved that they could fight bravely and well. Their success was not only received with joy at home, but it gave new courage to the war-weary men in the other Allied armies.

On July 18 Marshal Foch began the great drive which continued until the Germans asked for terms of peace. Every American soldier in France who was able to fight was put into the battle line. All conducted themselves with credit, but General Pershing gave special praise to the work of the First and Second Divisions. With the help of troops from Morocco these two American divisions forced the beginning of the German retreat. From that time until the close of the war the Germans were never again able to launch a drive of their own. A high officer of the German government speaking years later of those days said, "The history of the world was played out in three days."

The troops of the Second Division had the greatest difficulty in reaching their positions in time for the attack. The road to the front was blocked with vehicles of all sorts. It rained steadily, and the night was so dark that the men could not see an arm's length ahead. Some of the soldiers became lost in the woods as they were attempting to move up to the jumping-off trenches. The time for the attack was set at 4:35 A.M. The troops who were to go "over the top" first broke into a dead run for the last ten minutes of the trip. As the Allied guns burst into a roar at 4:35 the weary men rushed into the jumping-off trenches, scrambled "over the top," formed for the attack, and plunged through driving rain toward the enemy's lines.

On through July the Allied drive continued, with the Americans bearing their share of the fighting. On August 3 the world learned that the Second Battle of the Marne had ended in a severe defeat for the Germans.

[425]

General Pershing was at last in a position to form
the First American Army, for which he had long
planned.   He brought his men together and prepared
to attack what was known as the Saint-Mihiel section
of the battle line.   In 1914 the Germans had captured
the region around the town of Saint-Mihiel.   At this
point their line curved out into French territory somewhat like a great horseshoe.   The Americans proposed
to recapture the region and straighten the line.

The attack began in the early morning hours of
September 12.   The Germans had strung heavy tangles
of barbed wire which had to be removed before the
Americans could reach the enemy lines.   The few
tanks — little moving forts — that were to be had

went ahead to crush these tangles. Following them went men who with wire cutters opened a path for the soldiers. Overhead the airplanes dropped bombs on the enemy. Taken by surprise, the Germans soon began to retreat. In a little more than twenty-four hours of fighting the American Army had recaptured Saint-Mihiel and straightened the battle line. Seven thousand Americans had been killed or wounded, but the Germans had lost 200 square miles of territory, 16,000 prisoners, and 450 guns

This victory was important. To the war-weary Allies it gave new hope. To Americans it was a cause for pride. To the enemy it brought despair.

Marshal Foch was now ready for a further drive along the entire battle line. The American Army under General Pershing was given the section which lay between the Argonne Forest and the Meuse River. There at half past five on the morning of September 26 the Americans started their attack against the German lines. For forty-seven days they struggled to smash the defenses of the enemy. The attack, starting on a front twenty-four miles long, spread until at the end the battle was raging along a ninety-mile line.

[428]

The BATTLE LINES of the WESTERN FRONT 1917-18

The Germans fought desperately, but it was a losing fight. Step by step they were driven back, not only in this section but all along the front. Their request for terms of peace brought to a close the Allied drive of which the battle fought by the Americans in the Argonne-Meuse section was a part. On November 11, 1918, the Germans signed an armistice, which means that they agreed to stop fighting. The World War was at an end.

**President Wilson tries to make a lasting peace.** — Even before America entered the war, President Wilson had dreamed of helping to make a peace which would prevent all future wars. During the months while America was fighting he stated this idea over and over again in his speeches. He felt that a lasting peace could be made only when nations stopped thinking of the land or money that they might get as a result of the war. He wanted to set up a plan by which all the nations of the world could work together. The plan

[430]

that he proposed was to establish a League of Nations which would settle quarrels and keep peace in the world.

A great meeting called a Peace Conference was arranged, at which a treaty of peace was written. Each of the Allied nations sent representatives to this conference, which was held at Versailles, a place not far from Paris. President Wilson went to this conference, hoping to make plans for a League of Nations and to secure a lasting peace.

Certainly the people of Europe were tired of war. Everywhere that President Wilson went the people crowded around him to hear more about his plans for peace. However, some of the leading men in the European countries had quite different ideas from those held by the American President. One wanted to see Germany punished; another hoped to receive money for the damages done by the invading army; many wanted more land because they had fought on the winning side. Wilson soon found that while most of the representatives agreed with him that a lasting peace was to be desired, very few of them were willing to give up any of their own wants to secure it.

Those were weary months for the American President as one after another of his ideas was refused by the conference. One hope he held, however. If he could get a League of Nations established, other difficulties could be made right later. Since the other representatives were willing to try his plan, the treaty of peace provided for the setting up of a League of Nations.

[431]

When at last he came home, Mr. Wilson faced a new problem. The Constitution of the United States says that a treaty must be approved by at least two thirds of the Senators. The President had not appointed a Senator as a representative to the Peace Conference. He had made no effort to win the support of the Senators to his plan. Now he found many of them refusing to approve the treaty because it provided for a League of Nations.

There began a long struggle between the President and the Senate. Some of the Senators favored the League, but more did not. Some proposed accepting the treaty and the plan of the League with certain changes. Mr. Wilson refused to accept any of the proposed changes.

In the autumn of 1919 the President decided to make a trip over the United States to explain his plan to the people. If he could arouse their support, he hoped that they would influence the Senators to vote for the treaty. Warned that he was far from well, Mr. Wilson still insisted upon making the trip. Before it was completed he became so ill that he had to return to Washington at once. Although he grew much better, he was never again strong and well.

In the end the Senate refused to accept the treaty or to allow the United States to enter the League of Nations. However, the League was established but this country has never been a member. The United States made a separate treaty of peace with Germany.

[432]

It was a splendid dream which Woodrow Wilson dreamed, but the world was not ready for it.

The World War did not end all wars. Neither did it make the world safe for democracy. Because it failed to do these things for which America fought, some people have said that no good came of it. However, those who take this point of view have not looked at the whole picture. By taking part in this war the United States came to have a larger place in world affairs. The experience gained in the World War was of some help to the nation when a quarter of a century later it had to fight a still greater war. Moreover, the years of peace that followed the end of the fighting in 1918 did give some small nations of Europe a chance to enjoy better government than they had ever known before. The World War of 1914–1918 was the opening fight in a long battle that is still under way. Justice and freedom can prevail on the earth only when that battle ends in victory.

## The Nation Has a Period of Peace

**America tries to forget the war.** — The effect of a great war is always felt for many years after the fighting ceases. You will remember that it required a long period of time for the South to recover from the War between the States. The nation was still suffering from the effects of the World War when, a quarter of century later, it was plunged into another conflict.

A soldier who came back from France often showed no desire to talk of battles, and when questioned by friends sometimes replied, "Let's not talk about it. I want to forget the war." This feeling of the returned soldier came in a way to be the feeling of people all over the country. They wanted to return to the old safe days before the world had been disturbed by a great conflict. America wanted to forget the war.

In seeking to forget, Americans plunged into a whirl of moneymaking and pleasure seeking such as the coun-

[434]

try had never known before. Soon after the close of the war there had been a short period when prices were high and wages paid to workers were low. Many of the returned soldiers had trouble finding work. But after a year or two conditions became better and business began a period of rapid growth.

From 1923 to 1929 the factories of the United States poured out great quantities of goods. Advertisements in papers and magazines, on billboards, and over the radio told people every day that they needed automobiles, electric refrigerators, radios, new furniture, and a thousand other articles that Machine Age methods were producing. If they did not have the money to pay for these things, they could be bought by paying a small sum when making the purchase and a certain amount each week or month until all was paid.

Since people were constantly wanting more things, they needed to make more money. Business was good, but many people who had not done so before began to search for other ways to make money. They found it by buying stock issued by some of the great business companies of the country. Buying stock means that a person having some money that he would like to use to make more money buys a share in a company or industry. The men who manage the company or industry use this money in making their business larger, and they pay the owner of the stock for the use of his money. The buying and selling of stocks is carried on in a place called a stock exchange.

In the money-mad nineteen twenties stocks rose higher and higher in value. More and more people bought, hoping to sell as the price advanced and thus make a quick profit. This fever for easy money spread like a disease. Even people who had worked hard all their lives and saved a little money each week often took all their savings to buy stock. About 1928 some bankers began to warn people that this condition could not go on forever, but no one paid much attention to the warnings.

[436]

Both for the soldiers and for the people who stayed at home the period of the war was an exciting time. For the soldier there were battles to think about, while for those at home there were always "drives" to be put over or other kinds of war work to do. Then the war and all its excitement ended. This sudden change left many people feeling restless. They wanted to forget the war but they still wanted to do exciting things.

With plenty of money and all of the comforts of the Machine Age it was natural that some restless Ameri-

cans spent a great deal of their time seeking pleasure. During the nineteen twenties there was much dancing and playing of games. Travel by automobile became very popular in all parts of the country. In almost every home in America a radio brought the latest programs. Millions of people attended motion-picture theaters. For many Americans making money and having a pleasant time seemed the two most important things in life.

Americans showed their desire to forget the war in another way. Mr. Wilson's dream had been to give America a large place in world affairs. He had hoped to see his country play an important part in keeping the peace of the world. By 1920 Americans had shown quite plainly that they did not want to take such a place as Mr. Wilson had hoped to have them occupy. They had fought one war and they had no desire to do anything that might draw them into another. Not only did America refuse to become a member of the League of Nations, but in later years the people showed little interest in joining the World Court. This was another plan which called for the nations of the world to work together.

One thing was done, however, which for a time seemed to favor world peace. In 1921 President Warren G. Harding called a conference which met in Washington D. C. At this meeting representatives of several nations discussed the matter of reducing the size of their navies. Great Britain, the United States,

[438]

and Japan finally agreed to a plan which did limit the number of battleships which each might have. However, some years later the plan was given up, and the nations again increased the size of their navies.

The United States also took part in other conferences which discussed limiting the number of tanks, submarines, guns, and other war materials that nations might own. However, none of these conferences succeeded in preventing war.

Another effort was made to do away with wars when a treaty was prepared saying that nations signing it agreed not to go to war but to settle disputes by peaceful means. A very large number of nations including our own signed this treaty but within a dozen years or less most of them were at war.

Immigrants from foreign countries had always come to America in large numbers. Much of the work in factories and on farms had been performed by them. In 1921 the United States passed a law which limited the number of people who could in the future come to America from foreign lands.

The farmers were one group of people who failed to share in the prosperous times enjoyed by most Americans after the World War. They had received very good prices for their farm products during the war. Urged by the Government to raise large amounts of food, many of them had gone into debt to buy more land and tools. When the war stopped, the larger crops were not needed, prices went ˙down, and the farmers were left to pay for land and tools as best they could. All through the years in which others prospered they continued to have a hard time because the prices which their products would bring were not large enough for them to buy the manufactured goods that they needed.

Just at the close of the war two new measures that had wide influence were put into effect. Both were passed much earlier than they otherwise would have been because of feeling aroused by the war. One of these measures gave all women twenty-one years of age or older the right to vote. The other said that no liquor should be made, sold, or shipped in the United States. This latter measure was done away with in 1933, and the law now allows the sale of liquor in the United States except in states or communities that forbid it.

During the prosperous years that followed the war there was a great increase in crime of all kinds. Many of those who broke the law were young boys and girls in their teens.

**A depression comes in America.** — As was suggested earlier, the great rise in the value of stocks could not go on forever. By 1928 some people had begun to fear that there was trouble ahead, but most of those who were making money went merrily on their way.

In October, 1929, the crash came. Stocks fell in value, and millions of dollars were lost by the citizens of America. Things moved rapidly from bad to worse. Factories closed, throwing men and women out of work. Banks and business houses failed, thus causing more loss of money. People could not pay their taxes, which meant that there was less money for supporting schools and paying the expenses of government. Farmers got even less than they had before for their products. Things became so bad that many American citizens needed help to feed their families properly.

Such a condition as this, called a *depression*, is not new in the world. It usually follows war. The United States had had several other periods of business depression but never one so bad as this. Things were made worse by the fact that it was a world depression. All of the countries which fought in the World War and some that did not had suffered greatly.

[441]

The depression which had begun in the United States in the fall of 1929 dragged on. By the early part of 1933 thirteen million persons in this country were out of work. The Government had made some efforts to meet the needs of the times, but it had not succeeded in putting these idle workers back at their jobs.

In the fall of 1932 Franklin D. Roosevelt was elected President of the United States. In his speeches when he was running for office Mr. Roosevelt had promised to give the poor man (whom he called the "forgotten man") a "New Deal" in government. Because he used this term often the laws passed during the early years that he was President were often spoken of as the "New Deal." These laws had two purposes. One was to help end the depression. The other purpose was to create better conditions of living for working people.

A number of measures were taken to provide work. Camps were set up where young men lived and helped to take care of forests. Many useful jobs such as repairing roads and streets, building playgrounds, improving parks, cleaning public buildings, teaching children under school age, sewing, and preparing guidebooks to places of interest were done by persons who had no other work. For these tasks they received a small wage. Boys and girls were given jobs around high schools and colleges so that they could earn enough to stay in school. Some of those who had left school were paid a small amount while they were learning a trade.

[442]

A public building program was aided by the Government. This provided work for many men. Such a program had begun while President Hoover was in office, but it was continued and made larger under President Roosevelt. As a result of this government aid schools, hospitals, electric light and power plants, post offices, sewers, highways, bridges, and many other public works were built.

In certain places groups of houses were built, which could be rented or bought by people who had only a small amount of money. People who wished to buy or build their own homes were also given help in borrowing money.

Farmers who had had a hard time for years were in still worse condition after the depression struck the nation. A number of measures were put into effect to improve their condition. One purpose of these measures was to secure better prices for farm products. Another was to help farmers secure loans of money when these were greatly needed. Some laws were intended to aid very poor farm families to secure better living and working conditions.

[443]

Many people lost their money in the early years of the depression because banks failed. A law was passed which said that the government would protect each person's bank deposit up to the amount of $5,000. This measure made banks much stronger.

Another law intended to improve the condition of many citizens provided a plan for paying old-age pensions. It also furnished sums of money to be used in aiding the blind, children without parents, and certain others in need. Still another part of this measure allowed persons who were out of work to receive a sum of money each week for a certain number of weeks.

The right of laboring men to form unions that could make bargains with those who hired the men had been disputed by some people. This right was established by a law passed in 1935. Unions have added many new members in recent years. They have often made bargains which have secured for the workers higher wages, shorter hours, and better conditions. When labor unions have not been able to secure terms that they wished, they have often gone on strike. This means that they have refused to continue to work until their terms are met.

Dams and power plants were built in several parts of the United States during recent years. One of the largest of these undertakings was in the Tennessee River Valley. Preventing floods, providing electric power, and furnishing water to irrigate dry lands were some of the benefits that dams made possible.

[444]

## A Second World War Is Fought

**The world moves toward war.** — While the United States was struggling to get out of the depression, some nations were having even a worse time than ours. When people have no jobs and are hungry, they are likely to listen to anyone who claims to have a plan for making things better. That was exactly what happened in a number of European countries. In Italy, where the people were in great difficulties long before the depression reached America, a leader appeared who promised a new and better way of life to the Italians if they would follow him. This man, Benito Mussolini, secured control of the government of Italy in 1922 and began putting his ideas into practice. In Germany Adolf Hitler gained control of the affairs of government in 1933. He promised to make Germany a mighty nation. In each of these countries conditions did improve, for people were put to work and so could make a living. But it soon became clear that this work was all directed toward preparing the nation for war.

While the First World War was being fought, a revolution had broken out in Russia. This uprising was led by the Communist Party. In time this party secured complete control of affairs in Russia, with its leader as the head of the government. When an earlier leader died in 1924 Joseph Stalin became the head of the Russian government. Under the Communist rule Russia built many factories and power plants, opened new mines, produced more on its farms, and made other changes that gave people better living conditions. But Russia also was preparing itself in case war should come.

In the United States people had no desire to go to war again. Even after European nations had begun to fight many American citizens believed that this country could stay out of the war. They thought that the oceans which lie on either side of the country would protect us from attack. People who believed this bitterly opposed any preparations for war in this country. They felt that the United States could and should remain neutral. But President Roosevelt (who had

[446]

been elected a second time in 1936 and a third time in 1940) thought the nation might be drawn into the war and so should prepare to defend itself.

One bright spot in all this talk of war was the growing friendship between the United States and the Latin American countries. These are the countries that lie South of the United States in North America and all the countries in South America. These nations have not always had a friendly feeling for the United States. But all our Presidents in recent years have tried to create better feeling between these countries and ours. President Roosevelt called this a "good-neighbor" policy. This effort of the past several years has led to a better understanding between the United States and most of the Latin American countries.

**Nations take up arms.** — In Japan also men who believed in making war took over the control of the government. It was this nation that took the first step in a long chain of acts that led to a Second World War. In 1931 Japan seized Manchuria, a section of northeastern China.

In 1935 Mussolini sent Italian forces into Ethiopia, an independent country in Africa. Eight months later the country was conquered.

The next year Hitler ordered German soldiers to move into the Rhineland, a strip of territory lying along the French boundary. The treaty of peace at the end of the First World War had stated that German soldiers should never enter the Rhineland again.

[447]

A year later Japan attacked China, and thus began a war which continued for eight years.

The steps that led directly to war in Europe came rapidly after that. Germany seized Austria in 1938 and within a few months also came into control of Czecho-Slovakia. The next year German armies marched into Poland. This led Britain and France to declare war on Germany which they did on September 3, 1939. This was the beginning of the Second World War.

Poland was conquered in two weeks. Denmark fell without a fight early in 1940, and Norway was invaded. The German armies roared across western Europe. This was a new type of warfare, quite different from

the trench fighting of the First World War. Overhead German airplanes whizzed, dropping bombs and machine gunning those below. On the ground tanks and armored cars plunged ahead sweeping aside the French and British who opposed them. Belgium, Luxemburg, and the Netherlands were quickly crushed. By June Paris was in German hands and France surrendered.

Italy at once came into the war on the side of Germany, and a few months later sent its armies into Greece. The brave people of this country fought so well that it was necessary for Germany to come to Italy's aid before the Greeks were conquered.

While all this was happening Russia and Finland had fought a short war. The Finns fought well but victory went to the larger nation. Russia also took control of three small independent countries on the Baltic Sea.

The fighting spread to Africa where British troops forced the Italians out of Ethiopia. German forces invaded Africa, hoping to seize the Suez Canal, which is controlled by the British.

During the last half of 1940 and the early part of 1941 the Germans poured millions of tons of bombs on

[449]

Britain. Planes flew over the English Channel wave after wave. Hitler hoped to knock the British out of the war by this bombing attack, but that stout-hearted people stood firm.

In the spring of 1941 Hitler sent his armies into the Balkans. Hungary, Rumania, and Bulgaria entered the war on the side of Germany and Italy. Yugoslavia fought the German invaders. Though the Germans established control over the country, they never succeeded in fully conquering it. A large number of men escaped to the mountains and from secret camps continued to attack the Germans at every opportunity.

At about this same time British and Free-French armies occupied Iraq and Syria in Asia. The Free-French were men who had escaped from France and formed a movement pledged to fight for the freedom of their homeland. Their leader was General Charles de Gaulle.

In June, 1941, Germany suddenly attacked Russia. These nations had seemed to be friendly; so this move on Hitler's part was somewhat of a surprise. Finland then entered the war on Germany's side During that

[450]

summer and fall the Russian armies were forced back almost to the gates of their great cities, Moscow and Leningrad. In the winter, however, the Russians began to gain back some of the ground they had lost.

**The United States enters the war.** — December 7, 1941, began like any other peaceful winter Sunday in the United States. But when the day ended, the whole course of American history had been changed. In the early morning of that day airplanes came flying across the Pacific Ocean toward the great American naval base at Pearl Harbor in the Hawaiian Islands. These were Japanese planes, each carrying a load of bombs, which were dropped squarely upon American ships and planes and upon the quarters where soldiers slept. Three hundred or more men were killed. The damage to planes and ships was very great.

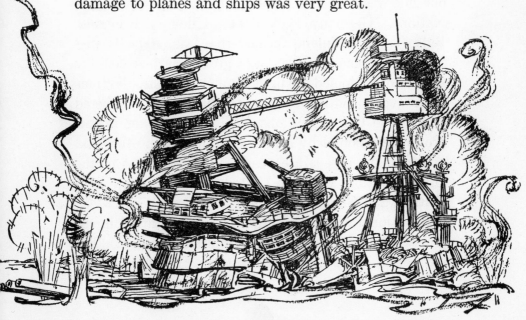

That same day and the next the Japanese also attacked the Philippines, Guam, Wake, and Midway Islands, all American territory. At the same time they struck at Malaya and Hong Kong in Asia, both held by the British. Neither the United States nor Great Britain was at war with the Japanese when these sneak attacks were made.

On December 8, 1941, the Congress of the United States declared war upon Japan. Whatever differences the American people had had over the wisdom of preparing for war were now swept away. All were united in one common purpose — to destroy the enemy. Congress also declared war against Germany and Italy. Britain at the same time went to war with Japan.

The struggle had truly become a World War. On one side were the Axis Powers; on the other the United Nations. Germany, Italy, Japan, Hungary, Rumania, Bulgaria, and Finland formed the Axis. The United Nations became a very large group, as one country after another joined the fight against the Axis. Nations from every continent on the globe were numbered among the United Nations. All the countries in this group were bound by a pledge to help each other and not to make a separate peace. The strongest of the United Nations were the United States, Russia, Great Britain, and China.

A national defense program had been started in the United States after the war in Europe began. The Army and Navy were made larger. For the first time

[452]

in the nation's history men were drafted into the army while the country was at peace. Congress passed a law that made it possible for this country to send supplies to nations fighting the Axis. New bases were secured for the use of the airplanes and ships guarding the Panama Canal and our Atlantic coast. Factories began to turn out great numbers of airplanes, guns, tanks, and other war materials.

**The nation prepares for action.** — After the United States entered the war all the efforts to build a great fighting force were speeded up still further. All branches of service were made larger. Laws were passed which made it possible for women to enter the various branches of the service. As in other wars women served as nurses. Training of this vast number of young people went on all over the United States. Not only camps but colleges and universities became training centers.

The making of many articles was stopped altogether so that materials, labor, and factories could be used to produce war goods. Thousands of men and women who had never before worked in factories or plants took jobs. Day and night, month in and month out the plants, shops, mills, and factories of America turned out the materials of war. Never before in all the

[453]

world's history had such vast amounts of goods been produced in so short a time.

Back of the factory were the farms, the forests, the mines, and all the other places that supplied raw products. In these places too other American citizens were giving their best efforts to help win the war. Swiftly, as the finished goods came forth, they were carried by trucks, trains, ships, and planes to the fighting fronts. Materials produced in the United States were shared with all the United Nations.

Fighting a war costs vast sums of money. To secure this taxes were greatly increased and bonds were sold. Boys and girls shared in the support of the war by buying War Savings Stamps.

People who stayed at home prepared for possible attack. Among other things they learned how to protect themselves during an air raid, studied first aid, and watched for enemy airplanes. Children and grownups both helped collect paper, iron, tin, and other materials needed for war. They also gave money for war relief, Red Cross, the United Service Organizations, and other purposes. As in earlier wars women sewed, knitted, and made hospital dressings.

In order that meat, butter, sugar, gasoline, tires, and certain other scarce articles might be shared equally by all the people such goods were rationed. Good citizens were careful not to waste anything that they used.

**The nation fights the Axis Powers in Europe.** — While the United States made ready its armed forces the war in Europe and North Africa still raged. As rapidly as American soldiers were trained, they were sent to Great Britain. The first Americans to take an active part in the war in Europe were the air forces. These men, stationed in Britain, flew over Europe and dropped bombs on territory held by the Germans.

In November, 1942, American forces landed in North Africa. Joining with the other United Nations fighters already there, the Americans helped free Africa from the Axis. General Dwight D. Eisenhower was in command of the drive that brought victory.

With North Africa conquered the next move of United Nations troops was across the Mediterranean. Three small islands were occupied. In July, 1943, Sicily was invaded and after a few weeks was conquered. The opening days of September brought the invasion of Italy. That nation soon surrendered, but the German armies there fought hard to stop the invaders. Mussolini escaped to safety in German territory.

The advance north through Italy was slow and painful. The German army in northern Italy held out until the closing days of the war, in the spring of 1945. When the German hold on Italy was broken Mussolini fell into the hands of the Italians and was killed by his own people.

The war between Russia and Germany, begun in 1941, continued with bitter fighting. During the summer of 1942 the Germans made another sweep far

[455]

AXIS-CONTROLLED AREAS
*in*
EUROPE *and* AFRICA

Axis-controlled areas at greatest extent,
1941 and 1942

Axis-controlled areas at surrender, May 1945

MILES
0    200    400    600    800

into Russia, somewhat like their advance of the year before. After hard fighting the tide was turned. Thereafter the Russians continued most of the time to push the Germans back. Their battle line extended from the Baltic to the Black Sea.

The Russians were not content, however, with driving the Germans out of Russia. They were determined to follow the enemy and destroy the Germans on their own ground. Russian armies, headed for Germany, poured across Poland. Month after month the battle raged, with the Germans slowly falling back toward their own boundaries. By 1944 they were fighting on German soil.

Demands for a "second front" in Europe began early in 1942. The Russians wished some of Germany's fighting strength drawn to other battle zones. The conquered people wanted relief from their terrible suffering under German rule. But a "second front" could not be undertaken until the United States had moved great numbers of men and billions of pounds of materials to Great Britain. Two years passed before the United Nations were fully prepared for the attack. Then, after the most careful preparation, a "second front" was opened on June 6, 1944, by the invasion of the Normandy Peninsula in France. An American, General Dwight D. Eisenhower, was supreme commander of the invasion forces.

Air, sea, and land forces worked together. For weeks before the invasion, bombing planes had attacked such important points in the invasion area as railroad yards and bridges. The bombing became heavier as D Day (the day of the invasion) came nearer. When the thousands of boats and vessels used in the invasion gathered in the English Channel, planes flew back and forth guarding them. A few hours before the men hit the Normandy beaches, thousands of fighting men were carried back of the German lines by plane. First down were the paratroopers who came down by parachute. Then the gliders that had been towed behind many of the planes were landed. Besides carrying men the gliders were loaded with guns, jeeps, and other things needed by the troops. From planes flying over the beaches came messages which told naval commanders where their guns could find hidden German defenses.

It was the Navy's job to get men and materials across the English Channel and to silence enemy fire on shore with their big guns. The naval vessels stood by during the invasion ready to lend aid with their guns and to return wounded men and prisoners to Britain.

Ahead of the main body of invasion troops went the British Commandos and American Rangers. It was their job to wreck all possible enemy defenses. They did their work with daring and high courage.

Perhaps you can better understand the meaning of invasion if you will try to imagine that you are with the men who landed on the Normandy beaches in the early morning of that June day.

[458]

It is shortly after midnight. The English Channel is alive with boats of every sort. From many ports they come, several thousand of them, following now the lanes that have been cleared for them by mine sweepers. On board are men who have had long months of training for this hour. Most of them are eager for the great adventure just ahead.

Silently the vessels move to their positions. Overhead zoom the planes carrying the air-borne troops. There are so many that they stretch out for miles. Still the Germans have not discovered the great fleet in the channel. Their guns fire at the air-transport planes, but the vessels are not disturbed. Silently they wait for the time agreed upon. Men grow uneasy. Waiting is harder than action. Some are seasick for the channel is rough. The hum of other planes passing over head is heard. These are the bombers.

At last three o'clock comes and beaches break into a mighty roar of exploding bombs. American and British flyers have turned the shore into what seems like a giant display of fireworks. German guns reply; blazing planes fall to earth.

Small boats and landing barges gather around the larger vessels. The men begin to go over the side. The water is rough; it is risky business getting into the boats. Riding them through these rolling waves is still worse.

Dawn has come bringing the hour when the naval guns take their turn at blasting the shore. It seems

that every inch of the beach must be raked by the terrible, blinding fire from the several hundred guns. Behind this curtain of fire and smoke the boats and barges must make for shore. Each boat has a spot on the beach where it is supposed to land. The enemy has set up all manner of things to make landing difficult. Posts, wires, steel pillars, tree trunks all clutter the beaches. Trained men go ahead blasting a way through this jungle.

Now at last the landing boats come into shallow water. Some ram into the sand. From these men race

[460]

ashore, firing as they run, and tanks roll out to thunder into the battle. From other boats men leap into the rough water, struggling ashore as best they can. Some are knocked flat by the waves. Some crawl forward the last part of the way to keep out of enemy fire. Others crouch behind posts still standing on the beaches until they can follow a tank on to the shore. Here a bullet finds its mark and a man sinks into the water. There on shore another falls wounded.

As day stretches on, the beaches become a vast moving mass of men and machines. Here men are shooting

and being shot. Doctors move about binding up wounds. Injured men are carried out to the boats. Bulldozers come lumbering ashore and make ready to prepare an airfield the minute the beachhead is secure. Foot soldiers march on to open attacks at other points. Prisoners arrive. Planes zoom through the sky. Guns roar and shells burst. Action! Noise! Destruction! Death! These form the pattern of invasion. By means of them the United Nations have opened "a second front."

The Germans fought hard but they could not stop the American, British, and Canadian troops. The beachheads were made secure; the Normandy Peninsula was held; a move to take the Brittany Peninsula raced to a successful finish; the drive to secure complete control of France rolled forward. A large German army was bottled up in the northern part of the country. Then on August 15 came a second invasion of France. Troops of the United Nations landed on the southeastern coast. Among these were many French soldiers who had come to help free their homeland. Shortly before this a division of French troops had gone into action in northern France. Paris, the principal city of France was soon freed, and the drive for Germany was begun.

Heavy bombing of European cities was under way by 1942. Each month saw an increase in the might of these air attacks. One by one the cities of Germany were struck and in many cases were largely destroyed.

[462]

The Germans lost control of the air. They were not able to continue the heavy air raids made on Britain in the early months of the war. However, in 1944 the Germans tried two new bombs. These bombs, known as V-1 and V-2, were launched from the northwestern shores of the European mainland. They were directed toward Britain where they caused great destruction. Both the V-1 and the V-2 bombs traveled under their own power instead of being carried in airplanes. Both burst when they struck the earth or some other object. The United Nations armies moving toward Germany destroyed as rapidly as they could the fields from which the V-1 and V-2 bombs were launched.

The drive against Germany continued with fighting on two fronts. On the east the Russians pushed steadily forward. Hungary, Rumania, Finland, and Bulgaria gave up the struggle. Not only did these little countries quit fighting for Germany, but they began fighting against that nation. By the early months of 1945 the Russians were closing in on Berlin, the capital of Germany.

While the Russians had been pushing on to Berlin from the east, troops of other United Nations had moved toward Berlin from the west. American soldiers made up a large part of the forces on this front. In December, 1944, the steady progress toward Berlin was halted briefly. German forces attacked so strongly that the United Nations troops were thrown back for a time. But this attack, sometimes called the "Battle of

[463]

the Bulge," proved to be Germany's last stand. By the early months of 1945 United Nations fighters had taken again the ground they had lost and were racing for Berlin.

In April Russian and American armies met near the center of Germany. This meeting of the two armies split the German forces into two parts.

Early in May it was reported that Hitler was dead. The next day Berlin fell. The surrender of other cities followed quickly. On May 7, 1945, came the moment that the people of the United Nations had worked and fought to achieve. Germany surrendered.

The next day, V-E Day (Victory-in-Europe Day), was announced by the heads of the principal United Nations. All over the world people rejoiced. In their churches they gave thanks for the victory won. But in the midst of their gladness the men and women of the United Nations remembered that there was still an-

[464]

other victory to be won. In the Pacific fighting forces were still locked in a deadly struggle.

Russia, Great Britain, France, and the United States each ruled a part of Germany after the surrender. General Dwight D. Eisenhower was in command of the part controlled by the United States.

**The nation fights Japan.** — The attack on Pearl Harbor marked the beginning of an all-out war in the Pacific as well as in Europe. The Japanese intended to make themselves masters of Asia and the islands of the Far Pacific. They had already succeeded in occupying all the eastern part of China before they struck at American and British territory.

Though bravely defended by American marines Wake and Guam Islands fell to the Japanese. The Philippines held out for several months, the defending force holding the Bataan Peninsula even when the rest of the islands were in Japanese control. But in spite of a brave defense the Philippines were fully occupied by the Japanese in the spring of 1942.

The British too suffered severe losses of territory. Hong Kong, on the Chinese coast, Malaya, and a part of Burma were taken. So also were the Netherlands Indies, rich island possessions of the Netherlands.

China suffered greatly. Much of the country was in the hands of the enemy. The Japanese made new attacks from time to time. Worse still the only road that Free China had to the outside world was closed when the Japanese moved into Burma. This meant that all war supplies sent to China had to be flown over the Himalayas, the world's highest mountains. You will recall that a rapid flying service was set up between the United States and India. Goods delivered by this route were loaded into other planes and flown "over the hump," as the airmen called this jump over the mountains.

Many Pacific islands not previously controlled by Japan were seized by them in the early months of the war. On these air bases were built. Landings on New Guinea threatened Australia. Landings in the Aleutians threatened North America. As you will remember, the United States met this latter threat by sending large forces to Alaska and to some of the Aleu-

tian Islands. In 1943 the Japanese withdrew entirely from the Aleutians.

In August, 1942, American forces landed on Tulagi and Guadalcanal, two islands in the Solomon group. Months of bitter, bloody fighting followed, but by February, 1943, their hold on the islands was secure. This action prepared the way for a great movement of fighting forces that could end only when the United Nations were in control of all Japanese territory.

This war in the Pacific usually followed a pattern which was repeated again and again as new islands were conquered. The first step was severe bombing. After a period of "softening up" with bombs, troops made a landing and established a beachhead. In doing

this they usually had support from bombing planes and often from the big guns of naval vessels as well. Fighting their way foot by foot, often at great price in lives, the soldiers or marines gained control of the island. The last step was to make the newly won territory ready as a base from which planes could go out against other islands.

At the same time that land battles were being fought the American Navy was sinking Japanese ships wherever these were found. Such defeats as those suffered in 1942 in the Battle of the Coral Sea and in the attempt to take Midway Island cost the Japanese navy heavily. The American Navy did its work so well that these losses continued throughout the war. One of the greatest losses of ships was suffered by the Japanese in 1944 off the Philippine Islands. The week by week loss of supply and troop ships also weakened their fighting ability. In some cases when islands were strongly defended by the Japanese, they were by-passed. With the Navy guarding the seas, supply ships could not reach these troops. Without food or materials of war they were unable to fight.

How well the movement toward Japan went you can see by looking at your map. American fighting forces invaded one island after another. Troops of other United Nations also fought in some of these invasions. But all troops had a common purpose, to carry the war to Japanese soil. In the Solomons, the Marshalls, the Gilberts, the Admiralties, the Mariannas, the

[468]

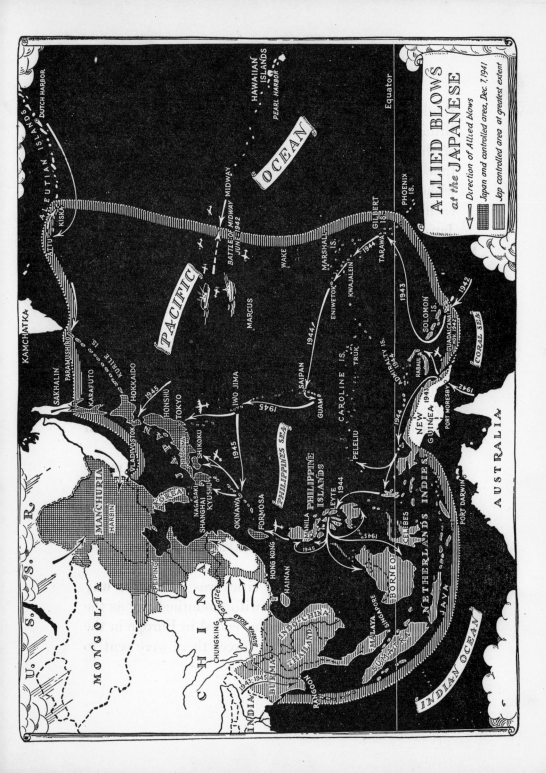

ALLIED BLOWS at the JAPANESE

→ Direction of Allied blows
▓ Japan and controlled area, Dec. 7, 1941
▒ Jap controlled area at greatest extent

Ryukyus, the Philippines, on New Guinea, New Britain, and various other islands, the fighting forces of the United Nations established themselves. Each time that they captured an island they could, if they wished, build a new airfield and supply base. Thus each island conquered was another step on the road to Japan.

It was with special joy that American forces once more gained control of territory that had been lost by the United States in the early days of the war. The final success in this respect was the regaining of the Philippines. American troops invaded the Philippines in October, 1944, and marched into Manila, the capital of the Islands, some four months later. General Douglas MacArthur was in command of the Philippine invasion. Thus he made good the promise that he had made three years earlier when he left the Islands. Then he had said to the Filipinos, "I will return."

The fight against Japan went forward on the mainland of Asia as well as on the islands and the ocean. United Nations forces fought in Burma. With the help of the American air force the Chinese kept up the fight against the Japanese invaders in their own country.

The bombing of Japanese cities was well under way by 1944. This was kept up with mounting fury as the months passed. After the war ended in Europe in the spring of 1945, American air forces there were sent to take part in the Pacific war.

[470]

The final blow in the air war against Japan came in August, 1945. An American bomber dropped an atomic bomb on a city in Japan. This was a new type of bomb never before used in war. It proved to be thousands of times more powerful than any other weapon ever used. The city on which it fell was almost wholly destroyed. A few days later a second atomic bomb was dropped. The Japanese city on which it fell was reduced to ruins.

While Japan was still trying to determine the damage done by the atomic bomb, Russia joined the war. Russian soldiers at once began fighting Japanese troops who were on the mainland of Asia.

Before the atomic bomb was dropped, the heads of the governments of Russia, Great Britain, and the United States called upon Japan to surrender or be destroyed. These men stated the terms of surrender which they would require of the enemy. On August 14, 1945, Japan accepted these terms and surrendered. The world celebrated V-J Day (Victory-in-Japan Day). The President of the United States declared a two-day holiday. Bells rang; whistles blew; bonfires blazed; children shouted; men and women paraded the streets laughing and singing. World War II was at an end.

The papers which stated the terms of surrender were signed on September 1 on board the United States battleship *Missouri*. American forces under the command of General Douglas MacArthur at once moved into Japan.

[471]

During the war General MacArthur had served as
Commander of United Nations forces in the Southwest
Pacific. Working with him to win the victory were
Admiral Chester W. Nimitz, Commander of the Pacific
fleet, and Admiral William F. Halsey, Jr., Commander
of the South Pacific fleet.

The American people were proud of the record which
their fighting men had made. Both officers and men
had fought with high courage and fine loyalty. On
land and sea, in the air, and in the depths of the ocean,
all around the globe, American men had fought and
died to make a free world.

**Americans call for a lasting peace.** — Even while
the war was being fought people in America talked of
the kind of peace they wanted. The United States
has never been a warlike nation. It did not want new
lands as a reward for victory. But it did want a peace
that would endure; a peace that would put an end for
all time to such wicked use of power as the Axis Nations
had practiced; a peace that promised a larger measure
of freedom and justice for all people.

During the war President Roosevelt helped to form a
plan by which the United Nations could work together
after the war was over. In 1944 President Roosevelt
[472]

was elected to serve his fourth term, but on April 12, 1945, he died very suddenly. The Vice President, Harry S. Truman, became President of the United States. The new president went forward with the plans that had been made by Roosevelt.

Men and women representing the various countries that were joined together as the United Nations met in April, 1945, in San Francisco. There they drew up a plan by which the nations could continue to work together when peace came. On June 26 the representatives of fifty nations signed this plan which was called the *United Nations Charter*.

Thus it happened that when the war ended the means by which the Nations could work together in peace was already set up. But the early months of peace showed that the people of the United Nations needed to know and understand each other better. The airplane, the radio, and other modern inventions have made the world one neighborhood. The problem that men must now solve is how they can live together as good neighbors in this world.

## A Word Game

This chapter contains many names, some of which are hard to spell and pronounce. Write these headings on a sheet of paper: Countries in Europe; Countries in Asia; American Presidents; American Commanders; Foreign Generals; Leaders in Other Countries; Places where Battles Were Fought. Under each heading list the names that belong there. Be sure that you can pronounce each name and that you spell it correctly.

Try to use each of these words correctly.

| | | | |
|---|---|---|---|
| submarine | trench | ration | atomic bomb |
| slogan | depression | invasion | rocket bomb |
| raids | labor union | stock exchange | beachhead |

This chapter also contains some words to add to the list of history terms in your notebook. These are *neutral, armistice, peace conference, indemnity, dominion, democracy.*

## A Map Study

On page 429 is a map showing the battle lines of the western front in the First World War. Study this as you read the part that the Americans took in this struggle. Locate the scenes of battles in which Americans took part.

On page 456 is a map showing territory in Europe, North Africa, and the Mediterranean controlled by the Axis at the height of its power. The map also shows the amount of territory held at the time of Germany's surrender. About what part of the total territory was left to Germany? Trace the steps by which this territory had been lost.

On page 469 is a map which shows the islands in the Pacific brought under control of the United Nations as they drove toward Japan. Note how these islands form stepping stones leading toward Japan.

[474]

## Some Things to Do

1. One of the best loved poems of the First World War is "In Flanders Fields." Among poems of the Second World War, "I Touched the Face of God" is very beautiful. Ask an older person to read these with you and help you to understand them.

2. Sing some of the songs popular in each war. Among these for the First World War were "Keep the Home Fires Burning," "There's a Long, Long Trail," and "Over There." Two that were often sung in the Second World War were "White Cliffs of Dover" and "Coming In on a Wing and a Prayer." Ask your music teacher to help you find others.

### Some Books to Read

Stories of the First World War are to be found in: *Shaggy, The Horse from Wyoming*, by Russell G. Carter, and in *War Horse*, by Fairfax Downey.

*Swing Shift*, by Howard M. Brier is a story of a boy who worked in a shipyard during the Second World War.

*Primrose Day*, by Carolyn Haywood, is an easy story of an English child who came to live in America because of the war. *The Wishing Window*, by Hortense Flexner, tells of French children forced out of their homes by war.

*Navy Wings of Gold* is the tale of three boys who enlisted in the Naval Air Corps, as told by Florence W. Taylor.

*Top Kick, U. S. Army Horse*, by Helen O. Watson, is a story of a horse in the Second World War.

To understand America, you must understand its many different people. In the stories listed below, you may read of other children living today in this land of ours.

*Blue Willow*, and *Sarah's Idea*, by Doris Gates
*Paradise Valley*, by Valenti Angelo
*Americans Every One*, by Lavinia R. Davis

[475]

*Up the Hill*, by Marguerite DeAngeli
*From Sea to Shining Sea*, by James G. Dyett
*Saturdays*, by Elizabeth Enright
*Ariminta*, and *Corner Key*, by Eva K. Evans
*Hash-ki, the Navajo*, by Florence Hayes
*Dixie Decides, Honey Jane*, and *Mr. Songcatcher and Company*, by May Justice
*Bayou Suzette*, by Lois Lenski
*Steppin and Family*, by Hope Newell
*Little Amish Schoolhouse*, by Ella M. Seyfrey
*Song of Tomorrow*, by Charlie M. Simon

## WORD LIST

### To the Pupil

The following list of words contains all that are likely to trouble you — indeed many more than are likely to trouble any one of you, for a great many of them are explained where they are first used in the text. The meanings that are given are those of the words as they are used in the text where you first find them. Most of these words, of course, have other meanings as well, sometimes many other meanings, which are not given here. For these other meanings you should consult a dictionary.

The following key or explanation shows you the meanings of the so-called diacritical (dī′à-krĭt′ĭ-kăl) marks that are used to tell you how to pronounce words:

āte, ärt, àsk, câre, ăm, ăorta, totăl, sodà; ēve, rĕlent, ĕnd, levĕl, givẽr; īce, ĭll; ōre, ŏbey, ŏff, fôrm, hŏt, cŏnfirm, nōōn, nŏŏk; ūse, ŭnite, tûrn, ŭp, discŭs; oil; our; ring; riṅk; bath; ba*th*e.

[476]

**aboard** (á-bōrd'), on a ship, train, airplane, etc.

**acid** (ăs'ĭd), a substance used in changing the fibers of plants into a form in which they can be made into cloth

**Admiralty Islands** (ăd'mĭ-răl-tĭ), a group of islands north of New Guinea in the Southwest Pacific Ocean

**advertise** (ăd'vĕr-tīz', ăd'vĕr-tīz'), to bring to the attention of the public

**advertisement** (ăd-vûr'tĭz-mĕnt), a printed notice which calls attention to an article or idea

**agony** (ăg'ō-nĭ), very great suffering

**agreement** (á-grē'mĕnt), an understanding

**ague** (ā'gū), a disease that causes the patient to have chills and fever

**air base** (âr bās), headquarters from which aircraft go out to carry out their work

**airplane carrier** (âr'plān' kăr'ĭ-ēr), a huge ship used to carry airplanes at sea, with a deck large enough for airplanes to land on and take off

**airport** (âr'pōrt'), a field prepared to launch, land, fuel, and otherwise care for airplanes

**aisle** (īl), a passage between rows of seats

**Alamo** (ä'lá-mō; ăl'-), a mission in San Antonio in which a company of Texas soldiers were killed by a Mexican army

**allegiance** (ă-lē'jăns), loyalty

**altitude** (ăl'tĭ-tūd), height

**ammunition** (ăm'ū-nĭsh'ŭn), bullets, powder, and the like, used in shooting guns and cannon

**annex** (ă-nĕks'), to add to a larger body

**annexation** (ăn'ĕk-sā'shŭn), the act of adding something to a larger body

**apartment house** (á-pärt'mĕnt hous), a building in which several or many families live, each in its own set of rooms

**Appomattox Court House** (ăp'ō-măt'-ŭks kōrt hous), the place in Virginia at which General Lee and General Grant met to arrange for the surrender of the Confederate Army

**Argonne Forest** (är'gŏn' fŏr'ĕst), a wooded region in France in which a battle was fought during the World War

**armistice** (är'mĭ-stĭs), a peace which lasts for a short time

**Articles of Confederation** (är'tĭ-k'lz, kŏn-fĕd'ēr-ā'shŭn), the plan of government under which Americans lived in the years between the close of the Revolutionary War and the adoption by the states of the Constitution

**atomic bomb** (á-tŏm'ĭk bŏm), a bomb so made that the atoms or parts of certain materials in the bomb break apart or explode with greater force than any other bomb ever used

**awe** (ô), wonder

**backwoodsman** (băk'wŏŏdz'măn), a man who lives in the forest

**balcony** (băl'kō-nĭ), a platform reaching out from a house at the level of an upper floor, and reached by a window or door opening from this upper floor

**bale** (bāl), a bundle of goods wrapped and tied for shipping

**bandanna handkerchief** (băn-dăn'á hăng'kēr-chĭf), a large colored handkerchief, usually red or blue

[477]

**banjo** (băn′jō), a stringed musical instrument

**baptize** (băp-tīz′), to perform a religious ceremony by dipping a person into water or by pouring or sprinkling water on him

**barbecue** (bär′bĕ-kū), an outdoor feast at which the meat of entire animals is roasted over an open fire

**barbed wire** (bärbd wīr), wire with sharp points on it

**battle front** (băt″l frŭnt), the line along which armies are drawn up for active fighting

**bayonet** (bā′ō-nĕt), a sharp pointed weapon fastened to the end of a gun

**beachhead** (bēch′ hĕd), a strip of land captured from the enemy and used as a base of operation in fighting a battle

**beacon light** (bē′kŭn; -k′n līt), a light used as a signal or as a guide by night

**bearing** (bâr′ĭng), a person's manner

**Belleau Wood** (bĕ′lō′), a wooded region in France where a battle was fought in the World War

**berth** (bûrth), a built-in place to sleep

**beseech** (bĕ-sēch′), to beg or to ask

**besieged** (bĕ-sējd′), surrounded by an armed force

**blackberry dumpling** (blăk′bĕr′ĭ dŭmp′lĭng), a dessert made by rolling blackberries, sugar, and butter inside dough and baking

**blockade** (blŏk-ād′), a condition in which one nation attempts to keep shipping from going into and out of ports belonging to another nation

**blockade runner** (blŏk-ād′ rŭn′ẽr), a person or a ship which slips past the enemy's ships to carry goods in or out of a blockaded port

**bomb** (bŏm), a hollow iron ball which is filled with a substance that explodes when the ball strikes

**bombardment** (bŏm-bärd′mĕnt; bŭm-), an attack made with gunfire or bombs

**boundary dispute** (bound′a-rĭ dĭs-pūt′), a difference between two persons, states, or nations as to where the dividing line between them is located

**brand** (brånd), a mark put on with a hot iron; the act of so marking

**brig** (brĭg), a ship having two masts

**bristle** (brĭs″l), short, stiff, coarse hair; to show that one is aroused and angry

**broad wife** (brôd wīf), a slave wife living on a plantation other than the one where her husband lives

**buckskin** (bŭk′skĭn), the tanned skin of a deer

**Buena Vista** (bwā′nä vēs′tä), a place in Mexico at which the American army won a battle during the Mexican War

**buffalo trace** (bŭf′a-lō trās) a path worn by the feet of buffalo moving over the prairies or through the woods

**bugle** (bū′g′l), a musical instrument of brass used to sound calls in the army

**bugler** (bū′glẽr), a person who blows a bugle

**bulldozer** (bool′dōz′ẽr), a huge machine used to level ground and put it in condition for roads, air bases, and the like

**bunk** (bŭnk), a narrow bed built against the wall

[478]

**bunkhouse** (bŭnk'hous'), the house in which a group of cowboys slept

**bustle** (bŭs''l), noisy hurry

**cable** (kā'b'l), a telegraph line laid on the bottom of the ocean

**calculating machine** (kăl'kŭ-lāt'ĭng mȧ-shēn'), a machine which can add, subtract, multiply, and divide

**calico** (kăl'ĭ-kō), a kind of cotton cloth which usually has a colored pattern printed on it

**caller** (kôl'ẽr), a person who calls out the figures to be performed in an old-fashioned square dance

**camera** (kăm'ẽr-ȧ), an instrument which takes pictures

**candidate** (kăn'dĭ-dāt), a person who is being considered for election to some office

**cannonade** (kăn'ŭn-ād'), the constant firing of cannon

**cantina** (kän-tē'nä), a leather box in which a pony express rider carried the mail

**capable** (kā'pȧ-b'l), having ability

**caravan** (kăr'ȧ-văn; kăr'ȧ-văn'), a company traveling together

**cargo** (kär'gō), load, freight

**celebration** (sĕl'ē-brā'shŭn), an occasion upon which special honor is paid to some person, deed, time, or place

**cellophane** (sĕl'ō-fān), a substance used for wrapping various articles

**celluloid** (sĕl'ŭ-loid), a hard substance used for making picture films, combs, and many other articles

**ceremony** (sĕr'ē-mō'nĭ), a special set of acts to be carried out on a certain occasion

**chap** (chăp), a young man

**Chapultepec** (chä-pōōl'tȧ-pĕk'), a steep hill just outside Mexico City

that was taken by the Americans during the Mexican War

**Château-Thierry** (shȧ'tō' tyĕ'rē'), a town in France in and near which a battle was fought in the World War

**Chickamauga** (chĭk'ȧ-mô'gȧ), a place where a battle was fought in the War between the States

**cholera** (kŏl'ẽr-ȧ), a dangerous disease

**chuck wagon** (chŭk wăg'ŭn), a wagon which carries a kitchen outfit and serves food to ranch hands

**churn** (chûrn), to stir or beat cream in order to cause butter to form; the vessel in which this is done

**circuit** (sûr'kĭt), a route or way over which a person or a group of persons travels at regular times

**circuit rider** (sûr'kĭt rīd'ẽr), a person who travels a circuit

**clearing** (klēr'ĭng), an open place from which trees have been cut in a forest

**clog dance** (klŏg dȧns), a dance in which the dancer beats the rhythm strongly with his feet

**coffin** (kŏf'ĭn), a box in which a dead person is buried

**colonist** (kŏl'ō-nĭst), settler in a new country

**commander** (kŏ-mȧn'dẽr), a person who commands; a general

**commander in chief**, a general who commands a whole army

**commission** (kŏ-mĭsh'ŭn), a group of persons appointed to do certain things

**Commonwealth of the Philippines** (kŏm'ŭn-wĕlth', fĭl'ĭ-pēnz, -pĭnz), the newly created Filipino nation

**communication** (kŏ-mū'nĭ-kā'shŭn), giving information through spoken or written messages

[479]

**Communist Party** (cŏm′ū-nĭst), a political party

**composition** (kŏm′pŏ-zĭsh′ŭn), a mixture of two or more substances

**compromise** (kŏm′prŏ-mīz), a settlement of a quarrel or dispute, which is made by each side giving up part of what it wants

**comrade** (kŏm′răd), a friend who shares in some undertaking

**concern** (kŏn-sûrn′), interest

**Concord coach** (kŏṅ′kẽrd kōch), a style of stagecoach that was popular in the United States for many years

**conductor** (kŏn-dŭk′tẽr), a person who collects tickets and has charge of a train

**Confederate States of America** (kŏn-fĕd′ẽr-ĭt stāts, ȧ-mĕr′ĭ-kȧ), the states which seceded from the United States in 1860–1861 and attempted to form a new nation

**conference** (kŏn′fẽr-ĕns), a meeting to discuss a particular subject

**conflict** (kŏn′flĭkt), a struggle

**confuse** (kŏn-fūz′), to make a mistake or throw out of order

**congratulate** (kŏn-grăt′ū-lāt), to express pleasure at another's good fortune or success

**constitution** (kŏn′stĭ-tū′shŭn), the principles of government by which the citizens of a country agree to live

**Constitutional Convention** (kŏn′stĭ-tū′shŭn-ȧl; -′l kŏn-vĕn′shŭn), the meeting held in 1787 at which the Constitution of the United States was written

**convention** (kŏn-vĕn′shŭn), a meeting called for a special purpose

**copilot** (kō-pī′lŭt), one who helps a pilot guide a ship, plane, or vessel

**corn pone** (kôrn pōn), a flat cake made of corn meal and water and baked on a griddle

**corn shredder** (kôrn shrĕd′ẽr), a machine which cuts cornstalks into small pieces before they are put in a silo

**cotton gin** (kŏt″n jĭn), a machine which separates cotton seeds from the lint

**crane** (krān), a machine for lifting heavy weights; an iron arm fastened to the wall of a fireplace for holding kettles over the fire

**creaking** (krēk′ĭng), squeaking

**creek** (krēk), a small stream

**cricket** (krĭk′ĕt), a black insect somewhat like a grasshopper

**crimson** (krĭm′z′n), deep, rich red

**cruelty** (krōō′ĕl-tĭ), a readiness to give pain to others

**deaf-mute** (dĕf′mūt′), a person who cannot hear or speak

**declaration of war** (dĕk′lȧ-rā′shŭn, wôr), a statement issued by a nation to tell that it has gone to war with another country

**de Gaulle, Charles** (dē gôl), the leader of the Free-French movement

**delicious** (dē-lĭsh′ŭs), delightful to taste or smell

**democracy** (dē-mŏk′rȧ-sĭ), a form of government in which citizens make their own laws and manage their own affairs

**Democrat** (dĕm′ŏ-krăt), a person who is a member of the Democratic Party, one of the large political parties of the United States

**depression** (dē-prĕsh′ŭn), a period when business is very bad, work is

[480]

scarce, and people generally have a hard time making a living

derrick (dĕr′ĭk), a machine used in lifting heavy objects

desperate (dĕs′pẽr-ĭt), very dangerous; beyond hope

dial telephone (dī′ăl tĕl′ĕ-fōn), a telephone which permits one person to call another without the help of a telephone operator

Diesel engine (dē′zĕl ĕn′jĭn), a type of oil-burning engine

dignity (dĭg′nĭ-tĭ), a quality which causes other people to treat one with respect

discourage (dĭs-kûr′ĭj), to take away hope

disruption (dĭs-rŭp′shŭn), breaking apart

dock (dŏk), a place where a boat or ship may be tied up to load and unload

dome (dōm), a high arched roof, the base of which is shaped like a circle

dominion (dŏ-mĭn′yŭn), rule or control; a territory or country under the control of one government

eighteenth century (ā′tēnth′ sĕn′chu̇-rĭ), the years from 1701 to 1800

electricity (ê-lĕk′trĭs′ĭ-tĭ), an unseen force which can be made to produce light, heat, and power

emancipate (ê-măn′sĭ-pāt), to free from slavery

Emancipation Proclamation (ê-măn′sĭ-pā′shŭn prŏk′lă-mā′shŭn), the paper, issued by President Lincoln, which announced that slaves held in seceding states were freed

encyclopedia (ĕn-sī′klŏ-pē′dĭ-à), a book which tells briefly about many different subjects

engineer (ĕn′jĭ-nēr′), a man who plans and builds machines, roads, bridges, canals, and the like

envelop (ĕn-vĕl′ŭp), to cover or wrap around

exhaust (ĕg-zȯst′), to use up

exhibit (ĕg-zĭb′ĭt), to show

exist (ĕg-zĭst′), to live or to be

failure (fāl′ûr), a lack of success

Federalist (fĕd′ẽr-ăl-ĭst), the name of a political party which was in power in the United States in the early days of the Republic

ferryboat (fĕr′ĭ-bōt′), a boat which carries passengers, wagons, cars, and goods across a river or bay

fiber (fī′bẽr), a threadlike piece of anything

fiddle (fĭd″l), a violin

fiddler (fĭd′lẽr), a person who plays a fiddle or violin

fife (fīf), a musical instrument somewhat like a flute, often played in war times

Filipino (fĭl′ĭ-pē′nō), a citizen of the Philippine Islands

film (fĭlm), a roll or sheet used in taking pictures

flagship (flăg′shĭp′), the ship of the commanding officer of a fleet

flagstaff (flăg′stȧf′), the pole from which a flag is flown

flapjack (flăp′jăk′), a thin, flat battercake

flatboat (flăt′bōt′), a boat with a flat bottom, used chiefly on rivers for hauling heavy freight

flax (flăks), a plant from whose stem linen thread is made

fleece (flēs), the wool of a sheep

foothill (fŏŏt′hĭl), a low hill at the foot of a mountain range

**foothold** (foŏt′hōld′), a place to support the feet when climbing

**frontier** (frŭn-tēr′; frŏn′tēr), the last edge of settled country

**gallant** (găl′ănt), noble; brave

**gallery** (găl′ēr-ĭ), a balcony looking down into a large hall

**galley** (găl′ĭ), a place where cooking is done on a boat, ship, or plane

**gamble** (găm′b′l), to play games to win money

**gambler** (găm′blēr), a person who plays games to win money

**garrison** (găr′ĭ-sŭn; -s′n), soldiers stationed in a fort

**gasp** (gȧsp), to catch the breath quickly

**germ** (jûrm), a plant or animal, so small that it cannot be seen, which causes disease

**gilded** (gĭl′dĕd; -dĭd), covered with a substance that looks like gold

**girdled** (gûr′dl′d), surrounded as with a girdle or belt

**glider** (glīd′ēr), a flying machine without a motor

**glimpse** (glĭmps), a very short look

**gold seeker** (gōld sēk′ēr), a person who hunts gold

**granary** (grăn′ȧ-rĭ; popularly grān′-ȧ-rĭ), a storehouse for grain

**granite** (grăn′ĭt), a very hard kind of rock

**Guadalcanal** (gwä′thäl-kä-näl′), an island in the South Pacific, one of the Solomon group

**Guerrière** (gâr′ĭ-âr″), a British ship which fought a battle during the War of 1812 with the American ship *Constitution*

**handy** (hăn′dĭ), able to do things easily with the hands

**hardship** (härd′shĭp), a condition which is hard to bear, for example, great cold

**harrow** (hăr′ō), a tool used to break plowed earth into fine pieces

**harsh** (härsh), rough

**hasty** (hās′tĭ), quick; hurried

**Hawaii** (hä-wī′ē), the largest of the Hawaiian Islands, a group located in the Pacific Ocean

**heartsick** (härt′sĭk′), unhappy; discouraged

**helmet** (hĕl′mĕt; -mĭt), a metal covering worn by a soldier to protect his head

**hemp** (hĕmp), a plant, the fibers from whose stems are made into rope, string, and coarse cloth

**hinder** (hĭn′dēr), to stop or hold back

**hobble** (hŏb″l), to tie the legs of an animal together so that he cannot run away

**homespun** (hōm′spŭn′), cloth woven from thread which was spun at home

**homesteader** (hōm′stĕd-ēr), a person who by meeting certain conditions gains the ownership of a piece of land granted by the government

**hominy** (hŏm′ĭ-nĭ), a kind of food made of corn

**hoop skirt** (hōōp skûrt), a very full skirt that is held out by big hoops

**horizon** (hŏ-rī′z′n), the line where the earth and sky seem to meet

**horror** (hŏr′ēr), very great fear or terror

**horse wrangler** (hôrs răng′glēr), a man who cares for the horses used by cowboys on a ranch

**hostess** (hōs′tĕs), a woman who entertains another person as her guest

**hull** (hŭl), the outer covering of a seed

[482]

husk (hŭsk), the outer covering of an ear of corn

husking bee (hŭsk′ĭng bē), a neighborhood gathering at which guests removed the husks from ears of corn and later spent the evening in dancing and feasting

husky (hŭs′kĭ), strong

hustle (hŭs″l), to rush or hurry

immigrant (ĭm′ĭ-grănt), a person who comes to a new country to live

impressment (ĭm-prĕs′mĕnt), seizing by force

improvement (ĭm-proov′mĕnt), the quality of becoming better

impulse (ĭm′pŭls), a sudden desire to act

inaugurate (ĭn-ô′gû-rāt), to install in office with a ceremony

inauguration (ĭn-ô′gû-rā′shŭn), the ceremony which is held when a high officer, such as the President of the United States, takes office

indemnity (ĭn-dĕm′nĭ-tĭ), money which is paid for damage that has been done

independence (ĭn-dĕ-pĕn′dĕns), the right to manage one's affairs; freedom from the control of others

industrious (ĭn-dŭs′trĭ-ŭs), liking to work

influenza (ĭn′floo-ĕn′zȧ), a disease that is often dangerous to life

insane (ĭn-sān′), out of one's mind

insult (ĭn-sŭlt′), to treat in a way that shows a lack of respect; (ĭn′sŭlt), a speech or action which shows a lack of respect for a person or thing

interfere (ĭn′tẽr-fēr′), to take a part in the affairs of someone else without the approval of that person

interpreter (ĭn-tûr′prĕ-tẽr), a person who translates words spoken in one language into another tongue

invade (ĭn-vād′), to enter with force or as an enemy

invader (ĭn-vād′ẽr), a person who enters by force

invasion (ĭn-vā′zhŭn), an entrance as an enemy and under arms; an attack

irrigate (ĭr′ĭ-gāt), to water dry land

Jesuit (jĕz′û-ĭt), a member of a certain Catholic religious brotherhood

joint occupation (joint ŏk-û-pā′shŭn), a plan by which two persons, states, or nations hold possession of property or land together

jumble (jŭm′b′l), to mix up; to confuse

jumping-off trench (jŭmp′ĭng ôf trĕnch), the first trench along a battle front, from which soldiers go out to make an attack

Justice of the Supreme Court (jŭs′tĭs, sû-prēm′ kōrt), a judge who sits in the highest court in the United States

keelboat (kēl′bōt′), a type of boat used on the rivers in pioneer days for fast transportation

kerosene (kĕr′ô-sēn′; kĕr′ô-sēn′), a kind of oil that is burned in lamps and stoves

Knights of Columbus (nīts, kô-lŭm′bŭs), a society of men, members of which are all Roman Catholics

Kuril Islands (koo′rĭl; koo-rēl′), a chain of islands belonging to Japan and lying northeast of the main body of the Japanese Islands

label (lā′bĕl; -b′l), a sign used to show what an article is

labor union (lā′bẽr ūn′yŭn), a body of workmen banded together to secure

[483]

their rights and protect their interests

**Lancaster Pike** (lăn′kăs-tēr pīk), the first paved road in the United States. It ran between Philadelphia and Lancaster, Pennsylvania.

**landlord** (lănd′lôrd′), the owner of a piece of property which is rented to someone else

**lank** (lăngk), tall and thin

**lantern** (lăn′tērn), a light which is protected from wind and rain, and may be carried about

**lariat** (lăr′ĭ-ăt), a long rope which when properly thrown will catch cows, horses, or other animals

**launch** (lônch; länch), to send out or to set forth

**League of Nations** (lēg, nā′shŭnz), a union of nations which was formed at the close of the World War for the purpose of preventing future wars

**legend** (lĕj′ĕnd; lē′jĕnd), a story from the past

**legislature** (lĕj′ĭs-lā′chŭr), a lawmaking body

**leisure** (lē′zhĕr; lĕzh′ĕr), time when a person is free from work

**lever** (lē′vēr; lĕv′ēr), a bar used for raising weights

**Liberty Bonds** (lĭb′ĕr-tĭ bŏndz), bonds sold by the United States government in order to raise money for World War I

**lifeboat** (līf′bōt′), an open boat carried on board a ship and used to carry passengers to safety in case the ship is wrecked

**linsey-woolsey** (lĭn′zĭ-wōōl′zĭ), a homemade cloth woven of linen and wool

**lint** (lĭnt), the soft, fluffy threads or fibers of certain plants

**longhorn** (lŏng′hôrn′), one of a long-horned breed of cattle, at one time common in the Southwest

**loom** (lōōm), a frame which holds the thread for weaving cloth

**lure** (lūr), that which strongly attracts

**Lusitania** (lū′sĭ-tā′nĭ-á), a ship which was sunk by a German submarine

**lusty** (lŭs′tĭ), strong; hearty

**machine gun** (má-shēn′ gŭn), a powerful gun which fires bullets one after another very rapidly

**malaria** (má-lâr′ĭ-á), a disease that causes the patient to have chills and fever

**Malaya** (má-lā′á), the most southern part of the Indo-China Peninsula in southeastern Asia

**mammy** (măm′ĭ), as used in the South, an old colored woman who has charge of white children

**Manila** (má-nĭl′á), the capital and chief city of the Philippine Islands

**manufacturer** (măn′û-făk′chŭr-ēr), a person who makes goods of some sort in large quantities

**Marconi, Guglielmo** (mär-kō′nĕ, gōōl-yĕl′mō), the inventor of the wireless telegraph

**mare** (mâr), a female horse

**Marne River** (märn rĭv′ēr), a river in France along which one of the famous battles of World War I was fought

**Marianas Islands** (mä′rĕ-ä′näs), a group of islands in the South Pacific, of which Guam Island is one

**mechanical** (mĕ-kăn′ĭ-kăl), belonging to or like a machine

**mess call** (mĕs kôl), the signal given in the army to call men to meals

**Meuse River** (mŭz rĭv′ēr), a river in France

**millrace** (mĭl′rās′), the stream of water that drives a mill wheel; the narrow passage through which this stream flows

**mimeograph** (mĭm′ĕ-ŏ-grăf′), a machine for making copies of written or typed material

**miserable** (mĭz′ēr-ȧ-b′l), unhappy; uncomfortable

**mission** (mĭsh′ŭn), the headquarters of a religious group who are seeking to win the people of the region to a new way of living

**missionary** (mĭsh′ŭn-ĕr′ĭ), a person who goes to a new region seeking to win the people there to a new religious belief

**moan** (mōn), a low cry such as is made by a person in pain

**moccasin** (mŏk′ȧ-sĭn), a soft covering made of skin and worn on the foot

**mochila** (mô-chē′lä), a square of leather to which were fastened their cantinas in which a pony express rider carried the mail

**Monterrey** (mŏn′tĕ-rā′), a city in Mexico

**Mormon** (môr′mŭn), a member of a church, the sacred book of which is called the Book of Mormon

**Morse code** (môrs kōd), a system of dots, dashes, and spaces used in sending telegrams

**mosquito** (mŭs-kē′tō), a small insect whose bite is painful

**mountaineer** (moun′tĭ-nēr′), a person who lives among the mountains

**mourners' bench** (mōr′nērz bĕnch), the seat, usually near the front of the church, to which people came during a revival meeting when they felt that they were sinners

**mournful** (mōrn′fŏŏl; -f′l), sad

**mowing machine** (mō′ĭng mȧ-shēn′), a machine used for cutting hay

**museum** (mŭ-zē′ŭm), a place where objects of interest are collected and kept

**mush** (mŭsh), a kind of food made by stirring corn meal into boiling water

**navigator** (năv′ĭ-gā′ter), one who directs the course of a ship, plane, balloon, or the like

**neutral** (nū′trăl), on neither side

**neutrality** (nû-trăl′ĭ-tĭ), a state of being on neither the one side nor the other in a war

**newcomer** (nū′kŭm′ēr), a person who has just come to a region

**New England Primer** (prĭm′ēr), a small book from which children learned to read in colonial schools

**newsboy** (nūz′boi′), a boy who sells papers on the streets

**nickname** (nĭk′nām′), a name not his own, by which a person is sometimes called

**nineteenth century** (nīn′tēnth′ sĕn′-chŭ-rĭ), the years from 1801 to 1900

**Northwest Territory** (nôrth′wĕst′ tĕr′ĭ-tō′rĭ), a name once given to the region lying northwest of the Ohio River

**notch** (nŏch), to cut a small hollow in a surface; the hollow thus cut

**Nova Scotia** (nō′vȧ skō′shȧ), a part of Canada, once known as Acadia

**nylon** (nī′lŏn), a kind of thread or cloth made from certain mineral elements; popularly said to be made of coal, air, and water

**oar** (ōr), a long pole, flattened into a

[485]

paddle at one end, which is used to row a boat

**oath of office** (ōth, ŏf′ĭs), a solemn promise made by a person who is taking up the duties of office

**operate** (ŏp′ēr-āt), to work; to run

**ordinance** (ôr′dĭ-năns), a law

**ore** (ōr), metal mixed with rock, sand, or soil as it comes from the earth

**organize** (ôr′găn-īz), to put into working order

**otter** (ŏt′ēr), a fur-bearing animal

**overflowing** (ō′vēr-flō′ĭng), flooding

**overseer** (ō′vēr-sē′ēr), one who directs and oversees the work of others

**packet boat** (păk′ĕt; -ĭt bōt), a fast-moving canalboat

**paddle wheel** (păd″l hwēl), a wheel with paddles on it, which pushes a boat through the water

**pane** (pān), a single sheet of glass used in a door or window

**parade** (pȧ-rād′), a procession

**pastime** (pȧs′tīm′), amusement; pleasure

**pawnshop** (pôn′shŏp′), a shop in which a person may borrow money, leaving articles which he owns with the understanding that they may be sold if he does not repay the loan

**Pawtucket** (pô-tŭk′ĕt), a city in Rhode Island

**peace conference** (pēs kŏn′fēr-ĕns), a meeting held to consider peace between nations

**peacock** (pē′kŏk′), a bird with a large, brightly colored tail, the feathers from which are sometimes used for making fans

**pealing** (pēl′ĭng), ringing

**peddler** (pĕd′lēr), a person who carries goods about and sells them from house to house

[486]

**pension** (pĕn′shŭn), a sum of money regularly paid to a person because of some past service

**perilous** (pĕr′ĭ-lŭs), dangerous

**Philippine Islands** (fĭl′ĭ-pēn; -pĭn), a group of islands in the western Pacific Ocean

**phonograph** (fō′nŏ-grȧf), a machine upon which can be played a record which reproduces sounds

**pilot** (pī′lŭt), one who guides a ship, plane, or boat

**pioneer** (pī′ŏ-nēr′), a person who goes before and prepares the way for others; a settler in a new part of the country

**placer miner** (plăs′ēr mīn′ēr), one who washes soil or sand where gold is found, to get the gold

**plantation** (plăn-tā′shŭn), a very large farm

**plea** (plē), a very earnest request

**plow** (plou), a tool for turning the soil; to turn the soil

**plucky** (plŭk′ĭ), full of courage

**plumbing** (plŭm′ĭng), the system of pipes that carry water and waste in a house

**political** (pŏ-lĭt′ĭ-kăl), having to do with opinions about matters of government

**politics** (pŏl′ĭ-tĭks), the science of government

**pork** (pōrk), the meat of the hog

**postal system** (pōs′tăl; -t'l sĭs′tĕm; -tĭm), a system for carrying mail over the country

**postmaster** (pōst′mȧs′tēr), a man who has charge of a post office

**postmaster general** (pōst′mȧs′tēr jĕn′ēr-ăl), the officer in the President's Cabinet who has charge of postal matters

**pottery** (pŏt′ẽr-ĭ), pots, dishes, vases, and the like made from clay and hardened by heat

**poverty** (pŏv′ẽr-tĭ), state of being poor or in need

**prairie** (prâr′ĭ), a large area of level, grass-covered land

**preservation** (prĕz′ẽr-vā′shŭn), preserving; keeping safe

**President's Cabinet** (prĕz′ĭ-dĕnts kăb′ĭ-nĕt; -nĭt), a group of persons who are appointed by the President of the United States to have charge of certain departments of government and to act as advisers to him about matters concerning these departments

**procession** (prŏ-sĕsh′ŭn), a line of marching people

**production** (prŏ-dŭk′shŭn), the act of producing or making

**protest** (prŏ-tĕst′), to object

**Protestant** (prŏt′ĕs-tănt), referring to any branch of the Christian Church other than the Roman or Greek Catholic

**prow** (prou), the forward pointed part of a boat or ship

**prowling** (proul′ĭng), wandering about, usually while hunting for something

**Puerto Rico** (pwĕr′tō rē′kō), an island in the West Indies

**Pullman sleeping car** (pŏol′măn slēp′ĭng kär), a railroad car so built that the seats can be made into beds

**puncheon** (pŭn′chŭn), a split log turned with the flat side up

**quaint** (kwānt), odd; strange

**Quezon Manuel** (kā′zŏn, mä′nŏō-ĕl′), the first president of the Commonwealth of the Philippines

**radar** (rā′där), method of detecting and locating objects by means of pulses of high-frequency radio waves sent out in beams from a transmitter and reflected from the object to a specially designed receiver

**rafter** (ràf′tẽr), a piece of wood placed to support a roof

**raid** (rād), a sudden attack

**rallying cry** (răl′ĭ-ĭng krī), a short saying which, when repeated, has the power to bring people together for action

**rampart** (răm′pärt; -pẽrt), a wide bank of earth thrown up around a fort to help defend it

**ranch** (rănch), in the West, a large farm

**rancher** (răn′chẽr), a person who owns, runs, or works on a ranch

**ranchman** (rănch′măn), a rancher

**range** (rānj), an area of unfenced grassy land where cattle grazed

**ration** (rā′shŭn; răsh′ŭn), to limit the amount any one person may have to that which is his share when all of a product is fairly divided

**rayon** (rā′ŏn), thread or cloth made from wood pulp or certain other plant parts

**reaper** (rēp′ẽr), a machine used for cutting grain

**rebellion** (rĕ-bĕl′yŭn), a fight against the government

**reception** (rĕ-sĕp′shŭn), a party usually attended by a large number of people

**recollection** (rĕk′ŏ-lĕk′shŭn), memory

**Red Cross** (rĕd krŏs), a society organized to care for people who have become sick, hurt, or homeless as the result of wars or accidents

**refinery** (rḗ-fīn′ẽr-ĭ), a plant where a crude product such as oil is made pure

**refrigerator** (rḗ-frĭj′ẽr-ā′tẽr), a device for keeping food and other articles cool

**regulate** (rĕg′ů-lāt), to control

**relay race** (rē′lā rās), a race in which several people run, each starting over his part of the course as the person before him finishes

**reporter** (rḗ-pōr′tẽr), a person who gathers news for a newspaper

**Republican** (rḗ-pŭb′lĭ-kăn), a person who is a member of the Republican Party, one of the large political parties of the United States

**reservation** (rĕz′ẽr-vā′shŭn), an area of land that is set aside for some particular use; for example, certain lands are held as reservations for Indian tribes.

**resources** (rḗ-sōrs′ĕz; rē′sōrs-ĕz), natural products provided by nature, such as coal, iron; a ready supply

**reunited** (rē′ů-nīt′ĕd), united again; joined together again

**revolution** (rĕv′ṓ-lū′shŭn), an uprising against the established order of things

**Revolutionary War** (rĕv′ṓ-lū′shŭn-ẽr′ĭ), the war fought by the English colonies in America to win their independence from Great Britain

**rhythm** (rĭth′m), movement with an accent or beat regularly repeated

**rivet** (rĭv′ĕt; -ĭt), a metal bolt used to fasten steel beams or plates together

**Rough Riders** (rŭf′ rīd′ẽrz), a company of soldiers who fought in the Spanish-American War. Theodore Roosevelt was an officer in this company.

**roundup** (round′ŭp), a cattle drive held to bring together cattle that have been running on the open range

**roustabout** (roust′á-bout′), a laborer who works on the docks

**rudder** (rŭd′ẽr), a piece at the rear end of a boat or ship which aids in steering a course

**ruffle** (rŭf″l), a strip of material gathered on one edge and used for trimming dresses, curtains, and the like

**rustling** (rŭs′lĭng), making a soft swishing sound

**Ryukyu Islands** (ṙyōō′kyōō′) a group of islands lying south of Japan

**Sacagawea** (sä-kä′gä-wā′ä), an Indian woman, often called the Bird Woman, who acted as a guide for Lewis and Clark on their exploring trip

**Sacramento River** (săk′rá-mĕn′tō), a river in California

**saddlebag** (săd″l-băg′), one of a pair of bags carried across a horse's back behind the saddle

**sagebrush** (sāj′brŭsh′), a plant that is common on the dry plains in the western part of the United States

**Saint-Mihiel** (săn′ mē′yĕl′), a town in France in and near which Americans fought in the World War

**Saipan** (sī-pän′), an island in the Marianas group in the South Pacific

**saloon** (sá-lōōn′), a place where strong drink is sold

**saloonkeeper** (sá-lōōn′ kēp′ẽr), a person who keeps a saloon and sells liquor

[488]

**salute** (sȧ-lūt′), an honor paid by raising the hand to the head or by firing guns

**Salvation Army** (săl-vā′shŭn är′mĭ), a group of people organized to carry on certain types of religious work and to help the unfortunate

**San Antonio** (săn ăn-tō′nĭ-ō), a city in Texas

**San Francisco** (săn frăn-sĭs′kō), a city in California

**San Juan Hill** (săn hwän′), a hill in Cuba up the side of which Theodore Roosevelt led the Rough Riders in an attack on the fort at the top

**Santa Anna, Antonio Lopez** (sän′tä ä′nä, än-tō′nyō lō′päth), a Mexican general who led his country's armies against the Americans in the Mexican War

**Santa Fe** (săn′tȧ fā′), an early Spanish settlement, now a city in New Mexico

**sapling** (săp′lĭng), a young tree

**scald** (skôld; skäld), to pour boiling liquid over

**Schenectady** (skĕ-nĕk′tȧ-dĭ), a city in New York

**schooner** (skōōn′ẽr), a sailing vessel

**scornful** (skôrn′fŏŏl; -f′l), filled with scorn or contempt

**scraper** (skrāp′ẽr), a tool used for scraping a surface

**scurry** (skûr′ĭ), to hurry; to run quickly

**scythe** (sīth), a tool used for cutting grass

**sea monster** (sē mŏn′stẽr), a large or unusual sea animal. The expression is sometimes used to describe strange and dangerous animals that were once believed to live in the sea.

**secede** (sĕ-sēd′), to withdraw

**sectional** (sĕk′shŭn-ăl; -′l), referring to a particular section or part

**Senator** (sĕn′ȧ-tẽr), an officer of government who serves in either the state or national Senate

**Serbia** (sûr′bĭ-ȧ), the name used before the World War for a small country in southeastern Europe which is now a part of Yugoslavia

**session** (sĕsh′ŭn), a single sitting of a convention or other body of people, or several meetings of such a body while assembled

**shabby** (shăb′ĭ), badly worn

**shingle** (shĭn′g′l), a small piece of wood or other material used with similar pieces to cover a roof

**shorthand** (shôrt′hănd′), a system of rapid writing which uses various small marks in place of letters, sounds, and words

**shrill** (shrĭl), having a high-pitched, sharp sound

**shutter** (shŭt′ẽr), a window covering

**sickle** (sĭk″l), a small tool having a curved blade set on a small handle, used for cutting grass, grain, etc.

**signal** (sĭg′năl), a sign

**sinew** (sĭn′ū), the tough cord that joins muscle to bone

**six-shooter** (sĭks shōōt′ẽr), a pistol or revolver firing six shots before needing to be reloaded

**skid** (skĭd), a piece of wood or metal on which something rests

**slate** (slāt), a writing surface made of a certain kind of rock, a piece of which is set in a wooden frame. Slates were widely used in schools in pioneer days.

**slavery** (slāv′ẽr-ĭ), the state of being a slave

[489]

sledge hammer (slĕj hăm'ẽr), a very large, heavy hammer

slogan (slō'găn), a saying used to arouse people to action

sloop (slo͞op), a kind of sailboat

smokestack (smōk'stăk'), a tall chimney

snug (snŭg), cozy; comfortable

sob (sŏb), a stifled cry of grief or sorrow

sod (sŏd), a layer of grass-covered earth containing the grass and its roots

sorrel (sŏr'ĕl), reddish-brown

spangled (spăṅ'g'ld), covered with small bright bits

spike (spīk), a large nail

spindle (spĭn'd'l), the stick used in spinning to twist and draw out the thread

spine (spīn), the backbone; a thorn

sprawl (sprôl), to sit or lie in awkward or careless manner

squat (skwŏt), short and squarely built; to settle on land which does not belong to one

steersman (stērz'măn), the man who steers or pilots a boat

stirrup (stĭr'ŭp), the support hanging from the saddle, in which a horseback rider places his foot

stock (stŏk), shares in a company

stock exchange (stŏk ĕks-chănj'; ĭks-), a place where stocks are bought and sold

storage battery (stōr'ĭj băt'ẽr-ĭ), a battery in which electrical energy is stored. By using such a battery it is possible to have electricity where there is no electric power line.

stubborn (stŭb'ẽrn), hard-headed; set in purpose

sturdy (stûr'dĭ), strong

submarine (sŭb'má-rēn'), a boat that can travel under water

Supreme Court (sú-prēm'; so͞o-prēm' kōrt), the highest court in the United States

surrender (sú-rĕn'dẽr), to give up; to yield; to lay down arms

survey (sẽr-vā'), to measure carefully and mark boundary lines

surveyor (sûr-vā'ẽr), a man who marks the boundary lines of land

sustain (sŭs-tān'), to keep up; to give support to

swirling (swûrl'ĭng), whirling; moving rapidly with a twisting motion

switchboard (swĭch'bōrd'), the device which makes it possible to make or break electrical circuits and thus to communicate by telephone

tank (tăṅk), a small steel-covered vehicle mounted on caterpillar wheels, used to make attacks in recent wars

tank car (tăṅk kär), a railroad car built for carrying liquids

taps (tăps), the signal given in the army to put out lights at night

Tarawa (tä-rä'wä), an island in the Gilbert group in the South Pacific

tavern (tăv'ẽrn), as used in the past, a public house which sold liquor and which provided rooms and meals for travelers

tax (tăks), charge made by a government on the property or income of its citizens to pay the expenses of government

technicolor (tĕk'nĭ-kŭl'ẽr), process of making colored motion-picture films

television (tĕl'ĕ-vĭzh'ŭn; tĕl'ĕ-vĭzh'-

[490]

ŭn), the sending of scenes or images by means of wire or radio; usually done at the same time that sound is also sent, the two being reproduced at the same time in a receiving set.

**thermometer** (thẽr-mŏm′ê-tẽr), an instrument for measuring the degree of heat or cold

**threat** (thrĕt), a sign or statement of possible danger

**tidewater** (tīd′wô′tẽr), the region along the Atlantic coast in which the ocean tides flow inland in the broad rivers

**tidy** (tī′dĭ), neat

**tilt** (tĭlt), slant; lean

**toll** (tōl), a sum of money paid for the right to pass over a bridge or road

**tollgate** (tōl′gāt′), a gate across a toll road or bridge at which toll is paid

**toll road** (tōl′rōd′), a road over which one can travel only after payment of a sum of money

**tourist camp** (tŏŏr′ĭst kămp), a camp, provided with cabins, baths, and sometimes other comforts, in which people traveling by automobile may stay overnight

**tow** (tō) to pull by a rope

**towline** (tō′līn′), the rope used in towing

**towpath** (tō′pȧth′), a path beside a canal along which a horse walked as it towed the canalboat

**tractor** (trăk′tẽr), an engine on wheels used in pulling wagons, plows, etc.

**trample** (trăm′p'l), to crush or step on heavily

**transportation** (trăns′pôr-tā′shŭn), means of being carried from one place to another

**transfer** (trăns-fûr′), to change from one person or thing to another

**treaty of peace** (trē′tĭ, pēs), a written agreement setting forth the terms by which a war is ended

**trench** (trĕnch), a deep ditch in which fighting men are sheltered while fighting

**Tulagi** (tōō-lä′gĕ), an island in the South Pacific, one of the Solomon group

**tumble-down** (tŭm′b'l-doun′), in a bad state of repair; old and worn

**turban** (tûr′băn), a headdress made of a scarf or handkerchief wrapped around the head

**twentieth century** (twĕn′tĭ-ĕth; -ĭth sĕn′chû-rĭ), the years 1901 to 2000

**twitch** (twĭch), to jerk

**uncomfortable** (ŭn-kŭm′fẽrt-ȧ-b'l), not comfortable; uneasy

**V-1 and V-2 bombs** (bŏmz), bombs developed by Germans during World War II. Each bomb travels under its own power and carries materials which explode when the bomb reaches the earth

**vacuum cleaner** (văk′û-ŭm klēn′ẽr), a machine driven by an electric motor and used for cleaning rugs, furniture, etc.

**vacuum tube** (văk′û-ŭm tūb), a glass tube that is used in radios

**vehicle** (vē′ĭ-k'l; vē′hĭ-), a wagon, automobile, or other means of travel used on land

**Veracruz** (vā′rä-krōōs′; vẽr′ȧ-krōōz′), a city in Mexico

**veranda** (vĕ-răn′dȧ), a large porch

**Versailles** (vẽr-sālz′; vẽr′sä′y′), the city near Paris, France, where the Peace Conference was held at the close of World War I

[491]

**vigilance committee** (vĭj′ĭ-lăns kŏ-mĭt′ĭ), a group of citizens who in a pioneer town where many people broke the law sometimes seized lawbreakers and punished them

**wail** (wāl), a mournful cry made because of grief or pain

**warehouse** (wâr′hous′), a storehouse where goods are kept

**warping** (wôrp′ĭng), curving

**well-to-do** (wĕl′-tōō-dōō′), having enough money to be comfortable

**Westward Movement** (wĕst′wĕrd mōōv′mĕnt), the moving toward the West of American pioneers, which began before the Revolutionary War and continued until the later years of the nineteenth century

**whaling** (hwāl′ĭng), hunting and catching whales, which are huge sea animals

**Whig** (hwĭg), a political party that was important in the United States many years ago; a member of this party

**whitewash** (hwĭt′wŏsh′), a liquid made of lime and water and used for whitening walls, fences, and the like

**wood pulp** (wŏŏd pŭlp), a mass of ground wood used in making paper, rayon, and other products

**wrestle** (rĕs″l), to try to throw another person to the ground in a contest

**yam** (yăm), the root of a vine that is used for food; a kind of sweet potato

**Y.M.C.A.**, the usual way of speaking of the Young Men's Christian Association, a society which has for its purpose the improvement of the social and religious life of young men

# INDEX